THIS BOOK BELONGS TO

My Book of
BIBLE
STORIES

D.R. © 2006
La Torre del Vigía, A.R.
Heraldo 104, Col. Clavería, 02080 México, D.F.
Publicado en inglés en México: 2006
Primera edición en inglés: 2006
Tercera reimpresión: 2007

Bible quotations in this book
are paraphrased. They are put
in simple language so that
young children can get the
sense of them. Citations at
the end of each story provide
the Bible source.

This publication is provided as part of a worldwide Bible educational work
supported by voluntary donations.

My Book of Bible Stories
English (*my*-E)

Esta obra terminó de imprimirse en enero de 2007, en la imprenta de La Torre
del Vigía, A.R., Av. Jardín 10, Fracc. El Tejocote, 56239 Texcoco, Edo. de Méx.
La reimpresión consta de 98.000 ejemplares.

Printed in Mexico   ISBN 970-787-043-5   Impreso en México

MY BOOK OF BIBLE STORIES

THIS is a book of true stories. They are taken from the world's greatest book, the Bible. The stories give you a history of the world from when God began to create until right up to our present day. They even tell about what God promises to do in the future.

This book gives you an idea of what the Bible is all about. It tells about people of the Bible and the things they did. It also shows the grand hope of everlasting life in a paradise earth that God has given to people.

There are 116 stories in the book. These are grouped in eight parts. A page at the beginning of each part tells briefly what is found in that part. The stories appear in the order that events occurred in history. This helps you to learn when, in relation to other events, things happened in history.

The stories are told in simple language. Many of you young children will be able to read them for yourselves. You parents will discover that your smaller children will delight to have these stories read to them over and over again. You will find that this book contains much of interest for young and old alike.

Bible citations are given at the end of each story. You are encouraged to read these portions of the Bible on which the stories are based.

CONTENTS

PART 4   ISRAEL'S FIRST KING TO CAPTIVITY IN BABYLON

PART 5   CAPTIVITY IN BABYLON
TO REBUILDING OF JERUSALEM'S WALLS

PART 6   BIRTH OF JESUS TO HIS DEATH

PART 7   JESUS' RESURRECTION TO PAUL'S IMPRISONMENT

PART 8   WHAT THE BIBLE FORETELLS COMES TRUE

Study Questions
for *My Book of Bible Stories*

The questions for each of the 116 stories listed above
are found beginning on the page after the end of Story 116.

PART 1

Creation to the Flood

From where did the heavens and earth come? How did the sun, moon and stars, as well as the many things on earth, come to be? The Bible gives the true answer when it says that they were created by God. So our book begins with Bible stories about creation.

The first creations of God, we learn, were spirit persons somewhat like himself. They were angels. But the earth was created for people like us. So God made the man and woman named Adam and Eve and put them in a beautiful garden. But they disobeyed God and lost the right to keep living.

In all, from Adam's creation until the great Flood, there were 1,656 years. During this time many bad persons lived. In heaven, there were the unseen spirit persons, Satan and his bad angels. On earth, there were Cain and many other bad persons, including some unusually powerful men. But there were also good people on earth—Abel, Enoch and Noah. In Part ONE we will read about all these people and events.

GOD BEGINS TO MAKE THINGS

ALL the good things we have come from God. He made the sun to give us light by day, and the moon and stars so we can have some light at night. And God made the earth for us to live on.

But the sun, the moon, the stars and the earth were not the first things God made. Do you know what was the first? God first made persons like himself. We can't see these persons, just as we can't see God. In the Bible these persons are called angels. God made the angels to live with himself in heaven.

The first angel God made was very special. He was God's first Son, and he worked with his Father. He helped God to make all other things. He helped God to make the sun, the moon, the stars and also our earth.

What was the earth like then? In the beginning no one could live on earth. There was nothing but one big ocean of water all over the land. But God wanted people to live on earth. So he began to get things ready for us. What did he do?

Well, first the earth needed light. So God made the light from the sun to shine on the earth. He made it so there could be both nighttime and daytime. Afterward God caused land to come up above the water of the ocean.

At first there was nothing on the land. It looked like the picture you see here. There were no flowers or trees or animals. There were not even any fish in the oceans. God had a lot more work to do to make the earth really nice for animals and people to live on.

Jeremiah 10:12; Colossians 1:15-17; Genesis 1:1-10.

A BEAUTIFUL GARDEN

LOOK at the earth here! How pretty everything is! Look at the grass and the trees, the flowers and all the animals. Can you pick out the elephant and the lions?

How did this beautiful garden come to be? Well, let's see how God got the earth ready for us.

First, God made green grass to cover the land. And he made all kinds of small plants and bushes and trees. These growing things help to make the earth pretty. But they do more than that. Many of them also give us foods that taste very good.

God later made fish to swim in the water and birds to fly in the sky. He made dogs and cats and horses; big animals and small animals. What animals live near your home? Shouldn't we be glad that God made all these things for us?

Finally, God made one part of the earth a very special place. He called this place the garden of Eden. It was just perfect. Everything about it was beautiful. And God wanted the whole earth to become just like this pretty garden he had made.

But look at the picture of this garden again. Do you know what God saw that was missing? Let's see.

Genesis 1:11-25; 2:8, 9.

WHAT is different in this picture? Yes, it is the people in it. They are the first man and woman. Who made them? It was God. Do you know his name? It is Jehovah. And the man and woman came to be called Adam and Eve.

This is how Jehovah God made Adam. He took some dust from the ground and with it he formed a perfect body, a man's body. Then he blew into the man's nose, and Adam came to life.

Jehovah God had a job for Adam. He told Adam to name all the different kinds of animals. Adam may have watched the animals for a long time so he could pick the best names for them all. While Adam was naming the animals he began to see something. Do you know what that was?

The animals all had mates. There were papa elephants and mama elephants, and there were papa lions and mama lions. But Adam had no one to be his mate. So Jehovah

made Adam fall into a deep sleep, and he took a rib bone from his side. Using this rib, Jehovah made a woman for Adam, and she became his wife.

How happy Adam was now! And think how happy Eve must have been to be put in such a beautiful garden to live! Now they could have children and live together in happiness.

Jehovah wanted Adam and Eve to live forever. He wanted them to make the whole earth as pretty as the garden of Eden. How happy Adam and Eve must have been when they thought about doing this! Would you have liked to share in making the earth a pretty garden? But the happiness of Adam and Eve did not last. Let's find out why.

Psalm 83:18; Genesis 1:26-31; 2:7-25.

SEE what's happening now. Adam and Eve are being put out of the beautiful garden of Eden. Do you know why?

It is because they did something very bad. And so Jehovah is punishing them. Do you know the bad thing Adam and Eve did?

They did something God told them not to do. God told them they could eat food from the trees of the garden. But from one tree God said not to eat, or else they would die. He kept that tree as his own. And we know it is wrong to take something that belongs to someone else, don't we? Well, what happened?

One day when Eve was alone in the garden, a snake spoke to her. Think of that! It told Eve to eat fruit from the tree from which God told them not to eat. Now, when Jehovah made snakes he did not make them so they could talk. So this can only mean that someone else was making the snake speak. Who was that?

It wasn't Adam. So it had to be one of the persons that Jehovah had made long before he made the earth. Those persons are angels, and we cannot see them. This one angel had become very proud. He began thinking that he should be a ruler like God. And he wanted people to obey him instead of obeying Jehovah. He was the angel that made the snake talk.

This angel was able to fool Eve. When he told her that she would become like God if she ate the fruit, she believed it. So she ate, and Adam did too. Adam and Eve disobeyed God, and that is why they lost their beautiful garden home.

But someday God will see to it that the whole earth is made as pretty as the garden of Eden. Later we will learn how you may share in making it this way. But now, let's find out what happened to Adam and Eve.   Genesis 2:16, 17; 3:1-13, 24; Revelation 12:9.

OUTSIDE the garden of Eden, Adam and Eve had many troubles. They had to work hard for their food. Instead of beautiful fruit trees, they saw lots of thorns and thistles grow around them. This is what happened when Adam and Eve disobeyed God and stopped being His friends.

But worse than that, Adam and Eve started to die. Remember, God warned them that they would die if they ate fruit from a certain tree. Well, the very day that

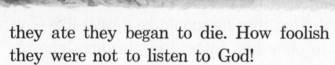

they ate they began to die. How foolish they were not to listen to God!

The children of Adam and Eve were all born after God put their parents out of the garden of Eden. This means that the children would also have to grow old and die.

If only Adam and Eve had obeyed Jehovah, life would have been happy for them and their children. They could all have lived forever in happiness on earth. No one would have had to grow old, get sick and die.

God wants people to live forever in happiness, and He promises that someday they will. Not only will the whole earth be beautiful, but all the people will be healthy. And everyone on earth will be a good friend with everyone else and with God.

But Eve was no longer a friend of God. So when she gave birth to her children, it was not easy for her. She had pain. Being disobedient to Jehovah certainly brought her a lot of sorrow, don't you agree?

Adam and Eve had many sons and daughters. When their first son was born, they named him Cain. They named their second son Abel. What happened to them? Do you know?

Genesis 3:16-23; 4:1, 2; Revelation 21:3, 4.

A GOOD SON, AND A BAD ONE 6

LOOK at Cain and Abel now. They have both grown up. Cain has become a farmer. He grows grains and fruits and vegetables.

Abel has become a keeper of sheep. He likes to take care of little lambs. They grow up into big sheep, and so Abel soon has a whole flock of sheep to watch over.

One day Cain and Abel bring a gift to God. Cain brings some food he has grown. And Abel brings the very best sheep he has. Jehovah is pleased with Abel and his gift. But he is not pleased with Cain and his gift. Do you know why?

It is not just that Abel's gift is better

than Cain's. It is because Abel is a good man. He loves Jehovah and his brother. But Cain is bad; he does not love his brother.

So God tells Cain that he should change his ways. But Cain does not listen. He is very angry because God liked Abel better. So Cain says to Abel, 'Let us go over into the field.' There, when they are all alone, Cain hits his brother Abel. He hits him so hard that he kills him. Wasn't that a terrible thing for Cain to do?

Even though Abel died, God still remembers him. Abel was good, and Jehovah never forgets a person like that. So one day Jehovah God will bring Abel back to life. At that time Abel will never have to die. He will be able to live here on earth forever. Won't it be fine to get to know persons like Abel?

But God is not pleased with persons like Cain. So after Cain killed his brother, God punished him by sending him far away from the rest of his family. When Cain went away to live in another part of the earth, he took with him one of his sisters, and she became his wife.

In time Cain and his wife began to have children. Other sons and daughters of Adam and Eve got married, and they also had children. Soon there were many people on the earth. Let's learn about some of them. Genesis 4:2-26; 1 John 3:11, 12; John 11:25.

A BRAVE MAN

AS THE number of people began to increase on the earth, most of them did bad things like Cain. But one man was different. He is this man named E'noch. E'noch was a brave man. The people all around him were doing very bad things, but E'noch still kept on serving God.

Do you know why those people back then did so many bad things? Well, think, Who caused Adam and Eve to disobey God and to eat the fruit that God said they should not eat? Yes, it was a bad angel. The Bible calls him Satan. And he is trying to get everyone to be bad.

One day Jehovah God had E'noch tell the people something they did not want to hear. It was this: 'God is someday going to destroy all the bad people.' The people were probably very angry to hear this.

They may even have tried to kill E'noch. So E'noch needed to be very brave to tell the people about what God was going to do.

God did not let E'noch live a long time among those bad people. E'noch lived to be only 365 years old. Why do we say "only 365 years"? Because men in those days were much stronger than now and lived much longer. Why, E'noch's son Me·thu'se·lah lived to be 969 years old!

Well, after E'noch died, the people just got worse and worse. The Bible says that 'everything they thought about was bad all the time,' and that 'the earth became filled with violence.'

Do you know one of the reasons why there was so much trouble on the earth in those days? It is because Satan had a new way of getting the people to do bad things. We will learn about this next.

Genesis 5:21-24, 27; 6:5;
Hebrews 11:5; Jude 14, 15.

GIANTS IN THE EARTH

I F SOMEONE were walking toward you and he was as tall as the ceiling in your house, what would you think? That person would be a giant! At one time there really were giants on the earth. The Bible shows that their fathers were angels from heaven. But how could that be?

Remember, the bad angel Satan was busy making trouble. He was even trying to get God's angels to be bad. In time, some of these angels started to listen to Satan. They stopped the work that God had for them to do in heaven. And they came down to earth and made human bodies for themselves. Do you know why?

The Bible says that it is because these sons of God saw the pretty women on earth and wanted to live with them. So they came to earth and married these women. The Bible says that this was wrong, because God made the angels to live in heaven.

When the angels and their wives had babies, these babies were different. At first they may not have looked very different. But they kept growing bigger and bigger, and getting stronger and stronger, until they became giants.

These giants were bad. And because they were so big and strong, they would hurt people. They tried to force everyone to be bad like themselves.

E'noch had died, but there was one man on earth now who was good. This man's name was Noah. He always did what God wanted him to do.

One day God told Noah that the time had come for Him to destroy all the bad people. But God was going to save Noah, his family and many of the animals. Let's see how God did this.

Genesis 6:1-8; Jude 6.

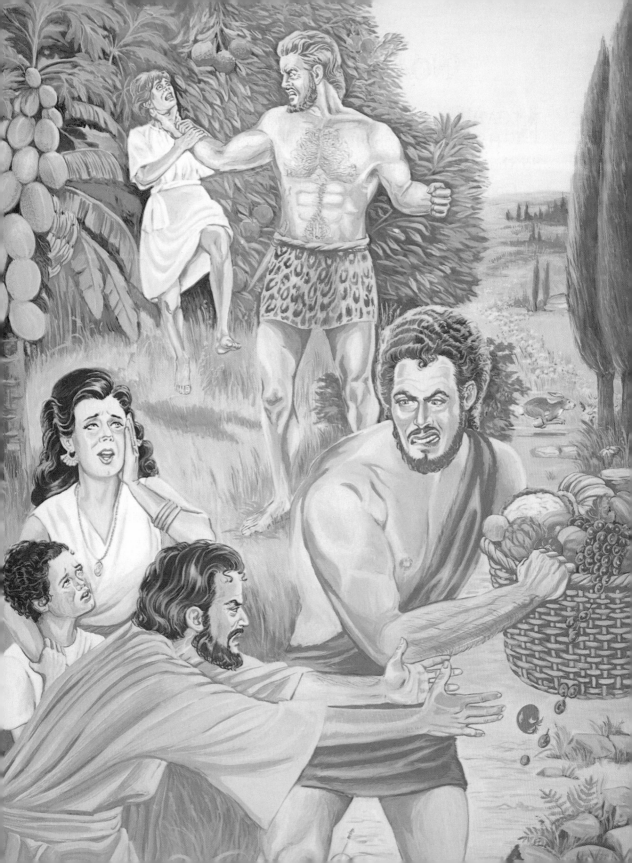

NOAH had a wife and three sons. His sons' names were Shem, Ham and Ja'pheth. And each of these sons had a wife. So there were eight persons in Noah's family.

God now had Noah do a strange thing. He told him to build a big ark. This ark was large like a ship, but it looked more like a big, long box. 'Make it three floors high,' God said, 'and put rooms in it.' The rooms were for Noah and his family, the animals, and the food all of them would need.

God also told Noah to fix up the ark so that no water could leak in. God said: 'I am going to send a great flood of water and destroy the whole world. Everyone not in the ark will die.'

Noah and his sons obeyed Jehovah and started building. But the other people just laughed. They kept on being bad. Nobody believed Noah when he told them what God was going to do.

It took a long time to build the ark because it was so big. Finally, after many years, it was finished. Now God told Noah to bring the animals into the ark. God said to bring in two of some kinds of animals, both a male and a female. But of other kinds of animals, God told Noah to bring in seven. God also told Noah to bring in all the different kinds of birds. Noah did just what God said.

Afterward, Noah and his family also went into the ark. Then God shut the door. Inside, Noah and his family waited. Just imagine you are there in the ark with them, waiting. Would there really be a flood as God said? Genesis 6:9-22; 7:1-9.

THE GREAT FLOOD

OUTSIDE the ark, the people went about their life the same as before. They still did not believe that the Flood would come. They must have laughed more than ever. But they soon stopped laughing.

All of a sudden water began to fall. It poured down from the sky as when you pour water from a bucket. Noah had been right! But it was too late now for anybody else to get into the ark. The door had been closed tight by Jehovah.

Soon all the low ground was covered. The water became like big rivers. It pushed over trees and rolled around big stones, and made a lot of noise. The people were afraid. They climbed up to higher ground. Oh, how they wished they had listened

to Noah and gotten into the ark when the door was still open for them! But now it was too late.

The water kept getting higher and higher. For 40 days and 40 nights the water poured out of the sky. It rose up the sides of the mountains, and soon even the tallest mountains were covered. So just as God had said, all the people and animals outside the ark died. But everyone inside was safe.

Noah and his sons had done a good job building the ark. The water lifted it up, and it floated right on top of the water. Then one day, after the rain stopped falling, the sun began to shine. What a sight it was! There was just one big ocean everywhere. And the only thing that could be seen was the ark floating on top.

The giants were gone now. No more would they be around to hurt people. All of them had died, along with their mothers and

the rest of the bad people. But what happened to their fathers?

The fathers of the giants were not really human people like us. They were angels that had come down to live as men on earth. So when the Flood came, they did not die with the rest of the people. They stopped using the human bodies they had made, and went back to heaven as angels. But they were no longer allowed to be part of the family of God's angels. So they became the angels of Satan. In the Bible they are called demons.

God now made a wind blow, and the waters of the flood began to go down. Five months later the ark came to rest on the top of a mountain. Many more days passed, and those inside the ark could look out and see the tops of the mountains. The waters kept on going down and down.

Then Noah let a black bird called a raven out of the ark. It would fly away for a while and then it would come back, because it could not find a good place to land. It kept doing this and each time it returned, it would rest on the ark.

Noah wanted to see if the waters had run off the earth, so next he sent a dove out of the ark. But the dove came back too because it did not find a place to stay. Noah sent it out a second time, and it brought back an olive leaf in its beak. So Noah knew that the waters had gone down. Noah sent out the dove a third time, and finally it found a dry place to live.

God now spoke to Noah. He said: 'Go out of the ark. Take your whole family and the animals with you.' They had been inside the ark for more than a whole year. So we can just imagine how happy they all were to be outside again and to be alive!

Genesis 7:10-24; 8:1-17; 1 Peter 3:19, 20.

PART 2

The Flood to the
Deliverance from Egypt

Only eight people survived the Flood, but in time they increased to number many thousands. Then, 352 years after the Flood, Abraham was born. We learn how God kept his promise by giving Abraham a son named Isaac. Then, of Isaac's two sons, Jacob was chosen by God.

Jacob had a big family of 12 sons and some daughters. Jacob's 10 sons hated their younger brother Joseph and sold him into slavery in Egypt. Later, Joseph became an important ruler of Egypt. When a bad famine came, Joseph tested his brothers to see whether they had a change of heart. Finally, Jacob's whole family, the Israelites, moved to Egypt. This happened 290 years after Abraham was born.

For the next 215 years the Israelites lived in Egypt. After Joseph died, they became slaves there. In time, Moses was born, and God used him to deliver the Israelites from Egypt. In all, 857 years of history are covered in Part TWO.

DO YOU know the first thing Noah did when he and his family came out of the ark? He made an offering or a gift to God. You can see him doing this in the picture below. Noah offered this gift of animals to thank God for saving his family from the great flood.

Do you think Jehovah was pleased with the gift? Yes, he was. And so he promised Noah that he would never destroy the world again by a flood.

Soon the land was all dried off, and Noah and his family began a new life outside the ark. God blessed them and told them: 'You must have many children. You must increase in numbers until people live all over the earth.'

But later, when people would hear about the great flood, they might be afraid that a flood like that would happen again. So God gave something that would remind people of his promise never to flood the whole earth again. Do you know what he gave to remind them? It was a rainbow.

A rainbow is often seen in the sky when the sun shines after it has rained. Rainbows may have many beautiful colors. Have you ever seen one? Do you see the one in the picture?

This is what God said: 'I promise that never again will all people and animals be destroyed by a flood. I am putting my rainbow in the clouds. And when the rainbow appears, I will see it and remember this promise of mine.'

So when you see a rainbow, what should it remind you of? Yes, God's promise that he will never destroy the world again by a great flood.   Genesis 8:18-22; 9:9-17.

MEN BUILD A BIG TOWER

12

MANY years passed. Noah's sons had lots of children. And their children grew up and had more children. Soon there were many people on the earth.

One of these persons was a great-grandson of Noah named Nim'rod. He was a bad man who hunted and killed both animals and men. Nim'rod also made himself a king to rule over other people. God did not like Nim'rod.

All the people at that time spoke one language. Nim'rod wanted to keep them all together so that he could rule them. So do you know what he did? He told the people to build a city and a big tower in it. See them in the picture making bricks.

Jehovah God was not pleased with this building. God wanted the people to move out and live all over the earth. But the people said: 'Come on! Let's build a city and a tower so high that its top will reach into the heavens. Then we will be famous!' The people wanted honor for themselves, not for God.

So God made the people stop building the tower. Do you know how he did it? By suddenly causing people to speak different languages, instead of just one. No longer did the builders understand one another. This is why their city came to be called Ba'bel, or Babylon, meaning "Confusion."

The people now began to move away from Ba'bel. Groups of persons who spoke the same language went to live together in other parts of the earth.

Genesis 10:1, 8-10; 11:1-9.

ABRAHAM – A FRIEND OF GOD

O NE of the places where people went to live after the Flood was called Ur. It became an important city with some nice homes in it. But the people there worshiped false gods. That was the way they did in Ba'bel too. The people in Ur and Ba'bel were not like Noah and his son Shem, who kept on serving Jehovah.

Finally, 350 years after the flood, faithful Noah died. It was just two years later that the man you see in this picture was born. He was a very special person to God. His name was Abraham. He lived with his family in that city of Ur.

One day Jehovah told Abraham: 'Leave Ur and your relatives, and go to a country I will show you.' Did Abraham obey God and leave behind all the comforts of Ur? Yes, he did. And it was because Abraham always obeyed God that he came to be known as God's friend.

Some of Abraham's family went along with him when he left Ur. His father Te'rah did. So did his nephew Lot. And, of course, Abraham's wife Sarah went too. In time they all arrived at a place called Ha'ran, where Te'rah died. They were far away from Ur.

After a while Abraham and his household left Ha'ran and came to the land called Ca'naan. There Jehovah said: 'This is the land that I will give to your children.' Abraham stayed in Ca'naan and lived in tents.

God began to help Abraham so that he came to have great flocks of sheep and other animals and hundreds of servants. But he and Sarah did not have any children of their own.

When Abraham was 99 years old, Jehovah said: 'I promise that you will become father to many nations of people.' But how could this happen, since Abraham and Sarah were now too old to have a child? Genesis 11:27-32; 12:1-7; 17:1-8, 15-17; 18:9-19.

CAN you see what Abraham is doing here? He has a knife, and it looks as if he is going to kill his son. Why would he ever do that? First, let's see how Abraham and Sarah got their son.

Remember, God promised them that they would have a son. But that seemed impossible, because Abraham and Sarah were so old. Abraham, however, believed that God could do what seemed impossible. So what happened?

After God made his promise, a whole year passed. Then, when Abraham was 100 years old and Sarah was 90 years old, they had a baby boy named Isaac. God had kept his promise!

But when Isaac had grown older, Jehovah tested Abraham's faith. He called: 'Abraham!' And Abraham answered: 'Here I am!' Then God said: 'Take your son, your only son, Isaac, and go to a mountain that I will show you. There kill your son and offer him up as a sacrifice.'

How sad those words made Abraham, because Abraham loved his son very much. And remember, God had promised that Abraham's children would live in the land of Ca'naan. But how could that happen if Isaac were dead? Abraham did not understand, but still he obeyed God.

When he got to the mountain, Abraham tied up Isaac and put him on the altar that he built. Then he took out the knife to kill his son. But just at that moment God's angel called: 'Abraham, Abraham!' And Abraham answered: 'Here I am!'

'Don't hurt the boy or do anything to him,' God said. 'Now I know that you have faith in me, because you have not held back your son, your only one, from me.'

What great faith Abraham had in God! He believed that nothing was impossible for Jehovah, and that Jehovah could even raise

Isaac from the dead. But it was not really God's will for Abraham to kill Isaac. So God caused a sheep to get caught in some nearby bushes, and he told Abraham to sacrifice it instead of his son.

Genesis 21:1-7; 22:1-18.

LOT'S WIFE LOOKED BACK

LOT and his family lived together with Abraham in the land of Ca'naan. One day Abraham said to Lot: 'There isn't land enough here for all our animals. Please, let us separate. If you go one way, then I will go the other.'

Lot looked over the land. He saw a very nice part of the country that had water and a lot of good grass for his animals. This was the District of the Jordan. So Lot moved his family and animals there. They finally made their home in the city of Sod'om.

The people of Sod'om were very bad. This upset Lot, because he was a good man. God was upset too. Finally, God sent two

angels to warn Lot that he was going to destroy Sod'om and the nearby city of Go·mor'rah because of their badness.

The angels told Lot: 'Hurry! Take your wife and your two daughters and get out of here!' Lot and his family were a little slow in going, and so the angels took them by the hand and led them out of the city. Then one of the angels said: 'Run for your lives! Don't look back. Run to the hills, so that you won't be killed.'

Lot and his daughters obeyed and ran away from Sod'om. They didn't stop for a moment, and they didn't look back. But Lot's wife disobeyed. After they had gone some distance from Sod'om, she stopped and looked back. Then Lot's wife became a pillar of salt. Can you see her in the picture?

We can learn a good lesson from this. It shows us that God saves those who obey him, but those who do not obey him will lose their lives. Genesis 13:5-13; 18:20-33; 19:1-29; Luke 17:28-32; 2 Peter 2:6-8.

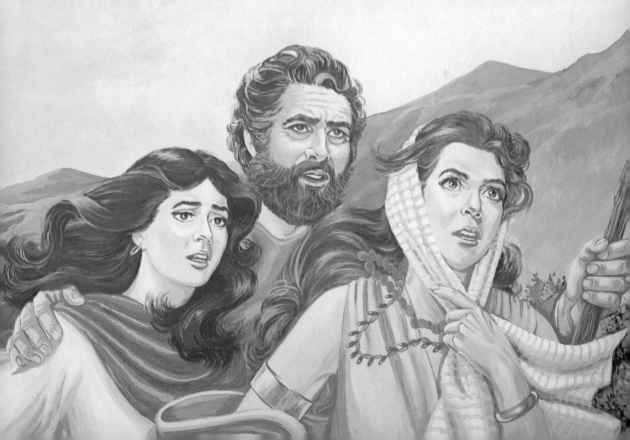

D O YOU know who the woman is in this picture? Her name is Re·bek'ah. And the man she is coming to meet is Isaac. She is going to become his wife. How did this happen?

Well, Isaac's father Abraham wanted to get a good wife for his son. He didn't want Isaac to marry one of the women in Ca'naan, because these people worshiped false gods. So Abraham called his servant and

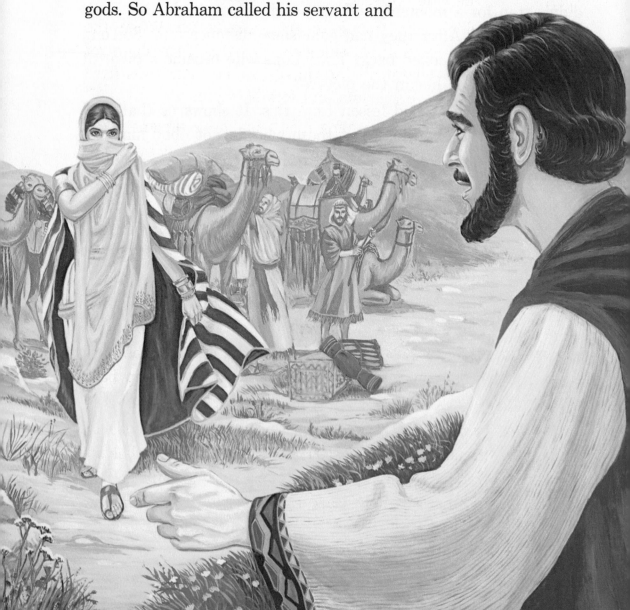

said: 'I want you to go back to where my relatives live in Ha'ran and get a wife for my son Isaac.'

Right away Abraham's servant took ten camels and made the long trip. When he got near the place where Abraham's relatives lived, he stopped at a well. It was late in the afternoon, the time when the women of the city would come to get water from the well. So Abraham's servant said a prayer to Jehovah: 'May the woman that gets some water for me and the camels be the one that you choose to be the wife of Isaac.'

Soon Re·bek'ah came along to get some water. When the servant asked her for a drink, she gave him one. Then she went and got enough water for all the thirsty camels. That was hard work because camels drink lots and lots of water.

When Re·bek'ah finished doing this, Abraham's servant asked her the name of her father. He also asked if he could stay overnight at their home. She said: 'My father is Be·thu'el, and there is room for you to stay with us.' Abraham's servant knew that Be·thu'el was the son of Abraham's brother Na'hor. So he knelt down and thanked Jehovah for leading him to Abraham's relatives.

That night Abraham's servant told Be·thu'el and Re·bek'ah's brother La'ban why he had come. They both agreed that Re·bek'ah could go with him and marry Isaac. What did Re·bek'ah say when she was asked? She said, 'Yes,' she wanted to go. So the very next day they got on the camels and began the long trip back to Ca'naan.

When they arrived, it was evening time. Re·bek'ah saw a man walking in the field. It was Isaac. He was glad to see Re·bek'ah. His mother Sarah had died just three years before, and he was still sad about this. But now Isaac came to love Re·bek'ah very much, and he was happy again.   Genesis 24:1-67.

THE two boys here are very different, aren't they? Do you know their names? The hunter is E'sau, and the boy taking care of the sheep is Jacob.

E'sau and Jacob were the twin sons of Isaac and Re·bek'ah. The father, Isaac, liked E'sau a lot, because he was a good hunter and would bring home food for the family to eat. But Re·bek'ah loved Jacob most, because he was a quiet, peaceful boy.

Grandfather Abraham was still alive, and we can just imagine how Jacob liked to listen to him talk about Jehovah. Abraham finally died at 175 years of age, when the twins were 15 years old.

When E'sau was 40 years old he married two women from the land of Ca'naan. This made Isaac and Re·bek'ah very sad, because these women did not worship Jehovah.

Then one day something happened that made E'sau very angry with his brother Jacob. The time came when Isaac was

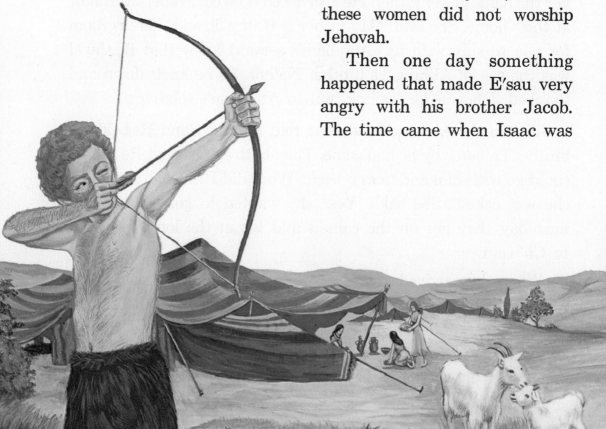

to give a blessing to his older son. Since E'sau was older than Jacob, E'sau expected to receive this blessing. But E'sau had earlier sold the right to receive the blessing to Jacob. Also, when the two boys were born God had said that Jacob would receive the blessing. And this is what happened. Isaac gave the blessing to his son Jacob.

Later, when E'sau learned about this he became angry with Jacob. He was so angry that he said he was going to kill Jacob. When Re·bek'ah heard about this, she was very worried. So she told her husband Isaac: 'It will be just terrible if Jacob also marries one of these women of Ca'naan.'

At that Isaac called his son Jacob and told him: 'Don't marry a woman from Ca'naan. Go instead to the house of your grandfather Be·thu'el in Ha'ran. Marry one of the daughters of his son La'ban.'

Jacob listened to his father, and right away began his long trip to where his relatives lived in Ha'ran.

Genesis 25:5-11, 20-34; 26:34, 35; 27:1-46; 28:1-5; Hebrews 12:16, 17.

DO YOU know who these men are Jacob is talking to? After traveling many days, Jacob met them by a well. They were taking care of their sheep. Jacob asked: 'Where are you from?'

'Ha′ran,' they said.

'Do you know La′ban?' Jacob asked.

'Yes,' they answered. 'Look, here comes his daughter Rachel with his flock of sheep.' Can you see Rachel there coming in the distance?

When Jacob saw Rachel with his uncle La′ban's sheep, he went and rolled the stone away from the well so the sheep could drink. Then Jacob kissed Rachel and told her who he was. She was very excited, and she went home and told her father La′ban.

La′ban was very happy to have Jacob stay with him. And when Jacob asked to marry Rachel, La′ban was

glad. However, he asked Jacob to work in his field seven years for Rachel. Because he loved Rachel so much Jacob did this. But when the time came for the marriage, do you know what happened?

La'ban gave his older daughter Le'ah to Jacob instead of Rachel. When Jacob agreed to work for La'ban seven more years, La'ban also gave him Rachel as his wife. In those times God allowed men to have more than one wife. But now, as the Bible shows, a man should have only one wife.

Genesis 29:1-30.

JUST look at this big family. These are Jacob's 12 sons. And he had daughters too. Do you know the names of any of the children? Let's learn some of them.

Le'ah gave birth to Reu'ben, Sim'e·on, Le'vi and Judah. When Rachel saw that she was not having any children, she was very sad. So she gave her maidservant Bil'hah to Jacob, and Bil'hah had two sons named Dan and Naph'ta·li. Then Le'ah also gave her maidservant Zil'pah to Jacob, and Zil'pah gave birth to Gad and Ash'er. Le'ah finally had two more sons, Is'sa·char and Zeb'u·lun.

At last Rachel was able to have a child. She named him Joseph. Later we will learn a lot more about Joseph, because he became a very important person. These were the 11 sons that were born to Jacob when he lived with Rachel's father La'ban.

Jacob also had some daughters, but the Bible gives the name of only one of them. Her name was Di'nah.

The time came when Jacob decided to leave La'ban and go back to Ca'naan. So he gathered together his big family and his great flocks of sheep and herds of cattle, and began the long trip.

After Jacob and his family had been back in Ca'naan for a while, Rachel gave birth to another son. It happened when they were on a trip. Rachel had a hard time, and she finally died while giving birth. But the little baby boy was all right. Jacob named him Benjamin.

We want to remember the names of the 12 sons of Jacob because the whole nation of Israel came from them. In fact, the 12 tribes of Israel are named after 10 sons of Jacob and two sons of Joseph. Isaac lived for many years after all these boys were born, and it must have made him happy to have so many grandsons. But let's see what happened to his granddaughter Di'nah.

Genesis 29:32-35; 30:1-26; 35:16-19; 37:35.

DINAH GETS INTO TROUBLE

DO YOU see who Di'nah is going to visit? She is going to see some of the girls who live in the land of Ca'naan. Would her father Jacob be happy about this? To help answer this question, try to remember what Abraham and Isaac thought about the women in Ca'naan.

Did Abraham want his son Isaac to marry a girl from Ca'naan? No, he did not. Did Isaac and Re·bek'ah want their son Jacob to marry a Ca'naan·ite girl? No, they did not. Do you know why?

It was because these people in Ca'naan worshiped false gods. They were not good people to have as husbands and wives, and they weren't good people to have as close friends. So we can be sure that Jacob would not be pleased that his daughter was making friends with these Ca'naan·ite girls.

Sure enough, Di'nah got into trouble. Can you see that Ca'naan·ite man in the picture who is looking at Di'nah? His name is She'chem. One day when Di'nah came on a visit, She'chem took Di'nah and forced her to lie down with him. This was wrong, because only married men and women are supposed to lie down together. This bad thing that She'chem did to Di'nah led to a lot more trouble.

When Di'nah's brothers heard about what had happened, they were very angry. Two of them, Sim'e·on and Le'vi, were so angry that they took swords and went into the city and caught the men by surprise. They and their brothers killed She'chem and all the other men. Jacob was angry because his sons did this bad thing.

How did all this trouble get started? It was because Di'nah made friends with people who did not obey God's laws. We will not want to make such friends, will we?   Genesis 34:1-31.

JOSEPH'S BROTHERS HATE HIM

SEE how sad and hopeless the boy is. This is Joseph. His brothers have just sold him to these men who are on their way to Egypt. There Joseph will be made a slave. Why have his half brothers done this bad thing? It is because they are jealous of Joseph.

Their father Jacob liked Joseph very, very much. He showed him favor by having a beautiful long coat made for him. When his 10 older brothers saw how much Jacob loved Joseph, they began to be jealous and to hate Joseph. But there was also another reason why they hated him.

Joseph had two dreams. In both of Joseph's dreams his brothers bowed down to him. When Joseph told his brothers these dreams, their hatred grew even more.

Now one day when Joseph's older brothers are taking care of their father's sheep, Jacob asks Joseph to go and see how they are getting along. When Joseph's brothers see him coming, some of them say: 'Let's kill him!' But Reu'ben, the oldest brother, says: 'No, don't you do that!' Instead they grab Joseph and throw him into a dried-up water hole. Then they sit down to decide what to do with him.

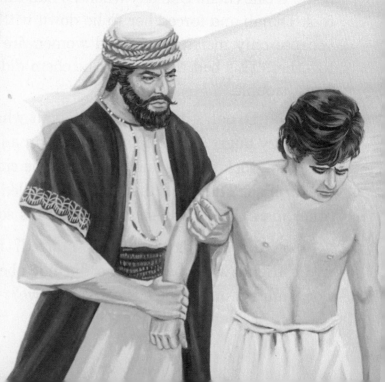

About this time some Ish'ma·el·ite men come along. Judah says to his half brothers: 'Let's sell him to the Ish'ma·el·ites.' And that's what they do. They sell Joseph for 20 pieces of silver. How mean and unkind that was!

What will the brothers tell their father? They kill a goat and again and again dip Joseph's beautiful coat into the goat's blood. Then they take the coat home to their father Jacob and say: 'We found this. Look at it, and see if it is not Joseph's coat.'

Jacob sees that it is. 'A wild animal must have killed Joseph,' he cries. And that is just what Joseph's brothers want their father to think. Jacob is very, very sad. He weeps for many days. But Joseph is not dead. Let's see what happens to him where he is taken.

Genesis 37:1-35.

JOSEPH is only 17 years old when he is taken down to Egypt. There he is sold to a man named Pot′i·phar. Pot′i·phar works for the king of Egypt, who is called Phar′aoh.

Joseph works hard for his master, Pot′i·phar. So when Joseph grows older, Pot′i·phar puts him in charge of his whole house. Why, then, is Joseph here in prison? It is because of Pot′i·phar's wife.

Joseph grows up to be a very good-looking man, and Pot′i·phar's wife wants him to lie down with her. But Joseph knows this is wrong, and he won't do it. Pot′i·phar's wife is very angry. So when her husband comes home, she lies to him and says: 'That bad Joseph tried to lie down with me!' Pot′i·phar believes his wife, and he is very angry with Joseph. So he has him thrown into prison.

The man in charge of the prison soon sees that Joseph is a good man. So he puts him in charge of all the other prisoners. Later Phar′aoh becomes angry with his cupbearer and his baker, and puts them into prison. One night they each have a special dream, but they do not know the meaning of their dreams. The next day Joseph says: 'Tell me your dreams.' And when they do, Joseph, with God's help, explains the meaning of their dreams.

To the cupbearer, Joseph says: 'In three days you will be let out of prison, and you will become Phar′aoh's cupbearer again.' So Joseph adds: 'When you get out, tell Phar′aoh about me, and help me to get out of this place.' But to the baker, Joseph says: 'In just three days Phar′aoh will have your head cut off.'

In three days it happens just as Joseph said. Phar′aoh has the baker's head cut off. The cupbearer, though, is let out of prison and begins to serve the king again. But the cupbearer forgets all about Joseph! He does not tell Phar′aoh about him, and Joseph has to stay in prison.

Genesis 39:1-23; 40:1-23.

TWO years pass, and Joseph is still in prison. The cupbearer has not remembered him. Then one night Phar'aoh has two very special dreams, and he wonders what they mean. Do you see him sleeping there? The next morning Phar'aoh calls his wise men and tells them the things that he has dreamed. But they are not able to tell him the meaning of his dreams.

Now the cupbearer at last remembers Joseph. He says to Phar'aoh: 'When I was in prison there was a man there who could tell the meaning of dreams.' Phar'aoh has Joseph brought out of prison right away.

Phar'aoh tells Joseph his dreams: 'I saw seven fat, beautiful cows. Then I saw seven very thin and bony cows. And the thin ones ate up the fat cows.

'In my second dream I saw seven heads of full, ripe grain growing on one stalk. Then I saw seven thin, dried-out heads of grain.

And the thin heads of grain began to swallow up the seven good heads of grain.'

Joseph says to Phar'aoh: 'The two dreams mean the same thing. The seven fat cows and the seven full heads of grain mean seven years, and the seven thin cows and the seven thin heads of grain mean seven more years. There will be seven years when a lot of food will grow in Egypt. Then there will be seven years when very little food will grow.'

So Joseph tells Phar'aoh: 'Choose a wise man and put him in charge of collecting food during the seven good years. Then the people will not starve during the following seven bad years when very little food will grow.'

Phar'aoh likes the idea. And he chooses Joseph to collect the food, and to store it up. Next to Phar'aoh, Joseph becomes the most important man in Egypt.

Eight years later, during the famine, Joseph sees some men coming. Do you know who they are? Why, they are his 10 older brothers! Their father Jacob has sent them to Egypt because they were running out of food back home in Ca'naan. Joseph recognizes his brothers, but they do not recognize him. Do you know why? It is because Joseph has grown older, and he is dressed in a different kind of clothes.

Joseph remembers that when he was a boy he dreamed about his brothers coming to bow down to him. Do you remember reading about that? So Joseph can see that it is God who has sent him down to Egypt, and for a good reason. What do you think Joseph does? Let's see.

Genesis 41:1-57; 42:1-8; 50:20.

JOSEPH TESTS HIS BROTHERS **24**

JOSEPH wants to know if his 10 older brothers are still mean and unkind. So he says: 'You are spies. You have come to find where our country is weak.'

'No, we are not,' they say. 'We are honest men. We are all brothers. We were 12. But one brother is no more, and the youngest is home with our father.'

Joseph pretends not to believe them. He keeps the brother named Sim'e·on in prison, and lets the others take food and go home. But he tells them: 'When you come back, you must bring your youngest brother with you.'

When they return home to Ca'naan, the brothers tell their father Jacob everything that happened. Jacob is very sad. 'Joseph is no more,' he cries, 'and now Sim'e·on is no more. I will not let you take my youngest son Benjamin.' But when their food begins to run out, Jacob has to let them take Benjamin to Egypt so they can get more food.

Now Joseph sees his brothers coming. He is very happy to see his younger brother Benjamin. Of course, none of them know that this important man is Joseph. Joseph now does something to test his 10 half brothers.

He has his servants fill up all their bags with food. But without letting them know, he also has his special silver cup put into Benjamin's bag. After they all leave and have gone a little distance on the road, Joseph sends his servants after them. When they catch up with them, the servants say: 'Why have you stolen our master's silver cup?'

'We have not stolen his cup,' the brothers all say. 'If you find the cup with any one of us, let that person be killed.'

So the servants search through all the bags, and they find the cup in Benjamin's bag, just as you see here. The servants say: 'The rest of you can go, but Benjamin must come with us.' What will the 10 half brothers do now?

They all return with Benjamin to Joseph's house. Joseph tells his brothers: 'You can all go home, but Benjamin must stay here as my slave.'

Judah now speaks up, and says: 'If I go back home without the boy, my father will die because he loves him very much. So please, keep me here as your slave, but let the boy go home.'

Joseph can see that his brothers have changed. They are not mean and unkind anymore. Let's find out what Joseph does now.

Genesis 42:9-38; 43:1-34; 44:1-34.

JOSEPH cannot control his feelings any longer. He tells all his servants to leave the room. When he is alone with his brothers, Joseph begins to cry. We can imagine how surprised his brothers are, because they do not know why he is crying. Finally he says: 'I am Joseph. Is my father still alive?'

His brothers are so surprised that they can't speak. They are afraid. But Joseph says: 'Please come closer.' When they do, he says: 'I am your brother Joseph, whom you sold into Egypt.'

Joseph continues to speak in a kind way: 'Do not blame yourselves because you sold me here. It was really God who sent me to Egypt to save people's lives. Phar'aoh has made me the ruler of the whole country. So now hurry back to my father and tell him this. And tell him to come and live here.'

Then Joseph throws his arms around his brothers, and he hugs and kisses them all. When Phar'aoh hears that Joseph's brothers have come, he tells Joseph: 'Let them take wagons and go get their father and their families and come back here. I will give them the best land in all Egypt.'

That is what they did. Here you can see Joseph meeting his father when he came to Egypt with his whole family.

Jacob's family had become very big. Altogether there were 70 when they moved to Egypt, counting Jacob and his children and grandchildren. But there were also the wives, and probably many servants too. These all settled in Egypt. They were called Israelites, because God had changed the name of Jacob to Israel. The Israelites became a very special people to God, as we will see later.

Genesis 45:1-28; 46:1-27.

DO YOU feel sorry for this sick man? His name is Job, and the woman is his wife. Do you know what she is saying to Job? 'Curse God and die.' Let's see why she would ever say a thing like that, and why Job suffered so much.

Job was a faithful man who obeyed Jehovah. He lived in the land of Uz, not far from Ca'naan. Jehovah loved Job very much, but there was someone who hated him. Do you know who?

It was Satan the Devil. Remember, Satan is the bad angel who hates Jehovah. He was able to get Adam and Eve to disobey Jehovah, and he thought he could get everybody else to disobey Jehovah too. But was he able to? No. Just think of the many faithful men and women we have learned about. How many can you name?

After Jacob and Joseph died in Egypt, Job was the person most faithful to Jehovah in all the earth. Jehovah wanted to let Satan know that he could not get everyone to be bad, so he said: 'Look at Job. See how faithful he is to me.'

'He is faithful,' Satan argued, 'because you bless him and he has many good things. But if you take these away, he will curse you.'

So Jehovah said: 'Go ahead. Take them away. Do all the bad

things you want to Job. We will see if he curses me. Only be sure that you do not kill him.'

First, Satan had men steal Job's cattle and camels, and his sheep were killed. Then he killed his 10 sons and daughters in a storm. Next, Satan struck Job with this terrible sickness. Job suffered very much. That is why Job's wife told him: 'Curse God and die.' But Job would not do it. Also, three false friends came and told him he had lived a bad life. But Job kept faithful.

This made Jehovah very happy, and afterward he blessed Job, as you can see in the picture. He healed him from his sickness. Job had 10 more beautiful children, and twice as many cattle, sheep and camels as he had before.

Will you always be faithful to Jehovah like Job? If you are, God will bless you too. You will be able to live forever when the whole earth will be made just as pretty as the garden of Eden.

Job 1:1-22; 2:1-13; 42:10-17.

A BAD KING RULES EGYPT

THE men here are forcing the people to work. Look at the man who is hitting one of the workers with a whip! The workers are of the family of Jacob, and are called Israelites. And the men forcing them to work are Egyptians. The Israelites have become slaves of the Egyptians. How did this happen?

For many years Jacob's big family lived at peace in Egypt. Joseph, who was the most important man in Egypt next to Phar'aoh the king, took care of them. But then Joseph died. And a new Phar'aoh, who did not like the Israelites, became king in Egypt.

So this bad Phar'aoh made the Israelites slaves. And he put men in charge of them who were mean and cruel. They forced

the Israelites to work very hard building cities for Phar'aoh. But still the Israelites kept growing in numbers. After a while the Egyptians became afraid that the Israelites would become too many and too strong.

Do you know what Phar'aoh did? He spoke to the women who helped the Israelite mothers when they gave birth to their babies, and said: 'You must kill every baby boy that is born.' But these were good women, and they would not kill the babies.

So Phar'aoh gave this command to all his people: 'Take the baby Israelite boys and kill them. Only let the baby girls live.' Wasn't that a terrible thing to command? Let's see how one of the baby boys was saved. Exodus 1:6-22.

HOW BABY MOSES WAS SAVED

SEE the little baby crying, and holding onto the lady's finger. This is Moses. Do you know who the pretty lady is? She is an Egyptian princess, Phar'aoh's own daughter.

Moses' mother hid her baby until he was three months old, because she didn't want him to be killed by the Egyptians. But she knew that Moses might be found, so this is what she did to save him.

She took a basket and fixed it so that no water would leak in. Then she put Moses into it, and placed the basket in the tall grass along the Nile River. Moses' sister, Mir'i·am, was told to stand nearby and see what would happen.

Soon Phar'aoh's daughter came down to the Nile River to bathe. Suddenly she saw the basket in the tall grass. She called to one of her servant girls: 'Go get that basket for me.' When the princess opened the basket, what a beautiful baby she saw! Little Moses was crying, and the princess felt sorry for him. She didn't want to have him killed.

Then Mir'i·am came up. You can see her in the picture. Mir'i·am asked Phar'aoh's daughter: 'Shall I go and call an Israelite woman to nurse the baby for you?'

'Please do,' the princess said.

So Mir'i·am ran quickly to tell her mother. When Moses' mother came to the princess, the princess said: 'Take this baby and nurse him for me, and I will pay you.'

So Moses' mother took care of her own child. Later when Moses was old enough, she took him to Phar'aoh's daughter, who adopted him as her own son. That is how Moses came to grow up in the house of Phar'aoh.

Exodus 2:1-10.

WHY MOSES RAN AWAY

LOOK at Moses running away from Egypt. Can you see the men chasing him? Do you know why they want to kill Moses? Let's see if we can find out.

Moses grew up in the house of Phar'aoh, the ruler of Egypt. He became a very wise and great man. Moses knew that he was not an Egyptian, but that his real parents were Israelite slaves.

One day, when he was 40 years old, Moses decided to go to see how his people were getting along. It was terrible how they were being treated. He saw an Egyptian beating an Israelite slave. Moses looked around, and when he didn't see anybody watching, he hit the Egyptian, and the Egyptian died. Then Moses hid his body in the sand.

The next day Moses went out to see his people again. He thought he could help them so they wouldn't have to be slaves anymore. But he saw two Israelite men fighting, so Moses said to the one who was in the wrong: 'Why are you beating up your brother?'

The man said: 'Who made you our ruler and judge? Are you going to kill me just as you killed that Egyptian?'

Moses now became afraid. He knew that people had found out what he had done to the Egyptian. Even Phar'aoh heard about it, and he sent men to kill Moses. That is why Moses had to run away from Egypt.

When Moses left Egypt, he went far away to the land of Mid'i·an. There he met the family of Jeth'ro, and married one of his daughters named Zip·po'rah. Moses became a shepherd and took care of Jeth'ro's sheep. For 40 years he lived in the land of Mid'i·an. He was now 80 years of age. Then one day, while Moses was taking care of Jethro's sheep, an amazing thing happened that changed Moses' whole life. Turn the page, and let's see what this amazing thing is.   Exodus 2:11-25; Acts 7:22-29.

THE BURNING BUSH

MOSES had come all the way to the mountain of Ho'reb to find grass for his sheep. Here he saw a bush on fire, but it wasn't burning up!

'This is strange,' Moses thought. 'I will go closer and get a better look.' When he did, a voice came from the bush, saying: 'Do not come any closer. Take off your sandals, because you are standing on holy ground.' It was God speaking by means of an angel, so Moses covered his face.

God then said: 'I have seen the suffering of my people in Egypt. So I am going to free them, and you are the one I am sending to lead my people out of Egypt.' Jehovah was going to bring his people to the beautiful land of Ca'naan.

But Moses said: 'I am nobody. How can I do this? But suppose I do go. The Israelites will say to me, "Who sent you?" Then what shall I say?'

'This is what you are to say,' God answered. ' "JEHOVAH the God of Abraham, the God of Isaac

and the God of Jacob has sent me to you."' And Jehovah added: 'This is my name forever.'

'But suppose they don't believe me when I say that you sent me,' Moses replied.

'What is in your hand?' God asked.

Moses answered: 'A stick.'

'Throw it on the ground,' God said. And when Moses did, the stick became a snake. Jehovah then showed Moses another miracle. He said: 'Put your hand inside your robe.' Moses did, and when he took his hand out, it was white like snow! The hand looked as if it had the bad sickness called leprosy. Next Jehovah gave Moses power to do a third miracle. Finally he said: 'When you do these miracles the Israelites will believe that I sent you.'

After that Moses went home and said to Jeth'ro: 'Please let me go back to my relatives in Egypt to see how they are.' So Jeth'ro said good-bye to Moses, and Moses began his trip back to Egypt. Exodus 3:1-22; 4:1-20.

WHEN Moses returned to Egypt, he told his brother Aaron all about the miracles. And when Moses and Aaron showed the Israelites these miracles, the people all believed that Jehovah was with them.

Then Moses and Aaron went to see Phar'aoh. They told him: 'Jehovah the God of Israel says, "Let my people go for three days, so they can worship me in the wilderness."' But Phar'aoh answered: 'I don't believe in Jehovah. And I'm not going to let Israel go.'

Phar'aoh was angry, because the people wanted time off from work to worship Jehovah. So he forced them to work even harder. The Israelites blamed Moses for how badly they were treated, and Moses felt sad. But Jehovah told him not to worry. 'I will make Phar'aoh let my people go,' Jehovah said.

Moses and Aaron went to see Phar'aoh again. This time they did a miracle. Aaron threw down his stick, and it became a big snake. But Phar'aoh's wise men also threw down sticks, and snakes appeared. But, look! Aaron's snake is eating up the snakes of the wise men. Still Phar'aoh would not let the Israelites go.

So the time came for Jehovah to teach Phar'aoh a lesson. Do you know how he did it? It was by bringing 10 plagues, or great troubles, on Egypt.

After many of the plagues, Phar'aoh sent for Moses, and said: 'Stop the plague, and I will let Israel go.' But when the plague would stop, Phar'aoh would change his mind. He would not let the people go. But, finally, after the 10th plague, Phar'aoh sent the Israelites away.

Do you know each of the 10 plagues? Turn the page and let's learn about them.   Exodus 4:27-31; 5:1-23; 6:1-13, 26-30; 7:1-13.

LOOK at the pictures. Each one shows a plague that Jehovah brought on Egypt. In the first picture you can see Aaron hitting the Nile River with his stick. When he did, the water in the river turned to blood. The fish died, and the river began to stink.

Next, Jehovah caused frogs to come up out of the Nile River. They were everywhere—in the ovens, the baking pans, in people's beds—everywhere. When the frogs died the Egyptians piled them up in great heaps, and the land stank with them.

Then Aaron hit the ground with his stick, and the dust turned into gnats. These are small flying bugs that bite. The gnats were the third plague on the land of Egypt.

The rest of the plagues hurt only the Egyptians, not the Israelites. The fourth was a plague of big flies that swarmed into the houses of all the Egyptians. The fifth plague was on the animals. Many of the cattle and sheep and goats of the Egyptians died.

Next, Moses and Aaron took some ashes and threw them into the air.

They caused bad sores on the people and the animals. This was the sixth plague.

After that Moses raised his hand toward the sky, and Jehovah sent thunder and hail. It was the worst hailstorm that Egypt ever had.

The eighth plague was a large swarm of locusts. Never before that time or since have there been so many locusts. They ate everything that the hail had not destroyed.

The ninth plague was of darkness. For three days thick darkness covered the land, but the Israelites had light where they were living.

Finally, God told his people to sprinkle the blood of a young goat or a young sheep on their doorposts. Then God's angel passed over Egypt. When the angel saw the blood, he did not kill anyone in that house. But in all the houses where there was no blood on the doorposts, God's angel killed the firstborn ones of both man and animals. This was the 10th plague.

After this last plague, Phar'aoh told the Israelites to leave. God's people were all ready to go, and that very night they started their march out of Egypt.   Exodus chapters 7 to 12.

LOOK at what is happening! That is Moses with his stick stretched out over the Red Sea. Those with him safely on the other side are the Israelites. But Phar'aoh and all his army are being drowned in the sea. Let's see how this came about.

As we learned, Phar'aoh told the Israelites to leave Egypt after God brought the 10th plague on the Egyptians. About 600,000 Israelite men left, as well as many women and children. Also, a large number of other people, who had become believers in Jehovah, left with the Israelites. They all took their sheep and goats and cattle with them.

Before they left, the Israelites asked the Egyptians for clothes and for things made of gold and silver. The Egyptians were very

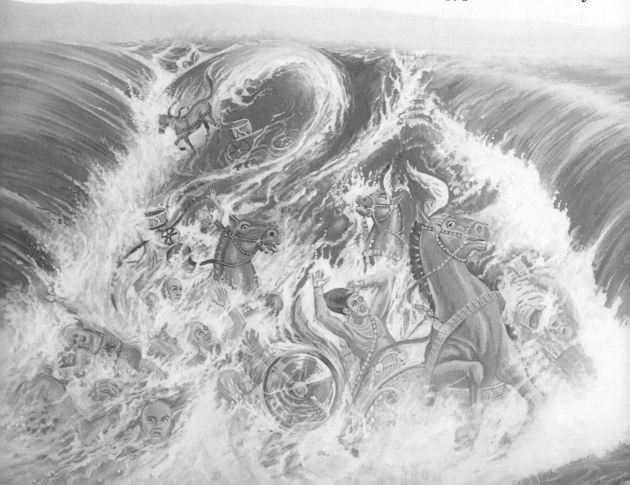

much afraid, because of that last plague upon them. So they gave the Israelites everything they asked for.

After a few days the Israelites came to the Red Sea. There they rested. In the meantime, Phar'aoh and his men began to feel sorry that they had sent the Israelites away. 'We have let our slaves go!' they said.

So Phar'aoh changed his mind once more. He quickly got his war chariot and his army ready. Then he began to chase after the Israelites with 600 special chariots, as well as all the other chariots of Egypt.

When the Israelites saw Phar'aoh and his army coming after them, they were very much afraid. There was no way to flee.

The Red Sea was on one side of them, and here the Egyptians were coming from the other direction. But Jehovah put a cloud between his people and the Egyptians. So the Egyptians were not able to see the Israelites to attack them.

Jehovah then told Moses to stretch his stick out over the Red Sea. When he did, Jehovah caused a strong east wind to blow. The waters of the sea were parted, and the waters were held up on both sides.

Then the Israelites began to march through the sea on dry ground. It took hours for the millions of people with all their animals to get safely through the sea to the other side. Finally the Egyptians were able to see the Israelites again. Their slaves were getting away! So they rushed into the sea after them.

When they did, God caused the wheels of their chariots to fall off. The Egyptians became very much afraid and began to cry out: 'Jehovah is fighting for the Israelites against us. Let's get out of here!' But it was too late.

This is when Jehovah told Moses to stretch his stick out over the Red Sea, as you saw in the picture. And when Moses did, the walls of water began to come back and cover the Egyptians and their chariots. The whole army had followed the Israelites into the sea. And not one of the Egyptians got out alive!

How happy all God's people were to be saved! The men sang a song of thanks to Jehovah, saying: 'Jehovah has won a glorious victory. He has thrown the horses and their riders into the sea.' Moses' sister Mir′i·am took her tambourine, and all the women followed her with their tambourines. And as they danced with joy, they sang the same song as the men were singing: 'Jehovah has won a glorious victory. He has thrown the horses and their riders into the sea.'

Exodus chapters 12 to 15.

PART 3

Deliverance from Egypt to Israel's First King

Moses led the Israelites from captivity in Egypt to Mount Sinai, where God gave them his laws. Later, Moses sent 12 men to spy out the land of Canaan. But 10 of them returned with a bad report. They caused the people to want to go back to Egypt. For their lack of faith, God punished the Israelites by having them wander for 40 years in the wilderness.

Finally, Joshua was chosen to lead the Israelites into the land of Canaan. To help them take the land, Jehovah caused miracles to happen. He made the Jordan River stop flowing, the walls of Jericho to fall down, and the sun to stand still for a whole day. After six years, the land was taken from the Canaanites.

Beginning with Joshua, Israel was ruled for 356 years by judges. We learn about many of them, including Barak, Gideon, Jephthah, Samson and Samuel. We also read about such women as Rahab, Deborah, Jael, Ruth, Naomi and Delilah. In all, Part THREE covers 396 years of history.

A NEW KIND OF FOOD

CAN you tell what the people are picking up off the ground? It is like frost. It is white, and it is thin and flaky. But it's not frost; it's something to eat.

It has been only about a month since the Israelites left Egypt. They are in the wilderness. Little food grows here, and so the people complain, saying: 'We wish that Jehovah had killed us in Egypt. At least there we had all the food that we wanted.'

So Jehovah says: 'I am going to cause food to rain down from the sky.' And this is what Jehovah does. The next morning when the Israelites see this white stuff that has fallen, they ask one another: 'What is it?'

Moses says: 'This is the food that Jehovah has given you to eat.' The people call it MANNA. It tastes like thin cakes made with honey.

'You are to pick up as much as each person can eat,' Moses tells the people. So each morning this is what they do. Then, when the sun gets hot, the manna left on the ground melts.

Moses also says: 'No one is to save any of the manna over to the next day.' But some of the people don't listen. Do you know what happens? The next morning the manna that they have saved is full of worms, and it begins to stink!

There is one day of the week, however, that Jehovah tells the people to gather twice as much manna. This is the sixth day. And Jehovah says to save some of it over to the next day, because he will not cause any to fall on the seventh day. When they save the manna over to the seventh day, it doesn't get full of worms and it doesn't stink! This is another miracle!

All the years that the Israelites are in the wilderness Jehovah feeds them with manna. Exodus 16:1-36; Numbers 11:7-9; Joshua 5:10-12.

JEHOVAH GIVES 35 HIS LAWS

לא תרצח | אנכי־יהוה
לא תנאף | לא יהיה
לא תגנב | לא תשא
לא תענה | זכור את
לא תחמד | כבד את

ABOUT two months after they leave Egypt, the Israelites come to Mount Si'nai, which is also called Ho'reb. This is the same place where Jehovah spoke to Moses from the burning bush. The people camp here and stay for a while.

As the people wait below, Moses climbs the mountain. Up there on top of the mountain, Jehovah tells Moses that He wants the Israelites to obey Him and to become His special people. When Moses comes down, he tells the Israelites what Jehovah has said. And the people say that they will obey Jehovah, because they want to be his people.

Jehovah now does a strange thing. He makes the top of the mountain smoke, and causes loud thunder. He also speaks to the people: 'I am Jehovah your God who brought you out of Egypt.' Then he commands: 'You must not worship any other gods except me.'

God gives the Israelites nine more commandments, or laws. The people are very afraid. They tell Moses: 'You speak to us, because we are afraid that if God speaks to us we may die.'

Later Jehovah tells Moses: 'Come up to me in the mountain. I will give you two flat stones on which I have written the laws that I want the people to keep.' So Moses again goes up into the mountain. For 40 days and nights he stays there.

God has many, many laws for his people. Moses writes these laws down. God also gives Moses the two flat stones. On these, God himself has written the 10 laws that he spoke to all the people. They are called the Ten Commandments.

The Ten Commandments are important laws. But so are the many other laws that God gives the Israelites. One of these laws is: 'You must love Jehovah your God with your whole heart, your whole mind, your whole soul and your whole strength.' And another is: 'You must love your neighbor as yourself.' God's Son, Jesus Christ, said that these are the two greatest laws that Jehovah gave to his people Israel. Later we will learn many things about God's Son and his teachings.

Exodus 19:1-25; 20:1-21; 24:12-18; 31:18; Deuteronomy 6:4-6; Leviticus 19:18; Matthew 22:36-40.

OH, OH! What are the people doing now? They are praying to a calf! Why are they doing this?

When Moses stays up on the mountain for a long time, the people say: 'We do not know what has happened to Moses. So let's make a god to lead us out of this land.'

'All right,' Moses' brother Aaron says. 'Take off your gold earrings, and bring them to me.' When the people do so, Aaron melts them down and makes a golden calf. And the people say:

'This is our God, who led us out of Egypt!' Then the Israelites have a big party, and worship the golden calf.

When Jehovah sees this, he is very angry. So he says to Moses: 'Hurry and go down. The people are acting very badly. They have forgotten my laws and are bowing down to a golden calf.'

Moses hurries down the mountain. And when he gets close, this is what he sees. The people are singing and dancing around the golden calf! Moses is so angry that he throws down the two flat stones with the laws on them, and they break into many, many pieces. He then takes the golden calf and melts it down. Then he grinds it into powder.

The people have done a very bad thing. So Moses tells some of the men to take their swords. 'The bad people who worshiped the golden calf must die,' Moses says. And so the men strike dead 3,000 people! Doesn't this show that we need to be careful to worship only Jehovah, and not any false gods? Exodus 32:1-35.

DO YOU know what this building is? It is a special tent for worshiping Jehovah. It is also called the tabernacle. The people

finished building it one year after they left Egypt. Do you know whose idea it was to build it?

It was Jehovah's idea. While Moses was up on Mount Si'nai, Jehovah told him how to build it. He said to make it so that it could easily be taken apart. In this way the parts could be carried to another place, and there be put together again. So when the Israelites moved from place to place in the wilderness, they carried the tent with them.

If you look inside the small room at the end of the tent, you can see a box, or chest. This is called the ark of the covenant. It had two angels or cherubs made of gold, one on each end. God again wrote the Ten Commandments on two flat stones, because Moses had broken the first ones. And these stones were kept inside the ark of the covenant. Also, a jar of manna was kept inside it. Do you remember what manna is?

Moses' brother Aaron is the one that Jehovah chooses to be the high priest. He leads the people in worshiping Jehovah. And his sons are priests too.

Now look at the bigger room of the tent. It is twice as big as the small room. Do you see the box, or little chest, with some smoke going up from it? This is the altar where the priests burn some sweet-smelling stuff called incense. Then there is the lampstand that has seven lamps. And the third thing in the room is a table. On it are kept 12 loaves of bread.

In the yard of the tabernacle there is a big bowl, or basin, that is filled with water. The priests use it for washing. There is also the big altar. Here the dead animals are burned as an offering to Jehovah. The tent is right in the middle of the camp, and the Israelites live in their tents all around it.

Exodus 25:8-40; 26:1-37; 27:1-8; 28:1; 30:1-10, 17-21; 34:1, 2; Hebrews 9:1-5.

LOOK at the fruit these men are carrying. See how big that bunch of grapes is. It takes two men to carry it on a pole. And see the figs and the pomegranates. Where did this beautiful fruit come from? From the land of Ca'naan. Remember, Ca'naan is where Abraham, Isaac and Jacob once lived. But because of the

famine there Jacob, with his family, moved to Egypt. Now, about 216 years later, Moses is leading the Israelites back to Ca'naan. They have come to a place in the wilderness called Ka'desh.

Bad people live in the land of Ca'naan. So Moses sends out 12 spies, and tells them: 'Find out how many people live there, and how strong they are. Find out if the ground is good for growing things. And be sure to bring back some of the fruit.'

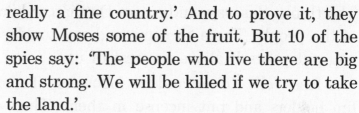

When the spies come back to Ka'desh, they tell Moses: 'It is really a fine country.' And to prove it, they show Moses some of the fruit. But 10 of the spies say: 'The people who live there are big and strong. We will be killed if we try to take the land.'

The Israelites are afraid when they hear this. 'It would have been better to die in Egypt or even here in the wilderness,' they say. 'We will be killed in battle, and our wives and children will be captured. Let's choose a new leader in place of Moses, and go back to Egypt!'

But two of the spies trust in Jehovah, and try to calm the people. Their names are Joshua and Ca'leb. They say: 'Don't be afraid. Jehovah is with us. It will be easy to take the land.' But the people don't listen. They even want to kill Joshua and Ca'leb.

This makes Jehovah very angry, and he tells Moses: 'None of the people from 20 years of age and over will go into the land of Ca'naan. They have seen the miracles that I did in Egypt and in the wilderness, but still they don't trust me. So they will wander in the wilderness for 40 years until the last person dies. Only Joshua and Ca'leb will go into the land of Ca'naan.'

Numbers 13:1-33; 14:1-38.

AARON'S ROD GROWS FLOWERS

SEE the flowers and ripe almonds growing from this rod, or stick. This is the rod of Aaron. These flowers and the ripe fruit grew out of Aaron's rod in just one night! Let's see why.

The Israelites have been wandering in the wilderness for a while now. Some of the people don't think Moses should be the leader, or that Aaron should be the high priest. Ko'rah is one who thinks this way, and so are Da'than, A·bi'ram and 250 leaders of the people. These all come and say to Moses: 'Why is it that you put yourself above the rest of us?'

Moses tells Ko'rah and his followers: 'Tomorrow morning take fire holders and put incense in them. Then come to Jehovah's tabernacle. We will see whom Jehovah will choose.'

The next day Ko'rah and his 250 followers come to the tabernacle. Many others come along to support these men. Jehovah is very angry. 'Get away from the tents of these bad men,' Moses says. 'Don't touch anything that belongs to them.' The people listen, and move away from the tents of Ko'rah, Da'than and A·bi'ram.

Then Moses says: 'By this you will know whom Jehovah has chosen. The ground will open and swallow up these bad men.'

As soon as Moses stops talking, the ground opens. Ko'rah's tent and belongings and Da'than and A·bi'ram and those with them go down, and the ground closes over them. When the people hear the cries of those falling into the ground, they shout: 'Run! The earth might swallow us too!'

Ko'rah and his 250 followers are still near the tabernacle. So Jehovah sends fire, and all of them are burned up. Then Jehovah tells Aaron's son E·le·a'zar to take the fire holders of the dead men and to make a thin covering for the altar with them. This altar covering is to serve as a warning to the Israelites that no one besides Aaron and his sons should act as priests for Jehovah.

But Jehovah wants to make very clear that it is Aaron and his sons whom he has chosen to be priests. So he tells Moses: 'Have a leader of each tribe of Israel bring his rod. For the tribe of Levi, have Aaron bring his rod. Then put each of these rods in the tabernacle in front of the ark of the covenant. The rod of the man that I have chosen as priest will grow flowers.'

When Moses looks the next morning, why, Aaron's rod has these flowers and ripe almonds growing out of it! So do you see now why Jehovah caused Aaron's rod to grow flowers?

Numbers 16:1-49; 17:1-11; 26:10.

Y EAR after year passes—10 years, 20 years, 30 years, 39 years! And the Israelites are still in the wilderness. But all these years Jehovah takes care of his people. He feeds them with manna. He leads them during the day with a pillar of cloud, and by night with a pillar of fire. And all during these years their clothes don't wear out and their feet don't get sore.

It is now the first month of the 40th year since leaving Egypt. The Israelites again camp at Ka'desh. This is where they were when the 12 spies were sent to spy out the land of Ca'naan nearly 40 years before. Moses' sister Mir'i·am dies at Ka'desh. And as before, there is trouble here.

The people can't find any water. So they complain to Moses: 'It would have been better if we had died. Why did you bring us out of Egypt into this terrible place where nothing will grow? There are no grain, no figs, no grapes, no pomegranates. There isn't even any water to drink.'

When Moses and Aaron go to the tabernacle to pray, Jehovah tells Moses: 'Gather the people together. Then in front of them all speak to that rock over there. Enough water will come out of it for the people and all their animals.'

So Moses gathers the people, and says: 'Listen, you who have no trust in God! Do Aaron and I have to get water out of this rock for you?' Then Moses strikes the rock twice with a stick, and a great stream of water comes pouring out of the rock. There is enough water for all the people and animals to drink.

But Jehovah is angry with Moses and Aaron. Do you know why? It is because Moses and Aaron said that *they* were going to bring water from the rock. But really Jehovah did it. And because Moses and Aaron didn't tell the truth about this, Jehovah says that he is going to punish them. 'You will not lead my people into Ca'naan,' he says.

Soon the Israelites leave Ka'desh. After a short while they come to Mount Hor. Here, up on top of the mountain, Aaron dies. He is 123 years of age at the time of his death. The Israelites are very sad, and so for 30 days all the people weep for Aaron. His son E·le·a'zar becomes the next high priest of the nation of Israel.

Numbers 20:1-13, 22-29; Deuteronomy 29:5.

DOES that look like a real snake wrapped around the pole? It isn't. The snake is made of copper. Jehovah told Moses to put it up on the pole so that the people could look at it and keep alive. But the other snakes on the ground are real. They have bitten the people and made them sick. Do you know why?

It is because the Israelites have spoken against God and Moses. They complain: 'Why did you bring us out of Egypt to die in this wilderness? There is no food or water here. And we can't stand to eat this manna anymore.'

But the manna is good food. By a miracle Jehovah has given it to them. And by a miracle he has given them water too. But the people aren't thankful for the way God has taken care of them. So Jehovah sends these poisonous snakes to punish the Israelites. The snakes bite them, and many of them die.

Finally the people come to Moses and say: 'We have sinned, because we have spoken against Jehovah and you. Now pray to Jehovah to take these snakes away.'

So Moses prays for the people. And Jehovah tells Moses to make this copper snake. He says to put it on a pole, and that anyone who is bitten should look at it. Moses does just what God says. And the people who were bitten look at the copper snake and they get well again.

There is a lesson to learn from this. All of us are, in a way, like those Israelites who were bitten by those snakes. We are all in a dying condition. Look around, and you will see that people grow old, get sick, and die. This is because the first man and woman, Adam and Eve, turned away from Jehovah, and we are all their children. But Jehovah has made a way so we can live forever.

Jehovah sent his Son, Jesus Christ, to earth. Jesus was hung on a stake, because many people thought he was bad. But Jehovah gave Jesus to save us. If we look to him, if we follow him, then we can have everlasting life. But we will learn more about this later. Numbers 21:4-9; John 3:14, 15.

A DONKEY TALKS

HAVE you ever heard of a donkey's talking? 'No,' you may say. 'Animals can't talk.' But the Bible tells about a donkey that did. Let's see how it happened.

The Israelites are almost ready to go into the land of Ca'naan. Ba'lak, the king of Mo'ab, is afraid of the Israelites. So he sends for a smart man named Ba'laam to come to curse the Israelites. Ba'lak promises to give Ba'laam a lot of money, so Ba'laam gets on his donkey and starts on his way to see Ba'lak.

Jehovah does not want Ba'laam to curse His people. So he sends an angel with a long sword to stand in the road to stop Ba'laam. Ba'laam can't see the angel, but his donkey does. So the donkey keeps trying to turn away from the angel, and finally just lies down on the road. Ba'laam is very angry, and beats his donkey with a stick.

Then Jehovah causes Ba'laam to hear his

donkey speak to him. 'What have I done to you so that you should beat me?' asks the donkey.

'You have made me look like a fool,' Ba'laam says. 'If I had a sword I would kill you!'

'Have I ever treated you like this before?' the donkey asks.

'No,' Ba'laam answers.

Then Jehovah lets Ba'laam see the angel with the sword standing on the road. The angel says: 'Why have you beaten your donkey? I have come to block your way, because you should not be going to curse Israel. If your donkey had not turned away from me, I would have struck you dead, but I would not have hurt your donkey.'

Ba'laam says: 'I have sinned. I did not know that you were standing on the road.' The angel lets Ba'laam go, and Ba'laam goes on to see Ba'lak. He still tries to curse Israel, but, instead, Jehovah makes him bless Israel three times. Numbers 21:21-35; 22:1-40; 23:1-30; 24:1-25.

MOSES wants to go into Ca'naan with the Israelites. So he asks: 'Let me cross the Jordan River, Jehovah, and see the good land.' But Jehovah says: 'That's enough! Don't mention this again!' Do you know why Jehovah said that?

It is because of what happened when

Moses struck the rock. Remember, he and Aaron did not honor Jehovah. They didn't tell the people that it was Jehovah who was bringing water from the rock. For this reason Jehovah said that he would not let them go into Ca'naan.

So a few months after Aaron dies, Jehovah tells Moses: 'Take Joshua, and stand him in front of E·le·a'zar the priest and the people. And there before them all, tell everybody that Joshua is the new leader.' Moses does just what Jehovah says, as you can see in the picture.

Then Jehovah tells Joshua: 'Be strong, and do not be afraid. You will lead the Israelites into the land of Ca'naan that I have promised them, and I will be with you.'

Later Jehovah tells Moses to climb high up to the top of Mount Ne'bo in the land of Mo'ab. From up there Moses can look across the Jordan River and see the beautiful land of Ca'naan. Jehovah says: 'This is the land that I promised to give to the children of Abraham, Isaac and Jacob. I have let you see it, but

I will not let you go into it.'

There on top of Mount Ne'bo Moses dies. He was 120 years of age. He was still strong, and his eyesight was still good. The people are very sad and cry because Moses is dead. But they are happy to have Joshua as their new leader.

Numbers 27:12-23;
Deuteronomy 3:23-29; 31:1-8,
14-23; 32:45-52; 34:1-12.

RAHAB HIDES THE SPIES

THESE men are in trouble. They must get away, or they will be killed. They are Israelite spies, and the woman helping them is Ra'hab. Ra'hab lives here in a house on the wall of the city of Jer'i·cho. Let's find out why these men are in trouble.

The Israelites are ready to cross the Jordan River into the land of Ca'naan. But before they do, Joshua sends out the two spies. He tells them: 'Go take a look at the land and the city of Jer'i·cho.'

When the spies come into Jer'i·cho, they go to the house of Ra'hab. But somebody tells the king of Jer'i·cho: 'Two Israelites came in here tonight to spy out the land.' When he hears this, the king sends men to Ra'hab, and they command her: 'The men that you have in your house, bring them out!' But Ra'hab has hidden the spies on her roof. So she says: 'Some men did come to my house, but I don't know where they were from. They left just as it was getting dark, before the city gate was closed. If you hurry, you can catch them!' And so the men go chasing after them.

After they leave, Ra'hab hurries up to the roof. 'I know that Jehovah will give you this land,' she tells the spies. 'We heard how he dried up the Red Sea when you were leaving Egypt, and how you killed the kings Si'hon and Og. I have been kind to you, so promise me, please, that you will be kind to me. Save my father and mother, and my brothers and sisters.'

The spies promise that they will, but Ra'hab must do something. 'Take this red cord and tie it in your window,' the spies say, 'and gather all your relatives into your house with you. And when we all return to take Jer'i·cho, we will see this cord in your window and will not kill anyone in your house.' When the spies go back to Joshua, they tell him everything that happened.

Joshua 2:1-24; Hebrews 11:31.

CROSSING THE JORDAN RIVER

LOOK! the Israelites are crossing the Jordan River! But where is the water? Because lots of rain falls at that time of year, the river was very full just a few minutes before. But now the water is all gone! And the Israelites are going across on dry land just as they did at the Red Sea! Where did all the water go? Let's see.

When the time came for the Israelites to cross the Jordan River, this is what Jehovah had Joshua tell the people: 'The priests should take the ark of the covenant and go ahead of us. When they put their feet into the waters of the Jordan River, then the waters will stop running.'

So the priests pick up the ark of the covenant, and carry it ahead of the people. When they come to the Jordan, the priests step right into the water. It is running very strong and deep. But as soon as their feet touch the water, the water begins to stop running! It is a miracle! Upstream Jehovah has dammed up the waters. So, soon there is no more water in the river!

The priests who are carrying the ark of the covenant go right out into the middle of the dry river. Can you see them in the picture? As they stand there, all the Israelites walk right across the Jordan River on dry land!

When everyone has gone across, Jehovah has Joshua tell 12 strong men: 'Go into the river where the priests are standing with the ark of the covenant. Pick up 12 stones, and stack them where you all stay tonight. Then, in the future, when your children ask what these stones mean, you should tell them that the waters stopped running when Jehovah's ark of the covenant crossed the Jordan. The stones will remind you of this miracle!' Joshua also sets up 12 stones where the priests had stood in the riverbed.

At last Joshua tells the priests carrying the ark of the covenant: 'Go up out of the Jordan.' And as soon as they do, the river begins running once more.

Joshua 3:1-17; 4:1-18.

WHAT'S making these walls of Jer′i·cho fall? It looks as if a big bomb has hit them. But in those days they didn't have bombs; they didn't even have guns. It is another miracle of Jehovah! Let's learn how it happened.

Listen to what Jehovah tells Joshua: 'You and your fighting men are to march around the city. March around it once each

day for six days. Carry the ark of the covenant with you. Seven priests should walk ahead of it and blow their horns.

'On the seventh day you should march around the city *seven* times. Then give a long sound on the horns, and have everyone shout with a great war cry. And the walls will fall down flat!'

Joshua and the people do what Jehovah says. While they march, everyone is silent. No one speaks a word. All that can be heard is the sound of the horns and the marching feet. The enemies of God's people in Jer'i·cho must have been afraid. Can you see that red cord hanging from a window? Whose window is that? Yes, Ra'hab has done what the two spies told her to do. All her family are inside watching with her.

Finally, on the seventh day, after marching around the city seven times, the horns sound, the fighting men shout, and the walls fall. Then Joshua says: 'Kill everyone in the city and burn it. Burn everything. Save only the silver, gold, copper and iron, and give them to the treasury of Jehovah's tent.'

To the two spies, Joshua says: 'Go into the house of Ra'hab, and bring her and all her family out.' Ra'hab and her family are saved, just as the spies had promised her. Joshua 6:1-25.

LOOK at what this man is burying in his tent! A beautiful robe, and a gold bar and some pieces of silver. He has taken them from the city of Jer′i·cho. But what should have been done with the things in Jer′i·cho? Do you remember?

They were supposed to have been destroyed, and the gold and silver were to have been given to the treasury of Jehovah's tabernacle. So these people have disobeyed God. They have stolen what belongs to God. The man's name is A′chan, and those with him are part of his family. Let's see what happens.

After A′chan steals these things, Joshua sends out some men to fight against the city of A′i. But they are beaten in battle. Some are killed, and the rest run away. Joshua is very sad. He lies down with his face to the ground and prays to Jehovah: 'Why have you let this happen to us?'

Jehovah answers: 'Get up! Israel has sinned. They have taken some of the things that were to be destroyed or to be given to Jehovah's tabernacle. They stole a beautiful robe and kept

it secret. I will not bless you until you destroy it, and the one who has taken these things.' Jehovah says that he will show Joshua who the bad man is.

So Joshua gathers all the people together, and Jehovah picks out the bad man A'chan. A'chan says: 'I have sinned. I saw a beautiful robe, and the bar of gold and the silver pieces. I wanted them so much that I took them. You will find them buried inside my tent.'

When these things are found and brought to Joshua, he says to A'chan: 'Why have you brought trouble on us? Now Jehovah will bring trouble on you!' At that all the people stone A'chan and his family to death. Doesn't that show that we should never take things that do not belong to us?

Afterward Israel goes out to fight against A'i again. This time Jehovah helps his people, and they win the battle.

Joshua 7:1-26; 8:1-29.

MANY of the cities in Ca'naan now get ready to fight against Israel. They think that they can win. But the people in the nearby city of Gib'e·on do not think so. They believe that God is helping the Israelites, and they do not want to fight against God. So do you know what the Gib'e·on·ites do?

They decide to make it look as if they live somewhere very far away. So some of the men put on ragged clothes and worn-out sandals. They load their donkeys with worn-out sacks, and take some old dry bread. Then they go to Joshua and say: 'We have come from a very distant land, because we heard about your great God, Jehovah. We heard all the things that he did for you in Egypt. So our leaders told us to get some food ready for a trip and to go and say to you: "We are your servants. Promise that you will not make

war with us." You can see that our clothes are worn out from the long trip and that our bread has become old and dry.'

Joshua and the other leaders believe the Gib′e·on·ites. So they make a promise not to fight against them. But three days later they learn that the Gib′e·on·ites really live nearby.

'Why did you tell us that you came from a distant land?' Joshua asks them.

The Gib′e·on·ites answer: 'We did so because we were told that your God Jehovah had promised to give all this land of Ca′naan to you. So we were afraid that you would kill us.' But the Israelites keep their promise, and they do not kill the Gib′e·on·ites. Instead they make them their servants.

The king of Jerusalem is angry because the Gib′e·on·ites have made peace with Israel. So he says to four other kings: 'Come and help me to fight Gib′e·on.' And that is what these five kings do. Were the Gib′e·on·ites wise to make peace with Israel, which now causes these kings to come to fight against them? We will see.

Joshua 9:1-27; 10:1-5.

THE SUN STANDS STILL

LOOK at Joshua. He is saying: 'Sun, stand still!' And the sun does stand still. It stays right there in the middle of the sky for a whole day. Jehovah makes it happen! But let's see why Joshua wants the sun to keep shining.

When the five bad kings in the land of Ca'naan start to fight against the Gib'e·on·ites, the Gib'e·on·ites send a man to ask Joshua for help. 'Come to us quickly!' he says. 'Save us! All the kings in the hill country have come up to fight against your servants.'

Right away Joshua and all his fighting men go. All night long they march. When they come to Gib'e·on, the soldiers of the five kings are afraid and begin to run away. Then Jehovah makes large hailstones fall from the sky, and more soldiers die from being hit by the hailstones than are killed by Joshua's fighting men.

Joshua can see that soon the sun will go down. It will be dark, and many of the soldiers of the five bad kings will get away. So that is why Joshua prays to Jehovah and then says: 'Sun, stand still!' And when the sun keeps shining, the Israelites are able to finish winning the fight.

There are many more bad kings in Ca'naan who hate God's people. It takes Joshua and his army about six years to defeat 31 kings in the land. When this is done, Joshua sees to it that the land of Ca'naan is divided out to those tribes yet needing territory.

Many years pass, and Joshua finally dies at 110 years of age. As long as he and his friends are alive, the people obey Jehovah. But when these good men die, the people start doing bad things and get into trouble. This is when they really need God's help.

Joshua 10:6-15; 12:7-24; 14:1-5; Judges 2:8-13.

WHEN the Israelites get into trouble, they cry out to Jehovah. Jehovah answers them by giving brave leaders to help them. The Bible calls these leaders judges. Joshua was the first judge, and some of the judges after him were named Oth'ni·el, E'hud and Sham'gar. But two of the people who help Israel are women named Deb'o·rah and Ja'el.

Deb'o·rah is a prophetess. Jehovah gives her information about the future, and then she tells the people what Jehovah says. Deb'o·rah is also a judge. She sits under a certain palm tree in the hill country, and people come to her to get help with their problems.

At this time Ja'bin is the king of Ca'naan. He has 900 war chariots. His army is so strong that many of the Israelites have been forced to

become servants of Ja′bin. The chief of King Ja′bin's army is named Sis′e·ra.

One day Deb′o·rah sends for Judge Ba′rak, and tells him: 'Jehovah has said: "Take 10,000 men and lead them to Mount Ta′bor. There I will bring Sis′e·ra to you. And I will give you victory over him and his army." '

Ba′rak tells Deb′o·rah: 'I will go if you too will go with me.' Deb′o·rah goes along, but she says to Ba′rak: 'You won't get credit for the victory, because Jehovah will give Sis′e·ra into the hand of a woman.' And this is what happens.

Ba′rak goes down from Mount Ta′bor to meet Sis′e·ra's soldiers. Suddenly Jehovah causes a flood, and many of the enemy soldiers are drowned. But Sis′e·ra gets off his chariot and runs away.

After awhile Sis′e·ra comes to the tent of Ja′el. She invites him in, and gives him some milk. This makes him sleepy, and soon he is fast asleep. Then Ja′el takes a tent pin and drives it into this bad man's head. Later, when Ba′rak comes, she shows him the dead Sis′e·ra! So you can see that what Deb′o·rah said came true.

Finally King Ja′bin is killed too, and the Israelites have peace again for awhile. Judges 2:14-22; 4:1-24; 5:1-31.

RUTH AND NAOMI

IN THE Bible you will find a book called Ruth. It is a story
about a family that lived during the time when Israel had
judges. Ruth is a young woman from the land of Mo'ab; she does
not belong to God's nation of Israel. But when Ruth learns about
the true God Jehovah, she comes to love him very much. Na'o·mi
is an older woman who helped Ruth to learn about Jehovah.

Na'o·mi is an Israelite woman. She and her husband and two
sons moved to the land of Mo'ab at a time when there was
little food to eat in Israel. Then one day Na'o·mi's husband died.
Later Na'o·mi's sons married two Mo'ab·ite girls named Ruth and
Or'pah. But after about 10 years, Na'o·mi's two sons died. How
sad Na'o·mi and the two girls were! What would Na'o·mi do now?

One day Na'o·mi decides to make the long trip back
home to her own people. Ruth and Or'pah want to stay

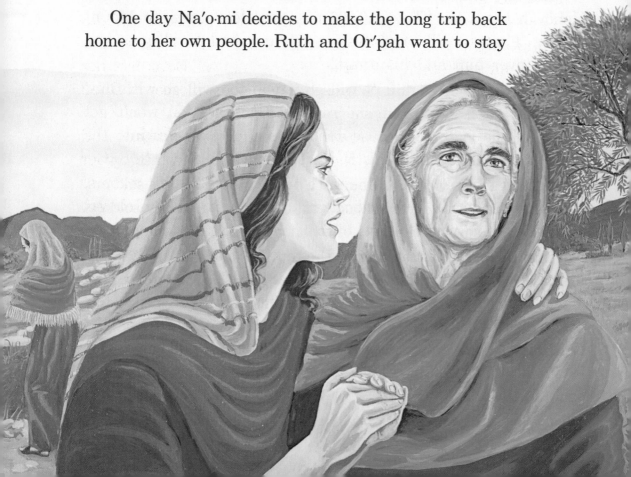

with her, and so they go along too. But after they have traveled awhile on the road, Na'o·mi turns to the girls and says: 'Go back home and stay with your mothers.'

Na'o·mi kisses the girls good-bye. At that they start to cry, because they love Na'o·mi very much. They say: 'No! We will go with you to your people.' But Na'o·mi answers: 'You must go back, my daughters. It will be better for you at home.' So Or'pah starts on her way home. But Ruth does not go.

Na'o·mi turns to her and says: 'Or'pah has left. You too go home with her.' But Ruth answers: 'Don't try to make me leave you! Let me go with you. Where you go I will go, and where you live I will live. Your people will be my people, and your God will be my God. Where you die I will die, and that is where I will be buried.' When Ruth says this, Na'o·mi doesn't try anymore to make her go home.

Finally the two women get to Israel. Here they settle down to live. Ruth right away begins working in the fields, because it is the time for gathering the barley. A man named Bo'az lets her gather barley in his fields. Do you know who the mother of Bo'az was? She was Ra'hab of the city of Jer'i·cho.

One day Bo'az tells Ruth: 'I have heard all about you, and how kind you have been to Na'o·mi. I know how you left your father and mother and your own country and how you came to live among a people you had never known before. May Jehovah be good to you!'

Ruth answers: 'You are very kind to me, sir. You have made me feel better by the nice way that you have spoken to me.' Bo'az likes Ruth very much, and it is not very long before they get married. How happy this makes Na'o·mi! But Na'o·mi is even happier when Ruth and Bo'az have their first son, named O'bed. Later O'bed becomes the grandfather of David, about whom we will learn a lot later on.   Bible book of Ruth.

GIDEON AND HIS 300 MEN

DO YOU see what is happening here? These are all fighting men of Israel. The men bending down are taking a drink. Judge Gid'e·on is the man standing close to them. He is watching how they drink the water.

Look closely at the different ways in which the men are drinking. Some are putting their face right down to the water.

But one is taking the water up in his hands, so that he can watch what is going on around him. This is important, for Jehovah told Gid′e·on to choose only the men who keep watching while they drink. The rest, God said, should be sent home. Let's see why.

The Israelites are in a lot of trouble again. The reason is that they have not obeyed Jehovah. The people of Mid′i·an have gained power over them and are hurting them. So the Israelites cry to Jehovah for help, and Jehovah listens to their cries.

Jehovah tells Gid′e·on to get an army, so Gid′e·on gathers together 32,000 fighting men. But there is an army of 135,000 men against Israel. And yet Jehovah tells Gid′e·on: 'You have too many men.' Why did Jehovah say that?

It is because if Israel won the war, they might think that they won by themselves. They might think that they didn't need Jehovah's help to win. So Jehovah says to Gid′e·on: 'Tell all the men who are afraid to go back home.' When Gid′e·on does this, 22,000 of his fighting men go home. That leaves him only 10,000 men to fight against all those 135,000 soldiers.

But, listen! Jehovah says: 'You still have too many men.' So he tells Gid′e·on to have the men drink at this stream and then to send home all the people who put their face down to the water to drink. 'I will give you the victory with the 300 men who kept watching while they drank,' Jehovah promises.

The time comes for the fight. Gid′e·on puts his 300 men in three groups. He gives to each man a horn, and a jar with a torch inside it. When it is about midnight, they all gather around the camp of enemy soldiers. Then, at the same time, they all blow their horns and break their jars, and shout: 'Jehovah's sword and Gid′e·on's!' When the enemy soldiers wake up, they are confused and afraid. They all begin to run, and the Israelites win the battle.   Judges chapters 6 to 8.

HAVE you ever made a promise and later found it hard to keep? The man in this picture did, and that is why he is so sad. The man is a brave judge of Israel named Jeph'thah.

Jeph'thah lives at a time when the Israelites are no longer worshiping Jehovah. They are again doing what is bad. So Jehovah lets the people of Am'mon hurt them. This makes the Israelites cry out to Jehovah: 'We have sinned against you. Please, save us!'

The people are sorry for the bad things that they have done. They show that they are sorry by worshiping Jehovah again. And so again Jehovah helps them.

Jeph'thah is chosen by the people to fight against the bad Am'mon·ites. Jeph'thah wants very much for Jehovah to help him

in the fight. So he promises Jehovah: 'If you will give me victory over the Am'mon·ites, the first person that comes out of my house to meet me when I return from the victory I will give to you.'

Jehovah listens to Jeph'thah's promise, and he helps him to win the victory. When Jeph'thah returns home, do you know who the first one is to come out to meet him? It is his daughter, who is his only child. 'Oh, my daughter!' Jeph'thah cries. 'What sadness you are bringing me. But I have made a promise to Jehovah, and I cannot take it back.'

When Jeph'thah's daughter learns about his promise, at first she is sad too. For it means that she will have to leave her father and friends. But she will spend the rest of her life serving Jehovah at his tabernacle in Shi'loh. So she tells her father: 'If you have made a promise to Jehovah, you must keep it.'

So Jeph'thah's daughter goes to Shi'loh, and she spends the rest of her life serving Jehovah at his tabernacle. Four days out of every year the women of Israel go to visit her there, and they have a happy time together. The people love Jeph'thah's daughter because she is such a good servant of Jehovah.

Judges 10:6-18; 11:1-40.

THE STRONGEST MAN

DO YOU know the name of the strongest man who ever lived? He is a judge named Samson. It is Jehovah who gives Samson his strength. Even before Samson is born, Jehovah tells his mother: 'Soon you will have a son. He will take a lead in saving Israel from the Phi·lis'tines.'

The Phi·lis'tines are bad people who live in Ca'naan. They have many fighting men, and they really hurt the Israelites. Once, when Samson is on his way to where the Phi·lis'tines live, a big lion comes roaring out to meet him. But Samson kills the lion with only his bare hands. He also kills hundreds of bad Phi·lis'tines.

Later Samson falls in love with a woman named De·li'lah.

The Phi·lis′tine leaders promise that each of them will give De·li′lah 1,100 pieces of silver if she tells them what makes Samson so strong. De·li′lah wants all that money. She is not a true friend of Samson, or of God's people. So she keeps asking Samson what it is that makes him so strong.

Finally, De·li′lah gets Samson to tell her the secret of his strength. 'My hair has never been cut,' he says. 'From the time that I was born, God chose me to be a special servant of his called a Naz′i·rite. If my hair was cut, I would lose my strength.'

Well, when De·li′lah learns this, she has Samson go to sleep on her lap. Then she calls a man to come in and cut his hair. When Samson wakes up, he has lost his strength. The Phi·lis′tines then come in and capture him. They put out both his eyes, and make him their slave.

One day the Phi·lis′tines have a big party to worship their god Dagon, and they bring Samson out of prison to make fun of him. In the meantime, Samson's hair has grown again. Samson says to the boy who is leading him by the hand: 'Let me touch the pillars that hold the building up.' Then Samson prays to Jehovah for strength, and takes hold of the pillars. He cries out: 'Let me die with the Phi·lis′tines.' There are 3,000 Phi·lis′tines at the party, and when Samson bends himself against the pillars the building falls down and kills all these bad people.

Judges chapters 13 to 16.

ISN'T this a good-looking little boy? His name is Samuel. And the man with his hand on Samuel's head is Israel's high priest E'li. That is Samuel's father El·ka'nah and his mother Han'nah who are bringing Samuel to E'li.

Samuel is only about four or five years old. But he will live here at Jehovah's tabernacle with E'li and the other priests. Why would El·ka'nah and Han'nah give someone so young as Samuel to serve Jehovah at the tabernacle? Let's see.

It was just a few years before this that Han'nah was very sad. The reason is that she could not have a baby, and she wanted one very, very much. So one day when Han'nah was visiting Jehovah's tabernacle, she prayed: 'O Jehovah, do not forget me! If you give me a son, I promise that I will give him to you so he can serve you all his life.'

Jehovah answered Han'nah's prayer, and months later she gave birth to Samuel. Han'nah loved her little boy, and she began teaching him about Jehovah when he was still very little. She told her husband: 'As soon as Samuel is old enough so he does not need to be nursed anymore, I will take him to the tabernacle to serve Jehovah there.'

This is what we see Han'nah and El·ka'nah doing in the picture. And because Samuel has been taught so well by his parents, he is glad to be able to serve Jehovah here at Jehovah's tent. Each year Han'nah and El·ka'nah come to worship at this special tent, and to visit their little boy. And each year Han'nah brings a new sleeveless coat that she has made for Samuel.

As the years go by, Samuel keeps on serving at Jehovah's tabernacle, and both Jehovah and the people like him. But high priest E'li's sons Hoph'ni and Phin'e·has are no good. They do many bad things, and get others to disobey Jehovah too. E'li should remove them from being priests, but he does not.

Young Samuel doesn't let any of the bad things going on at the tabernacle cause him to stop serving Jehovah. But because so few people really love Jehovah, it has been a long time since Jehovah has spoken to any human. When Samuel grows a little older this is what happens:

Samuel is asleep in the tabernacle when a voice wakes him up. He answers: 'Here I am.' And he gets up and runs to E'li, and says: 'You called me, and here I am.'

But E'li answers: 'I did not call you; go back to bed.' So Samuel goes back to bed.

Then there is a second call: 'Samuel!' So Samuel gets up and again runs to E'li. 'You called me, and here I am,' he says. But E'li answers: 'I did not call, my son. Lie down again.' So Samuel returns to bed.

'Samuel!' the voice calls a third time. So Samuel runs to E'li. 'Here I am, for you must have called me this time,' he says. E'li knows now that it must be Jehovah who is calling. So he tells Samuel: 'Go lie down once more, and if he calls again, you must say: "Speak, Jehovah, for your servant is listening."'

This is what Samuel says when Jehovah calls again. Jehovah then tells Samuel that he is going to punish E'li and his sons. Later Hoph'ni and Phin'e·has die in battle with the Phi·lis'tines, and when E'li hears what has happened he falls over, breaks his neck and dies too. So Jehovah's word comes true.

Samuel grows up, and becomes the last judge of Israel. When he grows old, the people ask him: 'Choose a king to rule over us.' Samuel does not want to do this, because really Jehovah is their king. But Jehovah tells him to listen to the people.

1 Samuel 1:1-28; 2:11-36; 4:16-18; 8:4-9.

PART 4

Israel's First King to Captivity in Babylon

Saul became Israel's first king. But Jehovah rejected him, and David was chosen to be king in his place. We find out many things about David. As a youth, he fought the giant Goliath. Later he fled from jealous King Saul. Then beautiful Abigail stopped him from doing a foolish thing.

Next, we learn many things about David's son Solomon, who took David's place as king of Israel. The first three kings of Israel each ruled for 40 years. After Solomon's death, Israel was divided into two kingdoms, a northern and a southern kingdom.

The northern 10-tribe kingdom lasted 257 years before it was destroyed by the Assyrians. Then 133 years later, the southern two-tribe kingdom was also destroyed. At this time the Israelites were taken captive to Babylon. So Part FOUR covers 510 years of history, during which time many exciting events pass before our view.

SAUL—ISRAEL'S FIRST KING

SEE Samuel pouring oil on the man's head. This is what they used to do to a person to show that he had been chosen as king. Jehovah tells Samuel to pour the oil on Saul's head. It is a special sweet-smelling oil.

Saul did not think that he was good enough to be king. 'I belong to the tribe of Benjamin, the smallest one in Israel,' he tells Samuel. 'Why do you say that I will be king?' Jehovah likes Saul because he does not pretend to be big and important. That is why He chooses him to be king.

But Saul is not poor or a small man. He comes from a rich family, and he is a very handsome, tall man. He is about a foot taller than anyone else in Israel! Saul is also a very fast runner, and he is a very strong man. The people are glad that Jehovah has chosen Saul to be king. They all begin to shout: 'Long live the king!'

The enemies of Israel are as strong as ever. They are still causing a lot of trouble for the Israelites. Soon after Saul is made king, the Am'mon·ites come up to fight against them. But Saul gathers a big army, and he wins the victory over the Am'mon·ites. This makes the people happy that Saul is king.

As the years go by, Saul leads the Israelites to many victories over their enemies. Saul also has a brave son named Jon'a·than. And Jon'a·than helps Israel to win many battles. The Phi·lis'tines are still the Israelites' worst enemy. One day thousands and thousands of Phi·lis'tines come to fight against the Israelites.

Samuel tells Saul to wait until he comes and makes a sacrifice, or gift, to Jehovah. But Samuel is slow in coming. Saul is afraid that the Phi·lis'tines will start the battle, so he goes ahead and makes the sacrifice himself. When Samuel finally comes, he tells Saul that he has been disobedient. 'Jehovah will choose another person to be king over Israel,' Samuel says.

Later Saul disobeys again. So Samuel tells him: 'It is better to obey Jehovah than to make a gift to him of the best sheep. Because you have not obeyed Jehovah, Jehovah will not keep you as king of Israel.'

We can learn a good lesson from this. It shows us how important it is to obey Jehovah always. Also, it shows that a good person, as Saul had been, can change and become bad. We never want to become bad, do we?

1 Samuel chapters 9 to 11; 13:5-14; 14:47-52; 15:1-35; 2 Samuel 1:23.

GOD CHOOSES DAVID

CAN you see what has happened? The boy has saved this little lamb from the bear. The bear came and carried off the lamb and was going to eat it. But the boy ran after them, and saved the lamb from the bear's mouth. And when the bear rose up, the boy grabbed the bear and struck it down dead! At another time he saved one of the sheep from a lion. Isn't he a brave boy? Do you know who he is?

This is young David. He lives in the town of Beth'le·hem. His grandfather was O'bed, the son of Ruth and Bo'az. Do you remember them? And David's father is Jes'se. David takes care of his father's sheep. David was born 10 years after Jehovah chose Saul to be king.

The time comes when Jehovah says to Samuel: 'Take some special oil and go to the house of Jes'se in Beth'le·hem. I have chosen one of his sons to be king.' When Samuel sees Jes'se's oldest son E·li'ab, he says to himself: 'This is surely the one that Jehovah has chosen.' But Jehovah tells him: 'Do not look at how tall and handsome he is. I have not chosen him to be king.'

So Jes'se calls his son A·bin'a·dab and brings him to Samuel. But Samuel says: 'No, Jehovah hasn't chosen him either.' Next, Jes'se brings his son Sham'mah. 'No, Jehovah hasn't chosen him either,' Samuel says. Jes'se brings seven of his sons to Samuel, but Jehovah doesn't choose any of them. 'Are these all the boys?' Samuel asks.

'There is still the youngest,' Jes'se says. 'But he is out taking care of the sheep.' When David is brought in, Samuel can see that he is a good-looking boy. 'This is the one,' Jehovah says. 'Pour the oil on him.' And this is what Samuel does. The time will come when David will become king of Israel. 1 Samuel 17:34, 35; 16:1-13.

DAVID AND GOLIATH

THE Phi·lis'tines again come to fight against Israel. David's three oldest brothers are now in Saul's army. So one day Jes'se tells David: 'Take some grain and loaves of bread to your brothers. Find out how they are getting along.'

When David arrives at the army camp, he runs to the battle line to look for his brothers. The Phi·lis'tine giant Go·li'ath comes out to make fun of the Israelites. He has been doing this every morning and evening for 40 days. He yells: 'Choose one of your men to fight me. If he wins and kills me, we will be your slaves. But if I win and kill him, you will be our slaves. I dare you to pick someone to fight me.'

David asks some of the soldiers: 'What will the man get who kills this Phi·lis'tine and frees Israel from this shame?'

'Saul will give the man many riches,' the soldier says. 'And he will give him his own daughter to be his wife.'

But all the Israelites are afraid of Go·li'ath because he is so big. He is more than 9 feet (about 3 meters) tall, and he has another soldier carrying his shield for him.

Some soldiers go and tell King Saul that David wants to fight Go·li'ath. But Saul tells David: 'You can't fight this Phi·lis'tine. You are just a boy, and he has been a soldier all his life.' David answers: 'I killed a bear and a lion that carried off my father's sheep. And this Phi·lis'tine will become like one of them. Jehovah will help me.' So Saul says: 'Go, and may Jehovah be with you.'

David goes down by a stream and gets five smooth stones, and puts them into his bag. Then he takes his sling and goes out to meet the giant. When Go·li'ath sees him, he can't believe it. He thinks it will be so easy to kill David.

'Just come to me,' Go·li'ath says, 'and I will give your body to the birds and animals to eat.' But David says: 'You come to me with a sword, a spear and a javelin, but I am coming to you with the name of Jehovah. This day Jehovah will give you into my hands and I will strike you down.'

At that David runs toward Go·li'ath. He takes a stone from his bag, puts it into his sling, and throws it with all his might. The stone flies straight into Go·li'ath's head, and he falls down dead! When the Phi·lis'tines see that their champion has fallen, they all turn and run. The Israelites run after them and win the battle.   1 Samuel 17:1-54.

WHY DAVID MUST RUN AWAY

AFTER David kills Go·li′ath, Israel's army chief Ab′ner brings him to Saul. Saul is very pleased with David. He makes him a chief in his army and takes him to live at the king's house.

Later, when the army returns from fighting the Phi·lis′tines, the women sing: 'Saul has killed thousands, but David tens of thousands.' This makes Saul jealous, because David is given more honor than Saul is. But Saul's son Jon′a·than is not jealous. He loves David very much, and David loves Jon′a·than too. So the two make a promise to each other that they will always be friends.

David is a very good player of the harp, and Saul likes the music that he plays. But one day Saul's jealousy causes him to do a terrible thing. While David is playing the harp, Saul takes his spear and throws it, saying: 'I will pin David to the wall!' But David dodges, and the spear misses. Later Saul misses David again with his spear. So David knows now that he must be very careful.

Do you remember the promise that Saul made? He said that he would give his daughter to be the wife of the man who killed Go·li'ath. Saul at last tells David that he can have his daughter Mi'chal, but first he must kill 100 of the enemy Phi·lis'tines. Think of that! Saul really hopes that the Phi·lis'tines will kill David. But they don't, and so Saul gives his daughter to be David's wife.

One day Saul tells Jon'a·than and all his servants that he wants to kill David. But Jon'a·than says to his father: 'Don't hurt David. He has never done anything wrong to you. Rather, everything he has done has been a great help to you. He risked his life when he killed Go·li'ath, and when you saw it, you were glad.'

Saul listens to his son, and he promises not to hurt David. David is brought back, and he serves Saul in his house again just as he did before. One day, however, while David is playing music, Saul again throws his spear at David. David dodges, and the spear hits the wall. This is the third time! David knows now that he must run away!

That night David goes to his own house. But Saul sends some men to kill him. Mi'chal knows what her father plans to do. So she tells her husband: 'If you don't get away tonight, tomorrow you will be dead.' That night Mi'chal helps David to escape through a window. For about seven years David must hide in one place after another so that Saul cannot find him. 1 Samuel 18:1-30; 19:1-18.

ABIGAIL AND DAVID

DO YOU know the pretty woman who is coming to meet David? Her name is Ab'i·gail. She has good sense, and she keeps David from doing a bad thing. But before learning about that, let's see what has been happening to David.

After David runs away from Saul, he hides in a cave. His brothers and the rest of his family join him there. About 400 men in all come to him, and David becomes their leader. David

then goes to the king of Mo'ab and says: 'Please let my father and mother stay with you until I see what happens to me.' Later David and his men begin hiding in the hills.

It is after this that David meets Ab'i·gail. Her husband Na'bal is a rich landowner. He has 3,000 sheep and 1,000 goats. Na'bal is a mean man. But his wife Ab'i·gail is very beautiful. Also, she knows how to do what is right. Once she even saves her family. Let's see how.

David and his men have been kind to Na'bal. They have helped to protect his sheep. So one day David sends some of his men to ask Na'bal for a favor. David's men come to Na'bal while he and his helpers are cutting the wool off the sheep. It is a feast day, and Na'bal has many good things to eat. So this is what David's men say: 'We have been kind to you. We have not stolen any of your sheep, but have helped to look after them. Now, please, give us some food.'

'I won't give my food to men like you,' Na'bal says. He speaks in a very mean way, and says bad things about David. When the men return and tell David about it, David is very angry. 'Put on your swords!' he tells his men. And they start on their way to kill Na'bal and his men.

One of Na'bal's men, who heard the mean words that Na'bal spoke, tells Ab'i·gail what happened. Right away Ab'i·gail gets some food ready. She loads it on some donkeys and starts on her way. When she meets David, she gets off her donkey, bows down and says: 'Please, sir, pay no attention to my husband Na'bal. He is a fool, and he does foolish things. Here is a gift. Please take it, and forgive us for what happened.'

'You are a wise woman,' David answers. 'You have kept me from killing Na'bal to pay him back for his meanness. Go home now in peace.' Later, when Na'bal dies, Ab'i·gail becomes one of David's wives.

1 Samuel 22:1-4; 25:1-43.

SAUL again tries to capture David. He takes 3,000 of his best soldiers and goes looking for him. When David learns about this, he sends spies out to learn where Saul and his men have camped for the night. Then David asks two of his men: 'Which of you will go to Saul's camp with me?'

'I will,' A·bish′ai answers. A·bish′ai is the son of David's sister Ze·ru′iah. While Saul and his men are sleeping, David and A·bish′ai creep silently into the camp. They pick up Saul's spear and his water jug, which is lying right beside Saul's head. No one sees or hears them because they are all fast asleep.

See David and A·bish′ai now. They have gotten away, and are safely on top of a hill. David shouts down to Israel's army chief: 'Ab′ner, why aren't you protecting your master, the king? Look! Where are his spear and his water jug?'

Saul wakes up. He recognizes David's voice, and asks: 'Is that you, David?' Can you see Saul and Ab′ner down there?

'Yes, my lord the king,' David replies to Saul. And David asks:

'Why are you trying to capture me? What bad thing have I done? Here is your spear, O king. Let one of your men come and get it.'

'I have done wrong,' Saul admits. 'I have acted foolishly.' At that David goes his way, and Saul returns home. But David says to himself: 'One of these days Saul will kill me. I should escape to the land of the Phi·lis'tines.' And that is what he does. David is able to fool the Phi·lis'tines and make them believe that he is now on their side.

Some time later the Phi·lis'tines go up to fight against Israel. In the battle, both Saul and Jon'a·than are killed. This makes David very sad, and he writes a beautiful song, in which he sings: 'I feel sad for you, my brother Jon'a·than. How dear you were to me!'

After this David returns to Israel to the city of He'bron. There is a war between the men who choose Saul's son Ish-bo'sheth to be king and the other men who want David to be king. But finally David's men win. David is 30 years old when he is made king. For seven and a half years he rules in He'bron. Some of the sons born to him there are named Am'non, Ab'sa·lom and Ad·o·ni'jah.

The time comes when David and his men go up to capture a beautiful city called Jerusalem. Jo'ab, another son of David's sister Ze·ru'iah, takes the lead in the fight. So David rewards Jo'ab by making him the chief of his army. Now David begins ruling in the city of Jerusalem.

1 Samuel 26:1-25; 27:1-7; 31:1-6;
2 Samuel 1:26; 3:1-21; 5:1-10;
1 Chronicles 11:1-9.

AFTER David begins ruling in Jerusalem, Jehovah gives his army many victories over their enemies. Jehovah had promised to give the land of Ca'naan to the Israelites. And now, with Jehovah's help, all the land that was promised to them finally becomes theirs.

David is a good ruler. He loves Jehovah. So one of the first things that he does after capturing Jerusalem is to bring Jehovah's ark of the covenant there. And he wants to build a temple in which to put it.

When David grows older, he makes a bad mistake. David knows that it is wrong to take something that belongs to someone else. But one evening, when he is on the roof of his palace, he looks down and sees a very beautiful woman. Her name is Bath-she'ba, and her husband is one of his soldiers named U·ri'ah.

David wants Bath-she'ba so much that he has her brought to his palace. Her husband is away fighting. Well, David makes love to her and later she finds she is going to have a baby. David is very worried and sends word to his army chief Jo'ab to have U·ri'ah put in the front of the battle where he will be killed. When U·ri'ah is dead, David marries Bath-she'ba.

Jehovah is very angry with David. So he sends his servant Nathan to tell him about his sins. You can see Nathan there talking to David. David is very sorry for what he has done, and so Jehovah does not put him to death. But Jehovah says: 'Because you have done these bad things, you will have a lot of trouble in your house.' And what trouble David has!

First, Bath-she'ba's son dies. Then David's firstborn son Am'non gets his sister Ta'mar alone and forces his love on her. David's son Ab'sa·lom is so angry about this that he kills Am'non. Later,

Ab'sa·lom wins the favor of many of the people, and he has himself made king. Finally, David wins the war against Ab'sa·lom, who is killed. Yes, David has a lot of trouble.

In between all of this, Bath-she'ba gives birth to a son named Solomon. When David is old and sick, his son Ad·o·ni'jah tries to make himself king. At that David has a priest named Za'dok pour oil on Solomon's head to show that Solomon will be king. Soon afterward David dies at 70 years of age. He ruled for 40 years, but now Solomon is the king of Israel.

2 Samuel 11:1-27; 12:1-18; 1 Kings 1:1-48.

SOLOMON is a teen-ager when he becomes king. He loves Jehovah, and he follows the good advice that his father David gave him. Jehovah is pleased with Solomon, and so one night he says to him in a dream: 'Solomon, what would you like me to give you?'

At this Solomon answers: 'Jehovah my God, I am very young and I don't know how to rule. So give me the wisdom to rule your people in a right way.'

Jehovah is pleased with what Solomon asks. So He says: 'Because you have asked for wisdom and not for long life or riches, I will give you more wisdom than anyone who has ever lived. But I will also give you what you did not ask for, both riches and glory.'

A short time later two women come to Solomon with a hard problem. 'This woman and I live in the same house,' explains one of them. 'I gave birth to a boy, and two days later she also gave birth to a baby boy. Then one night her baby died. But while I was asleep, she put her dead child next to me and took my baby. When I woke up and looked at the dead child, I saw that it was not mine.'

At this the other woman says: 'No! The living child is mine, and the dead one is hers!' The first woman answers: 'No! The dead child is yours, and the living one is mine!' This is the way the women argue. What will Solomon do?

He sends for a sword, and, when it is brought, he says: 'Cut the living baby in two, and give each woman half of it.'

'No!' cries the real mother. 'Please don't kill the baby. Give it to her!' But the other woman says: 'Don't give it to either of us; go on and cut it in two.'

Finally Solomon speaks: 'Don't kill the child! Give him to the first woman. She is the real mother.' Solomon knows this because the real mother loves the baby so much that she is willing to give him to the other woman so he won't be killed. When the people hear how Solomon solved the problem, they are glad to have such a wise king.

During the rule of Solomon, God blesses the people by making the soil grow plenty of wheat and barley, grapes and figs and other foods. The people wear fine clothes and live in good houses. There is more than enough of everything good for everybody.

1 Kings 3:3-28; 4:29-34.

BEFORE David died, he gave Solomon the plans from God for building Jehovah's temple. In the fourth year of his rule, Solomon begins building the temple, and it takes seven and a half years to finish it. Tens of thousands of men work on the temple, and the building costs lots and lots of money. This is because so much gold and silver are used in it.

The temple has two main rooms, just as the tabernacle had. But these rooms are twice the size of those in the tabernacle. Solomon has the ark of the covenant put in the inside room of the temple, and the other things that were kept in the tabernacle are put in the other room.

When the temple is finished, there is a big celebration. Solomon kneels in front of the temple and prays, as you can see in the picture. 'Not even all of heaven is large enough to hold you,' Solomon says to Jehovah, 'how much less, then, can this temple hold you. But, O my God, please listen to your people when they pray toward this place.'

When Solomon finishes his prayer, fire comes down from heaven. It burns up the animal sacrifices that have been made. And a bright light from Jehovah fills the temple. This shows that Jehovah is listening, and that he is pleased with the temple and Solomon's prayer. The temple, rather than the tabernacle, now becomes the place where the people come to worship.

For a long time Solomon rules in a wise way, and the people are happy. But Solomon marries many women from other countries who do not worship Jehovah. Can you see one of them worshiping before the idol? Finally his wives get Solomon to worship other gods too. Do you know what happens when Solomon does this? He no longer treats the people kindly. He becomes cruel, and the people are not happy anymore.

This makes Jehovah angry with Solomon, and he tells him: 'I will take the kingdom away from you and give it to another man. I will not do this in your lifetime, but during the rule of your son. But I won't take all the people of the kingdom away from your son.' Let's see how this happens.

1 Chronicles 28:9-21; 29:1-9; 1 Kings 5:1-18;
2 Chronicles 6:12-42; 7:1-5; 1 Kings 11:9-13.

THE KINGDOM IS DIVIDED

DO YOU know why this man is ripping his robe to pieces? Jehovah told him to do it. This man is God's prophet A·hi′jah. Do you know what a prophet is? He is a person that God tells ahead of time what is going to happen.

A·hi'jah is here speaking to Jer·o·bo'am. Jer·o·bo'am is a man that Solomon put in charge of doing some of his building work. When A·hi'jah meets Jer·o·bo'am here on the road, A·hi'jah does a strange thing. He takes off the new robe that he is wearing and tears it into 12 pieces. He tells Jer·o·bo'am: 'Take 10 pieces for yourself.' Do you know why A·hi'jah gives Jer·o·bo'am 10 pieces?

A·hi'jah explains that Jehovah is going to take the kingdom away from Solomon. He says that Jehovah is going to give 10 tribes to Jer·o·bo'am. This means that only two tribes will be left for Solomon's son Re·ho·bo'am to rule over.

When Solomon hears what A·hi'jah told Jer·o·bo'am, he becomes very angry. He tries to kill Jer·o·bo'am. But Jer·o·bo'am runs away to Egypt. After a while Solomon dies. He was king for 40 years, but now his son Re·ho·bo'am is made king. Down in Egypt Jer·o·bo'am hears that Solomon is dead, so he comes back to Israel.

Re·ho·bo'am is not a good king. He is even meaner to the people than his father Solomon had been. Jer·o·bo'am and some other important men go to King Re·ho·bo'am and ask him to be nicer to the people. But Re·ho·bo'am does not listen. In fact, he becomes even meaner than before. So the people make Jer·o·bo'am king over 10 tribes, but the two tribes of Benjamin and Judah keep Re·ho·bo'am as their king.

Jer·o·bo'am does not want his people to go to Jerusalem to worship at Jehovah's temple. So he makes two golden calves and gets the people of the 10-tribe kingdom to worship them. Soon the land becomes filled with crime and violence.

There is also trouble in the two-tribe kingdom. Less than five years after Re·ho·bo'am becomes king, the king of Egypt comes to fight against Jerusalem. He takes away many treasures from Jehovah's temple. So it is for only a short time that the temple remains the same as when it was built.   1 Kings 11:26-43; 12:1-33; 14:21-31.

AFTER King Jer·o·bo'am dies, each king who rules the northern 10-tribe kingdom of Israel is bad. King A'hab is the worst king of all. Do you know why? One big reason is his wife, wicked Queen Jez'e·bel.

Jez'e·bel is not an Israelite woman. She is the daughter of the king of Si'don. She worships the false god Ba'al, and she gets A'hab and many Israelites to worship Ba'al too. Jez'e·bel hates Jehovah and kills many of his prophets. Others have to hide in caves so that they won't be killed. If Jez'e·bel wants something, she will even kill a person to get it.

One day King A'hab is very sad. So Jez'e·bel asks him: 'Why are you sad today?'

'Because of what Na'both said to me,' A'hab answers. 'I wanted to buy his vineyard. But he told me I couldn't have it.'

'Don't worry,' Jez'e·bel says. 'I will get it for you.'

So Jez'e·bel writes letters to some chief men in the city where this man Na'both lives. 'Get some good-for-nothing men to say that Na'both has cursed God and the king,' she tells them. 'Then take Na'both out of the city and stone him to death.'

As soon as Jez'e·bel learns that Na'both is dead, she says to A'hab: 'Now go and take his vineyard.' Don't you agree that Jez'e·bel should be punished for doing such a terrible thing?

So, in time, Jehovah sends the man Je'hu to punish her. When Jez'e·bel hears that Je'hu is coming, she paints her eyes and tries to fix herself up to look pretty. But when Je'hu comes and sees Jez'e·bel in the window, he calls to the men in the palace: 'Throw her down!' The men obey, as you can see in the picture. They throw her down, and she dies. This is the end of wicked Queen Jez'e·bel.

1 Kings 16:29-33; 18:1-4; 21:1-16; 2 Kings 9:30-37.

D O YOU know who these men are and what they are doing? They are going out to battle, and the men there in front are singing. But you may ask: 'Why don't the singers have swords and spears to fight with?' Let us see.

Je·hosh'a·phat is king of the two-tribe kingdom of Israel. He lives at the same time as King A'hab and Jez'e·bel of the northern 10-tribe kingdom. But Je·hosh'a·phat is a good king, and his father A'sa was a fine king too. So for many years the people of the southern two-tribe kingdom enjoy a good life.

But now something happens to make the people afraid. Messengers report to Je·hosh'a·phat: 'A large army from the countries of Mo'ab, Am'mon and Mount Se'ir are coming to attack you.' Many Israelites gather at Jerusalem to seek Jehovah's

help. They go to the temple, and there Je·hosh′a·phat prays: 'O Jehovah our God, we do not know what to do. We are helpless against this large army. We look to you for help.'

Jehovah listens, and he has one of his servants tell the people: 'The battle is not yours, but God's. You will not have to fight. Just watch, and see how Jehovah will save you.'

So the next morning Je·hosh′a·phat tells the people: 'Have trust in Jehovah!' He then puts singers out in front of his soldiers, and as they march along they sing praises to Jehovah. Do you know what happens when they get near the battle? Jehovah causes the enemy soldiers to fight among themselves. And when the Israelites arrive, every enemy soldier is dead!

Wasn't Je·hosh′a·phat wise to trust in Jehovah? We will be wise if we trust in Him too.   1 Kings 22:41-53; 2 Chronicles 20:1-30.

IF YOU died, how would your mother feel if you were brought back to life? She would be very happy! But can a person who has died live again? Has it happened before?

Look at the man here, and the woman and the little boy. The man is the prophet E·li′jah. The woman is a widow of the city of Zar′e·phath, and the boy is her son. Well, one day the boy gets sick. He gets worse and worse until he finally dies. E·li′jah then tells the woman: 'Give the boy to me.'

E·li′jah takes the dead child upstairs and lays him on the bed. Then he prays: 'O Jehovah, make the boy live again.' And the boy starts to breathe! At that E·li′jah takes him back downstairs and says to the woman: 'Look, your son is alive!' This is why the mother is so happy.

Another important prophet of Jehovah is named E·li′sha. He serves as E·li′jah's helper. But in time Jehovah also uses E·li′sha to do miracles. One day E·li′sha goes to the city of Shu′nem, where a woman is very kind to him. Later this woman has a baby boy.

One morning, after the child has grown older, he goes out to join his father who is working in the field. Suddenly the boy cries out: 'My head hurts!' After he is taken home, the boy dies. How sad his mother is! Right away she goes and gets E·li′sha.

When E·li′sha arrives, he goes into the room with the dead child. He prays to Jehovah, and lies down over the body. Soon the boy's body becomes warm, and he sneezes seven times. How happy his mother is when she comes in and finds her boy alive!

Many, many people have died. This has made their families and friends very sad. We don't have the power to raise the dead. But Jehovah does. Later we will learn how he will bring many millions of people back to life. 1 Kings 17:8-24; 2 Kings 4:8-37.

A GIRL HELPS A MIGHTY MAN

DO YOU know what this little girl is saying? She is telling the lady about Jehovah's prophet E·li'sha, and the wonderful things that Jehovah helps him to do. The lady does not know about Jehovah because she is not an Israelite. Let's see, then, why the girl is in the lady's home.

The lady is a Syrian. Her husband is Na'a·man, the chief of the Syrian army. The Syrians had captured this little Israelite girl, and she was brought to Na'a·man's wife to be her servant.

Na'a·man has a bad sickness called leprosy. This sickness can even cause some of a person's flesh to fall off. So this is what the girl is telling Na'a·man's wife: 'I wish my master could go to Jehovah's prophet in Israel. He would heal him of his leprosy.' Later this is told to the lady's husband.

Na′a·man wants very much to be healed; so he decides to go to Israel. When he gets there, he goes to E·li′sha's house. E·li′sha has his servant go out and tell Na′a·man to go wash in the Jordan River seven times. This makes Na′a·man very angry, and he says: 'The rivers back home are better than any river in Israel!' After saying this, Na′a·man leaves.

But one of his servants tells him: 'Sir, if E·li′sha told you to do something hard, you would do it. Now why can't you just wash yourself, as he said?' Na′a·man listens to his servant and goes and dips himself in the Jordan River seven times. When he does, his flesh becomes firm and healthy!

Na′a·man is very happy. He returns to E·li′sha and tells him: 'Now I know for sure that the God in Israel is the only true God in all the earth. So, please, take this gift from me.' But E·li′sha answers: 'No, I will not take it.' E·li′sha knows that it would be wrong for him to take the gift, because it was Jehovah who had healed Na′a·man. But E·li′sha's servant Ge·ha′zi wants the gift for himself.

So this is what Ge·ha′zi does. After Na′a·man leaves, Ge·ha′zi runs to catch up with him. 'E·li′sha sent me to tell you that he would like some of your gift for friends who just came to visit,' Ge·ha′zi says. This, of course, is a lie. But Na′a·man doesn't know that it is a lie; so he gives Ge·ha′zi some of the things.

When Ge·ha′zi returns home, E·li′sha knows what he has done. Jehovah has told him. So he says: 'Because you did this bad thing, Na′a·man's leprosy will come upon you.' And it does, right away!

What can we learn from all of this? First, that we should be like the little girl and talk about Jehovah. It can do much good. Secondly, we should not be proud as Na′a·man was at first, but we should obey God's servants. And thirdly, we should not lie as Ge·ha′zi did. Can't we learn a lot from reading the Bible?

2 Kings 5:1-27.

JONAH AND THE BIG FISH

LOOK at the man in the water. He is in a lot of trouble, isn't he? That fish is about to swallow him! Do you know who this man is? His name is Jo'nah. Let's see how he got into so much trouble.

Jo'nah is a prophet of Jehovah. It is not long after the death of the prophet E·li'sha that Jehovah tells Jo'nah: 'Go to the great city of Nin'e·veh. The badness of the people there is very great, and I want you to speak to them about it.'

But Jo'nah does not want to go. So he gets on a boat that is going in the opposite direction from Nin'e·veh. Jehovah is not pleased with Jo'nah for running away. So He causes a big storm. It is so bad that the boat is in danger of sinking. The sailors are very much afraid, and they cry out to their gods for help.

Finally Jo'nah tells them: 'I worship Jehovah, the God who made the heaven and the earth. And I am running away from doing what Jehovah told me to do.' So the sailors ask: 'What should we do to you to stop the storm?'

'Throw me into the sea, and the sea will become calm again,' Jo'nah says. The sailors don't want to do it, but as the storm gets worse they finally throw Jo'nah overboard. Right away the storm stops, and the sea is calm again.

As Jo'nah sinks down into the water, the big fish swallows him. But he doesn't die. For three days and three nights he is in the belly of that fish. Jo'nah is very sorry that he did not obey Jehovah and go to Nin'e·veh. So do you know what he does?

Jo'nah prays to Jehovah for help. Then Jehovah makes the fish vomit Jo'nah out onto dry land. After that Jo'nah goes to Nin'e·veh. Doesn't this teach us how important it is that we do whatever Jehovah says?   Bible book of Jonah.

THIS is a picture of a paradise such as God may have shown to his prophet Isaiah. Isaiah lived shortly after Jo'nah did.

Paradise means "garden" or "park." Does it remind you of something we have already seen in this book? It looks much like the beautiful garden that Jehovah God made for Adam and Eve, doesn't it? But will the whole earth ever be a paradise?

Jehovah told his prophet Isaiah to write about the coming new paradise for God's people. He said: 'Wolves and sheep will live

together in peace. Young calves and baby lions will feed together, and little children will take care of them. Even a baby will not be harmed if it plays near a poisonous snake.'

'This can never happen,' many will say. 'There has always been trouble on earth, and there always will be.' But think about it: What kind of home did God give Adam and Eve?

God put Adam and Eve in a paradise. It is only because they disobeyed God that they lost their beautiful home, grew old and died. God promises that he will give people who love him the very things that Adam and Eve lost.

In the coming new paradise nothing will hurt or destroy. There will be perfect peace. All people will be healthy and happy. It will be just as God wanted it to be at the beginning. But we will learn later how God will bring this about. Isaiah 11:6-9; Revelation 21:3, 4.

GOD HELPS KING HEZEKIAH

DO YOU know why this man is praying to Jehovah? Why has he laid these letters in front of Jehovah's altar? The man is Hez·e·ki'ah. He is king of the southern two tribes of Israel. And he is in a lot of trouble. Why?

Because the As·syr'i·an armies have already destroyed the northern 10 tribes. Jehovah let this happen because those people were so bad. And now the As·syr'i·an armies have come to fight against the two-tribe kingdom.

The king of As·syr'i·a has just sent letters to King Hez·e·ki'ah. These are the letters that Hez·e·ki'ah has put here

before God. The letters make fun of Jehovah, and tell Hez·e·ki′ah to give up. So this is why Hez·e·ki′ah prays: 'O Jehovah, save us from the king of As·syr′i·a. Then all the nations will know that you alone are God.' Will Jehovah listen to Hez·e·ki′ah?

Hez·e·ki′ah is a good king. He is not like the bad kings of the 10-tribe kingdom of Israel, or like his bad father King A′haz. Hez·e·ki′ah has been careful to obey all of Jehovah's laws. So, after Hez·e·ki′ah finishes praying, the prophet Isaiah sends him this message from Jehovah: 'The king of As·syr′i·a will not come into Jerusalem. None of his soldiers will even come close to it. They will not shoot a single arrow at the city.'

Look at the picture on this page. Do you know who all these dead soldiers are? They are the As·syr′i·ans. Jehovah sent his angel, and in one night the angel killed 185,000 As·syr′i·an soldiers. So the king of As·syr′i·a gives up and goes back home.

The two-tribe kingdom is saved, and the people have peace for a while. But after Hez·e·ki′ah dies his son Ma·nas′seh becomes king. Ma·nas′seh and his son A′mon after him are both very bad kings. So again the land is filled with crime and violence. When King A′mon is murdered by his own servants, his son Jo·si′ah is made king of the two-tribe kingdom.

2 Kings 18:1-36; 19:1-37; 21:1-25.

JOSIAH is only eight years old when he becomes king of the southern two tribes of Israel. This is very young for one to be king. So at first some older persons help him to rule the nation.

When Jo·si'ah has been king for seven years he starts to seek Jehovah. He follows the example of good kings like David, Je·hosh'a·phat and Hez·e·ki'ah. Then, when he is still just a teen-ager, Jo·si'ah does a brave thing.

For a long time most of the Israelites have been very bad. They worship false gods. They bow down to idols. So Jo·si'ah goes out with his men and begins to remove false worship from the land. This is a big job because so many people worship false gods. You can see Jo·si'ah and his men here breaking up the idols.

Afterward, Jo·si'ah puts three men in charge of repairing Jehovah's temple. Money is collected from the people and given to these men to pay for the work that is to be done. While they are working on the temple, the high priest Hil·ki'ah finds something very important there. It is the very book of the law that Jehovah had Moses write a long, long time ago. It was lost for many years.

The book is taken to Jo·si′ah, and he asks that it be read to him. As he listens, Jo·si′ah can see that the people have not been keeping Jehovah's law. He feels very sad about this, and so he tears his clothes apart, as you can see here. He says: 'Jehovah is angry with us, because our fathers did not keep the laws written in this book.'

Jo·si′ah commands high priest Hil·ki′ah to find out what Jehovah is going to do to them. Hil·ki′ah goes to the woman Hul′dah, who is a prophetess, and asks her. She gives him this message from Jehovah to take back to Jo·si′ah: 'Jerusalem and all the people will be punished because they have worshiped false gods and the land has been filled with badness. But because you, Jo·si′ah, have done what is good, this punishment will not come until after your death.'   2 Chronicles 34:1-28.

A MAN WHO IS NOT AFRAID

SEE the people making fun of this young man. Do you know who he is? This is Jeremiah. He is a very important prophet of God.

Soon after King Jo·si'ah starts destroying the idols out of the land, Jehovah tells Jeremiah to be His prophet. However, Jeremiah thinks he is too young to be a prophet. But Jehovah says that He will help him.

Jeremiah tells the Israelites to stop doing bad things. 'The gods that the people of the nations worship are false,' he says. But many Israelites would rather worship idols than worship the true God Jehovah. When Jeremiah tells the people that God will punish them for their badness, they just laugh at him.

Years pass. Jo·si'ah dies, and three months later his son Je·hoi'a·kim becomes king. Jeremiah keeps telling the people: 'Jerusalem will be destroyed if you don't change your bad ways.' The priests grab Jeremiah and shout: 'You should be killed for saying these things.' Then they tell the princes of Israel: 'Jeremiah should be put to death, because he has spoken against our city.'

What will Jeremiah do now? He is not afraid! He tells all of them: 'Jehovah sent me to speak these things to you. If you don't change your bad ways of living, Jehovah will destroy Jerusalem. But be sure of this: If you kill me, you will be killing a man who has done no wrong.'

The princes let Jeremiah live, but the Israelites do not change their bad ways. Later Neb·u·chad·nez'zar, the king of Babylon, comes and fights against Jerusalem. Finally Neb·u·chad·nez'zar makes the Israelites his servants. He takes many thousands away to Babylon. Just think what it would be like to have strange people carry you off from your home to a strange land!

Jeremiah 1:1-8; 10:1-5; 26:1-16; 2 Kings 24:1-17.

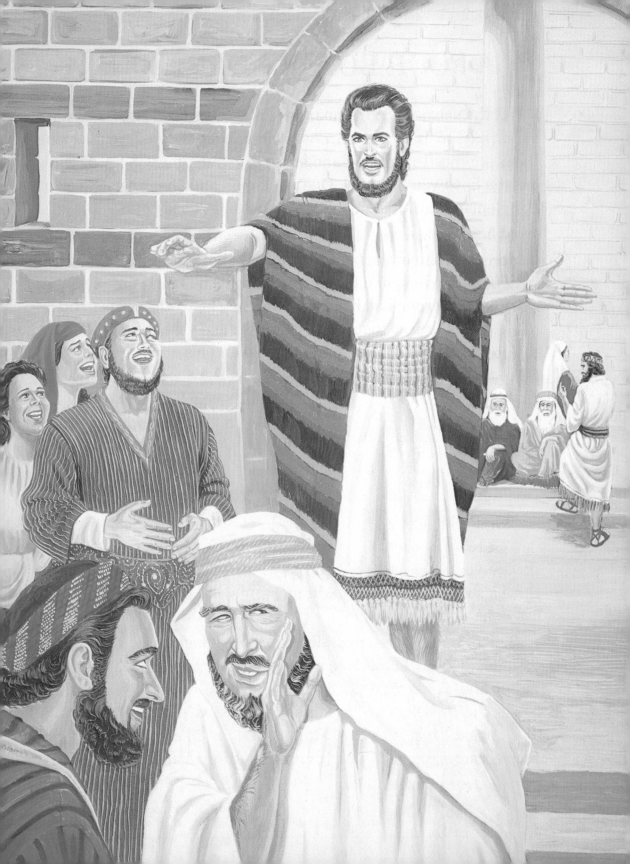

KING Neb·u·chad·nez'zar takes all the best educated Israelites away to Babylon. Afterward the king chooses from among them the most handsome and smartest young men. Four of these are the boys you see here. One is Daniel, and the other three the Babylonians call Sha'drach, Me'shach and A·bed'ne·go.

Neb·u·chad·nez'zar plans to train the young men to serve in his palace. After three years of training he will choose only the smartest ones to help him to solve problems. The king wants the boys to be strong and healthy while they are being trained. So he gives orders that his servants should give all of them the same rich food and wine that he and his family receive.

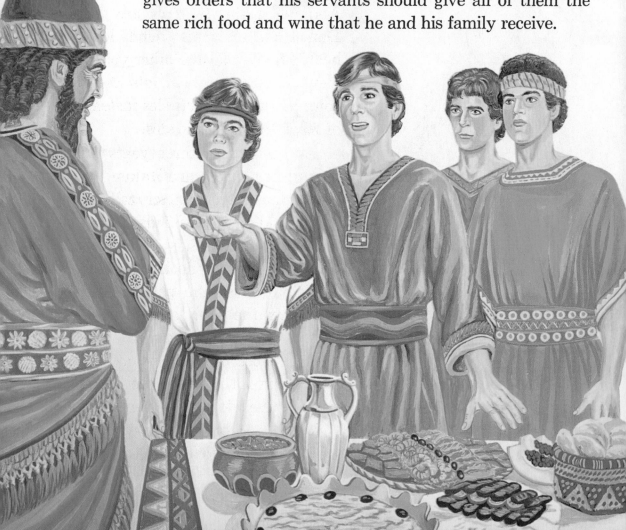

Look at young Daniel. Do you know what he is saying to Neb·u·chad·nez'zar's chief servant Ash'pe·naz? Daniel is telling him that he does not want to eat the rich things from the king's table. But Ash'pe·naz is worried. 'The king has decided what you are to eat and drink,' he says. 'And if you don't look as healthy as the other young men, he may kill me.'

So Daniel goes to the guardian that Ash'pe·naz has put in charge of him and his three friends. 'Please put us to the test for 10 days,' he says. 'Give us some vegetables to eat and water to drink. Then compare us with the other young men who are eating the king's food, and see who looks better.'

The guardian agrees to do this. And when the 10 days are up, Daniel and his three friends look healthier than all the other young men. So the guardian lets them continue to eat vegetables instead of what the king provides.

At the end of three years all the young men are taken to Neb·u·chad·nez'zar. After talking to them all, the king finds Daniel and his three friends to be the smartest ones. So he keeps them to help him in the palace. And whenever the king asks Daniel, Sha'drach, Me'shach and A·bed'ne·go questions or gives them hard problems, they know 10 times as much as any of his priests or wise men. Daniel 1:1-21.

IT IS over 10 years since King Neb·u·chad·nez'zar took all the best educated Israelites away to Babylon. And now look at what is happening! Jerusalem is being burned down. And the Israelites who weren't killed are being taken as prisoners to Babylon.

Remember, this is what Jehovah's prophets warned would happen if the people didn't change their bad ways. But the Israelites did not listen to the prophets. They kept right on worshiping false gods instead of Jehovah. So the people deserve to be punished. We know this because God's prophet Ezekiel tells us about the bad things that the Israelites were doing.

Do you know who Ezekiel is? He is one of the young men King Neb·u·chad·nez'zar took to Babylon over 10 years before this great destruction of Jerusalem took place. Daniel and his three friends, Sha'drach, Me'shach and A·bed'ne·go, were also taken to Babylon at the same time.

While Ezekiel is still in Babylon, Jehovah shows him the bad things happening back in Jerusalem at the temple. Jehovah does this by a miracle. Ezekiel is really still in Babylon, but Jehovah lets him see everything that is going on at the temple. And what Ezekiel sees is shocking!

'Look at the disgusting things that the people are doing here at the temple,' Jehovah tells Ezekiel. 'Look at the walls covered with pictures of snakes and other animals. And look at the Israelites worshiping them!' Ezekiel can see these things, and he writes down what is happening.

'Do you see what the Israelite leaders are doing in secret?' Jehovah asks Ezekiel. Yes, he can see this too. There are 70 men, and they are all worshiping false gods. They are saying: 'Jehovah is not seeing us. He has left the land.'

Then Jehovah shows Ezekiel some women at the north gate of the temple. They are sitting there worshiping the false god Tam'muz. And look at those men at the entrance of Jehovah's temple! There are about 25 of them. Ezekiel sees them. They are bowing to the east and worshiping the sun!

'These people have no respect for me,' Jehovah says. 'They not only do bad things but come right to my temple and do them!' So Jehovah promises: 'They will feel the force of my anger. And I will not be sorry for them when they are destroyed.'

It is only about three years after Jehovah shows Ezekiel these things that the Israelites rebel against King Neb·u·chad·nez'zar. So he goes to fight against them. After a year and a half the Babylonians break through the walls of Jerusalem and burn the city to the ground. Most of the people are killed or taken away as prisoners to Babylon.

Why has Jehovah let this terrible destruction happen to the Israelites? Yes, because they have not listened to Jehovah and they have not obeyed his laws. This shows how important it is for us always to do what God says.

At first a few people are allowed to stay in the land of Israel. King Neb·u·chad·nez'zar puts a Jew named Ged·a·li'ah in charge of these people. But then some Israelites murder Ged·a·li'ah. Now the people are afraid that the Babylonians will come and destroy them all because this bad thing has happened. So they force Jeremiah to come with them, and they run away to Egypt.

This leaves the land of Israel without any people at all. For 70 years no one lives in the land. It is completely empty. But Jehovah promises that he will bring his people back to the land after 70 years. In the meantime, what is happening to God's people in the land of Babylon where they have been taken? Let's see.

2 Kings 25:1-26; Jeremiah 29:10; Ezekiel 1:1-3; 8:1-18.

PART 5

Captivity in Babylon to Rebuilding of Jerusalem's Walls

While in captivity in Babylon, the Israelites had many tests of their faith. Sha'drach, Me'shach and A·bed'ne·go were thrown into a fiery hot furnace, but God brought them out alive. Later, after Babylon was defeated by the Medes and the Persians, Daniel was pitched into a lions' pit, but God also protected him by shutting the mouths of the lions.

Finally, the Persian king Cyrus freed the Israelites. They returned to their homeland just 70 years after they were taken away to Babylon as captives. One of the first things they did when they returned to Jerusalem was to begin building Jehovah's temple. However, enemies soon stopped their work. So it was about 22 years after returning to Jerusalem that they finally finished the temple.

Next, we learn about Ezra's trip back to Jerusalem to beautify the temple. This was some 47 years after the temple was finished. Then, 13 years after Ezra's trip, Nehemiah helped to rebuild Jerusalem's broken-down walls. Part FIVE covers 152 years of history down to this time.

DO YOU remember hearing about these three young men? Yes, they are the friends of Daniel who refused to eat what was not good for them. The Babylonians called them Sha'drach, Me'shach and A·bed'ne·go. But look at them now. Why aren't they bowing down to this huge image like everyone else? Let's find out.

Do you remember the laws that Jehovah himself wrote called the Ten Commandments? The first one of these is: 'You must not worship any other gods except me.' The young men here are obeying this law, even though it is not an easy thing to do.

Neb·u·chad·nez'zar, the king of Babylon, has called many important people to honor this image that he has set up. He has just finished saying to all the people: 'When you hear the sound of the horns, the harps and the other musical instruments, you are to bow down and worship this gold image. Anyone who does not bow down and worship will be thrown into a burning hot furnace right away.'

When Neb·u·chad·nez'zar learns that Sha'drach, Me'shach and A·bed'ne·go have not bowed down, he is very angry. He has them brought to him. He gives them another chance to bow down. But the young men trust in Jehovah. 'Our God whom we serve is able to save us,' they tell Neb·u·chad·nez'zar. 'But even if he does not save us, we will not bow down to your image of gold.'

At hearing this, Neb·u·chad·nez'zar is even more angry. There is a furnace nearby and he commands: 'Heat the furnace seven times hotter than it was before!' Then he has the strongest men in his army tie up Sha'drach, Me'shach and A·bed'ne·go and throw them into the furnace. The furnace is so hot that the strong men are killed by the flames. But what about the three young men whom they threw in?

The king looks into the furnace, and becomes very much afraid. 'Didn't we tie up three men and throw them into the burning hot furnace?' he asks.

'Yes, we did,' his servants answer.

'But I see four men walking around in the fire,' he says. 'They are not tied up, and the fire is not hurting them. And the fourth one looks like a god.' The king goes closer to the door of the furnace and cries out: 'Sha′drach! Me′shach! A·bed′ne·go! Come on out, you servants of the Most High God!'

When they come out, everyone can see that they have not been hurt. Then the king says: 'Let the God of Sha′drach, Me′shach and A·bed′ne·go be praised! He has sent his angel and saved them because they would not bow down and worship any god except their own.'

Isn't this a fine example of faithfulness to Jehovah for us to follow?   Exodus 20:3; Daniel 3:1-30.

WHAT is happening here? The people are having a big feast. The king of Babylon has invited a thousand important guests. They are using the gold cups and the silver cups and the bowls taken from Jehovah's temple in Jerusalem. But, suddenly, the fingers of a man's hand appear in the air and begin to write on the wall. Everyone is scared.

Bel·shaz′zar, the grandson of Neb·u·chad·nez′zar, is the king now. He shouts for his wise men to be brought in. 'Anyone who can read this writing and tell me what it means,' the king says, 'will be given many gifts and be made the third most important ruler in the kingdom.' But none of the wise men can read the writing on the wall, nor tell its meaning.

The king's mother hears the noise and comes into the big dining room. 'Please don't be so frightened,' she tells the king.

'There is a man in your kingdom that knows the holy gods. When your grandfather Neb·u·chad·nez'zar was king he made him the chief of all his wise men. His name is Daniel. Send for him, and he will tell you what all of this means.'

So right away Daniel is brought in. After refusing to take any gifts, Daniel begins to tell why Jehovah once removed Bel·shaz'zar's grandfather Neb·u·chad·nez'zar from being king. 'He was very proud,' Daniel says. 'And Jehovah punished him.'

'But you,' Daniel tells Bel·shaz'zar, 'knew all about what happened to him, and still you are proud just as Neb·u·chad·nez'zar was. You have brought in the cups and the bowls from Jehovah's temple and drunk out of them. You have praised gods made of wood and stone, and you have not honored our Grand Creator. That is why God has sent the hand to write these words.

'This is what is written,' Daniel says: 'ME'NE, ME'NE, TE'KEL and PAR'SIN.'

'ME'NE means that God has numbered the days of your kingdom and brought it to an end. TE'KEL means that you have been weighed on the scales and found to be no good. PAR'SIN means that your kingdom is given to the Medes and the Persians.'

Even while Daniel is speaking, the Medes and the Persians have begun to attack Babylon. They capture the city and kill Bel·shaz'zar. The handwriting on the wall comes true that very night! But what will happen to the Israelites now? We will soon find out, but first let's see what happens to Daniel. Daniel 5:1-31.

OH, OH! It looks as if Daniel is in a lot of trouble. But the lions are not hurting him! Do you know why? Who put Daniel in here with all these lions? Let's find out.

The king of Babylon is now a man named Da·ri′us. He likes Daniel very much because Daniel is so kind and wise. Da·ri′us chooses Daniel to be a chief ruler in his kingdom. This makes other men in the kingdom jealous of Daniel, so this is what they do.

They go to Da·ri′us and say: 'We have agreed, O king, that you should make a law saying that for 30 days no one should pray to any god or man except to you, O king. If anyone disobeys, then he should be thrown in with the lions.' Da·ri′us does not know why these men want this law made. But he thinks it is a good idea, so he puts the law into writing. Now the law cannot be changed.

When Daniel learns about the law, he goes home and prays, just as he always has done. The bad men knew that Daniel would not stop praying to Jehovah. They are happy, because it seems that their plan to get rid of Daniel is working.

When King Da·ri'us learns why these men wanted to make this law, he is very sorry. But he cannot change the law, so he has to give the command for Daniel to be thrown into the lions' pit. But the king tells Daniel: 'I hope that your God, whom you serve, will save you.'

Da·ri'us is so upset he can't sleep that night. The next morning he runs to the lions' pit. You can see him there. He cries out: 'Daniel, servant of the living God! Was the God whom you serve able to save you from the lions?'

'God sent his angel,' Daniel answers, 'and shut the mouths of the lions so that they did not hurt me.'

The king is very glad. He commands that Daniel be lifted out of the pit. Then he has the bad men who tried to get rid of Daniel thrown to the lions. Even before they reach the bottom of the pit, the lions grab them and break all their bones.

Then King Da·ri'us writes to all the people in his kingdom: 'I command that everyone should respect Daniel's God. He does great miracles. He saved Daniel from being eaten by the lions.'

Daniel 6:1-28.

GOD'S PEOPLE LEAVE BABYLON 80

NEARLY two years have passed since Babylon was captured by the Medes and the Persians. And look what is happening now! Yes, the Israelites are leaving Babylon. How did they get free? Who let them go?

Cy'rus, the king of Persia, did. Long before Cy'rus was born, Jehovah had his prophet Isaiah write about him: 'You will do just what I want you to do. The gates will be left open for you to capture the city.' And Cy'rus did take the lead in capturing Babylon. The Medes and the Persians came into the city at night through gates that had been left open.

But Jehovah's prophet Isaiah also said that Cy'rus would give

the command for Jerusalem and its temple to be built again. Did Cy'rus give this command? Yes, he did. This is what Cy'rus tells the Israelites: 'Go, now, to Jerusalem and build the temple of Jehovah, your God.' And this is just what these Israelites are on their way to do.

But not all the Israelites in Babylon can make the long trip back to Jerusalem. It is a long, long trip of about 500 miles (800 kilometers) and many are too old or too sick to travel so far. And there are other reasons why some people don't go. But Cy'rus tells those that don't go: 'Give silver and gold and other gifts to the people who are going back to build Jerusalem and its temple.'

So, many gifts are given to these Israelites who are on their way to Jerusalem. Also, Cy'rus gives them the bowls and the cups that King Neb·u·chad·nez'zar had taken from Jehovah's temple when he destroyed Jerusalem. The people have a lot of things to carry back with them.

After about four months of traveling, the Israelites get back to Jerusalem right on time. It is just 70 years since the city was destroyed, and the land was left completely empty of people. But though the Israelites are now back in their own country they will have some hard times, as we will learn next.

Isaiah 44:28; 45:1-4; Ezra 1:1-11.

TRUSTING IN GOD'S HELP

ALMOST 50,000 people make the long trip from Babylon to
Jerusalem. But when they arrive, Jerusalem is just a big
ruin. Nobody lives there. The Israelites have to build everything
all over again.

One of the first things that they build is an altar. This is a
place where they can make animal offerings, or gifts, to Jehovah.
A few months later the Israelites begin building the temple. But
enemies living in lands nearby don't want the Israelites to build it.
So they try to frighten them to make them stop. Finally, these
enemies get the new king of Persia to make a law to stop the
building work.

Years pass. Now it has been 17 years since the Israelites came
back from Babylon. Jehovah sends his prophets Hag′gai and
Zech·a·ri′ah to tell the people to start building again. The people
trust in God's help, and they obey the prophets. They start to
build again, even though a law says that they are not to do it.

So a Persian official named Tat′te·nai comes and asks the
Israelites what right they have to build the temple. The Israelites
tell him that when they were in Babylon, King Cy′rus told them:
'Go, now, to Jerusalem and build the temple of Jehovah, your God.'

Tat′te·nai sends a letter to Babylon and asks if Cy′rus, who is
now dead, really said that. Soon a letter from the new king of
Persia comes back. It tells that Cy′rus really said it. And so the
king writes: 'Let the Israelites build the temple of their God. And
I command you to help them.' In about four years the temple is
finished, and the Israelites are very happy.

Many more years pass. It is now almost 48 years since the
temple was finished. The people in Jerusalem are poor, and the
city and God's temple do not look very pretty. Back in Babylon,

the Israelite Ez'ra learns about the need to fix up God's temple. So do you know what he does?

Ez'ra goes to see Ar·ta·xerx'es, the king of Persia, and this good king gives Ez'ra many gifts to take back to Jerusalem. Ez'ra asks the Israelites in Babylon to help him carry these gifts to Jerusalem. About 6,000 people say they will go. They have a lot of silver and gold and other precious things to carry with them.

Ez'ra is worried, because there are bad men along the way. These men might take away their silver and gold, and kill them. So Ez'ra calls the people together, as you can see in the picture. Then they pray to Jehovah to protect them on their long trip back to Jerusalem.

Jehovah does protect them. And after four months of traveling, they arrive safely in Jerusalem. Doesn't this show that Jehovah can protect those who trust in him for help?   Ezra chapters 2 to 8.

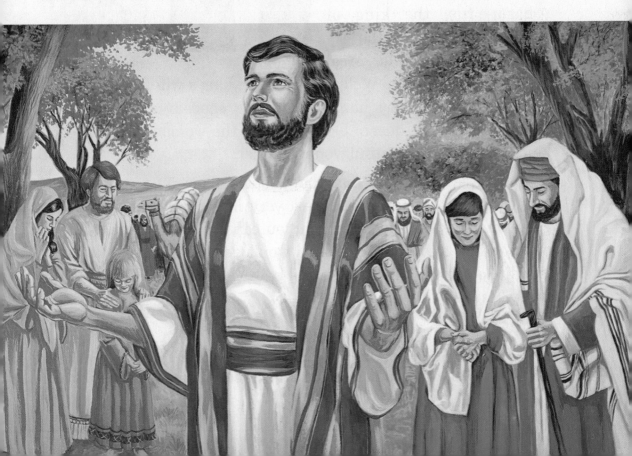

LET'S go back a few years before Ez'ra went to Jerusalem. Mor'de·cai and Esther are the most important Israelites in the kingdom of Persia. Esther is the queen, and her cousin Mor'de·cai is second only to the king in power. Let's see how this came about.

Esther's parents died when she was very small, and so Mor'de·cai has raised her. A·has·u·e'rus, the king of Persia, has a palace in the city of Shu'shan, and Mor'de·cai is one of his servants. Well, one day the king's wife Vash'ti does not obey him, so the king chooses a new wife to be his queen. Do you know the woman he chooses? Yes, beautiful young Esther.

Do you see this proud man that people are bowing down to? This is Ha'man. He is a very important man in Persia. Ha'man wants Mor'de·cai, whom you can see sitting here, to bow down to him also. But Mor'de·cai won't do it. He doesn't think it is right to bow down to such a bad man. This makes Ha'man very angry. And so this is what he does.

Ha'man tells the king lies about the Israelites. 'They are bad people who don't obey your laws,' he says. 'They should be put to death.' A·has·u·e'rus does not know that his wife Esther is an

Israelite. So he listens to Ha'man, and he has a law made that on a certain day all Israelites are to be killed.

When Mor'de·cai hears about the law, he is very upset. He sends a message to Esther: 'You must tell the king, and beg him to save us.' It is against the law in Persia to go see the king unless you're invited. But Esther goes in without being invited. The king holds out his gold rod to her, which means that she is not to be killed. Esther invites the king and Ha'man to a big meal. There the king asks Esther what favor she wants from him. Esther says that she will tell him if he and Ha'man will come to another meal the next day.

At that meal Esther tells the king: 'My people and I are to be killed.' The king is angry. 'Who dares to do such a thing?' he asks.

'The man, the enemy, is this bad Ha'man!' Esther says.

Now the king is really angry. He commands that Ha'man be killed. Afterward, the king makes Mor'de·cai second in power only to himself. Mor'de·cai then sees to it that a new law is made that allows the Israelites to fight for their lives on the day they are supposed to be killed. Because Mor'de·cai is such an important man now, many people help the Israelites, and they are saved from their enemies. Bible book of Esther.

L OOK at all the work going on here. The Israelites are busy building the walls of Jerusalem. When King Neb·u·chad·nez'zar destroyed Jerusalem 152 years before, he knocked down the walls and burned the city's gates. The Israelites did not build the walls again when they first came home from Babylon.

How do you think the people have felt living here all these years without walls around their city? They have not felt safe. Their enemies could easily come in and attack them. But now this man Ne·he·mi'ah is finally helping the people to build the walls again. Do you know who Ne·he·mi'ah is?

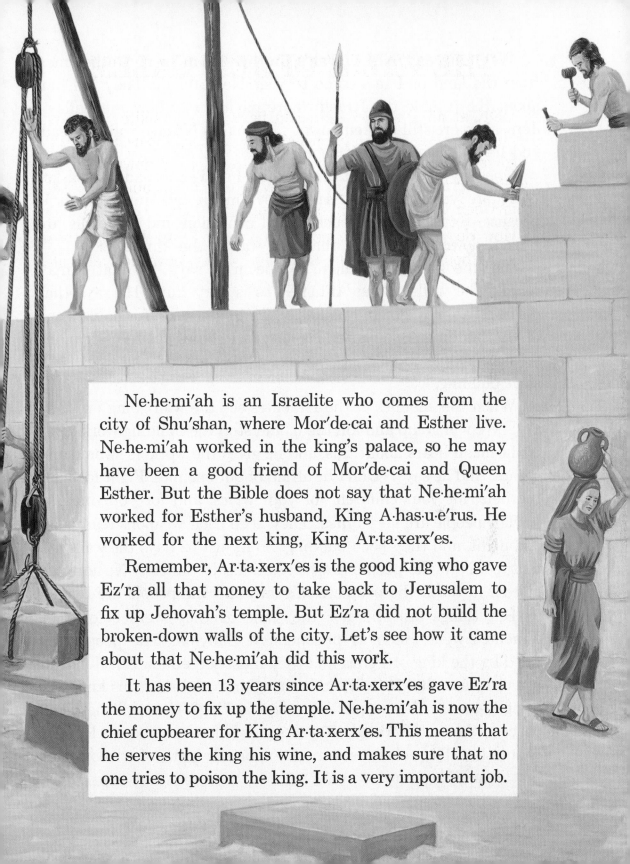

Ne·he·mi′ah is an Israelite who comes from the city of Shu′shan, where Mor′de·cai and Esther live. Ne·he·mi′ah worked in the king's palace, so he may have been a good friend of Mor′de·cai and Queen Esther. But the Bible does not say that Ne·he·mi′ah worked for Esther's husband, King A·has·u·e′rus. He worked for the next king, King Ar·ta·xerx′es.

Remember, Ar·ta·xerx′es is the good king who gave Ez′ra all that money to take back to Jerusalem to fix up Jehovah's temple. But Ez′ra did not build the broken-down walls of the city. Let's see how it came about that Ne·he·mi′ah did this work.

It has been 13 years since Ar·ta·xerx′es gave Ez′ra the money to fix up the temple. Ne·he·mi′ah is now the chief cupbearer for King Ar·ta·xerx′es. This means that he serves the king his wine, and makes sure that no one tries to poison the king. It is a very important job.

Well, one day Ne·he·mi′ah's brother Ha·na′ni and other men from the land of Israel come to visit Ne·he·mi′ah. They tell him about the trouble the Israelites are having, and how the walls of Jerusalem are still broken down. This makes Ne·he·mi′ah very sad, and he prays to Jehovah about it.

One day the king notices that Ne·he·mi′ah is sad, and asks: 'Why are you looking so sad?' Ne·he·mi′ah tells him that it is because Jerusalem is in such a bad condition and the walls are broken down. 'What is it that you want?' the king asks.

'Let me go to Jerusalem,' Ne·he·mi′ah says, 'so that I may rebuild the walls.' King Ar·ta·xerx′es is very kind. He says that Ne·he·mi′ah may go, and he helps him to get wood for doing some of the building. Soon after Ne·he·mi′ah comes to Jerusalem, he tells the people about his plans. They like the idea, and say: 'Let's start building.'

When the enemies of the Israelites see the wall going up, they say: 'We will go up and kill them, and stop the building work.' But Ne·he·mi′ah hears about this, and he gives the workers swords and spears. And he says: 'Don't be afraid of our enemies. Fight for your brothers, for your children, for your wives, and for your homes.'

The people are very brave. They keep their weapons ready day and night, and they keep building. So in just 52 days the walls are finished. Now the people can feel safe inside the city. Ne·he·mi′ah and Ez′ra teach the people God's law, and the people are happy.

But things are still not the same as they were before the Israelites were taken as prisoners to Babylon. The people are ruled by the king of Persia and they must serve him. But Jehovah has promised that he will send a new king, and that this king will bring peace to the people. Who is this king? How will he bring peace to the earth? About 450 years pass before any more is learned about this. Then there is a most important birth of a baby. But that is another story.

Nehemiah chapters 1 to 6.

PART 6

Birth of Jesus to His Death

The angel Gabriel was sent to a fine young woman named Mary. He told her that she would have a child who would rule as king forever. The child, Jesus, was born in a stable, where shepherds visited him. Later, a star guided men from the East to the young child. We learn who caused them to see that star, and how Jesus was saved from the efforts to kill him.

Next, we find Jesus, when he was 12 years old, talking with the teachers in the temple. Eighteen years later Jesus was baptized, and he then began the Kingdom preaching and teaching work that God sent him to earth to do. To help him in this work, Jesus chose 12 men and made them his apostles.

Jesus also did many miracles. He fed thousands of people with only a few small fishes and a few loaves of bread. He healed the sick and even raised the dead. Finally, we learn about the many things that happened to Jesus during the last day of his life, and how he was killed. Jesus preached for about three and a half years, so PART 6 covers a period of a little more than 34 years.

AN ANGEL VISITS MARY

84

THIS pretty woman is Mary. She is an Israelitess, who lives in the town of Naz'a·reth. God knows that she is a very fine person. That is why he has sent his angel Ga'bri·el to speak to her. Do you know what Ga'bri·el has come to tell Mary? Let's see.

'Good day, you highly favored one,' Ga'bri·el says to her. 'Jehovah is with you.' Mary has never seen this person before. She is worried, because she doesn't know what he means. But right away Ga'bri·el calms her fears.

'Don't be afraid, Mary,' he says. 'Jehovah is very pleased with you. That is why he is going to do a wonderful thing for you. You will soon have a baby. And you are to call him Jesus.'

Ga'bri·el goes on to explain: 'This child will be great, and he will be called Son of the Most High God. Jehovah will make him king, as David was. But Jesus will be a king forever, and his kingdom will never end!'

'How can this all be?' Mary asks. 'I am not even married. I have not lived with a man, so how can I have a baby?'

'God's power will come upon you,' Ga'bri·el answers. 'So the child will be called God's Son.' Then he tells Mary: 'Remember your relative Elizabeth. People said that she was too old to have children. But soon now she will have a son. So you see, there is nothing that God can't do.'

Right away Mary says: 'I am Jehovah's slave girl! May it happen to me just as you have said.' The angel then leaves.

Mary hurries off to visit Elizabeth. When Elizabeth hears Mary's voice, the baby inside Elizabeth jumps for joy. Elizabeth is filled with God's spirit, and she says to Mary: 'You are specially blessed among women.' Mary stays with Elizabeth about three months, and then goes back home to Naz'a·reth.

Mary is about to get married to a man named Joseph. But when Joseph learns that Mary is going to have a baby, he doesn't think he should marry her. Then God's angel says to him: 'Don't be afraid to take Mary to be your wife. For it is God who has given her a son.' So Mary and Joseph get married, and they wait for Jesus to be born.

Luke 1:26-56; Matthew 1:18-25.

JESUS BORN IN A STABLE

85

DO YOU know who this little baby is? Yes, it is Jesus. He has just been born in a stable. A stable is where animals are kept. Mary is laying Jesus in the manger, which is the place that holds the food for donkeys and other animals to eat. But why are Mary and Joseph here with the animals? This is no place for a baby to be born, is it?

No, it isn't. But this is why they are here: The ruler of Rome, Caesar Au·gus'tus, made a law that everyone must return to the

city where he was born to have his name written in a book. Well, Joseph was born here in Beth'le·hem. But when he and Mary arrived, there wasn't a room for them anywhere. So they had to come here with the animals. And on this very day Mary gave birth to Jesus! But, as you can see, he is all right.

Can you see the shepherds coming to see Jesus? They were

in the fields at night taking care of their sheep, and a bright light shone all around them. It was an angel! The shepherds were very much afraid. But the angel said: 'Don't be afraid! I have good news for you. Today, in Beth'le·hem, Christ the Lord was born. He will save the people! You will find him wrapped in cloths and lying in a manger.' Suddenly many angels came and began praising God. So right away these shepherds hurried to look for Jesus, and now they have found him.

Do you know why Jesus is so special? Do you know who he *really* is? Remember, in the first story of this book we told about God's first Son. This Son worked with Jehovah in making the heavens and the earth and everything else. Well, this is who Jesus is!

Yes, Jehovah took the life of his Son from heaven and put it inside Mary. Right away a baby began to grow inside her just as other babies grow inside their mothers. But this baby was God's Son. Finally Jesus was born here in a stable in Beth'le·hem. Can you see now why the angels were so happy to be able to tell people that Jesus had been born?

Luke 2:1-20.

CAN you see that bright star one of these men is pointing to? When they left Jerusalem, the star appeared. These men are from the East, and they study the stars. They believe that this new star is leading them to someone important.

When the men got to Jerusalem, they asked: 'Where is the child who is to be king of the Jews?' "Jews" is another name for Israelites. 'We first saw the child's star when we were in the East,' the men said, 'and we have come to worship him.'

When Herod, who is king at Jerusalem, heard about this he got upset. He did not want another king to take his place. So Herod called the chief priests and asked: 'Where will the promised king be born?' They answered: 'The Bible says in Beth'le·hem.'

So Herod called the men from the East, and said: 'Go make a search for the young child. When you find him, let me know. I want to go and worship him too.' But, really, Herod wanted to find the child to kill him!

Then the star moves ahead of the men to Beth′le·hem, and it stops over the place where the child is. When the men go into the house, they find Mary and little Jesus. They bring out gifts and give them to Jesus. But later Jehovah warns the men in a dream not to go back to Herod. So they return to their own country by another road.

When Herod learns that the men from the East have left for home, he gets very angry. So he gives the command for all the boys in Beth′le·hem two years of age and under to be killed. But Jehovah warns Joseph ahead of time in a dream, and Joseph leaves with his family for Egypt. Later, when Joseph learns that Herod has died, he takes Mary and Jesus back home to Naz′a·reth. This is where Jesus grows up.

Who do you think made that new star to shine? Remember, the men first went to Jerusalem after seeing the star. Satan the Devil wanted to kill God's Son, and he knew that King Herod of Jerusalem would try to kill him. So Satan is the one who must have made that star shine.

Matthew 2:1-23; Micah 5:2.

YOUNG JESUS IN THE TEMPLE

LOOK at the young boy talking to these older men. They are teachers in God's temple at Jerusalem. And the boy is Jesus. He has grown up quite a bit. Now he is 12 years old.

The teachers are very surprised that Jesus knows so much about God and the things written in the Bible. But why aren't Joseph and Mary here too? Where are they? Let's find out.

Every year Joseph brings his family to Jerusalem for the special celebration called the Passover. It's a long trip from Naz'a·reth to Jerusalem. No one has a car, and there are no trains. They didn't have them in those days. Most of the people walk, and it takes them about three days to get to Jerusalem.

By now Joseph has a big family. So there are some younger brothers and sisters of Jesus to look after. Well, this year Joseph and Mary have left with their children on the long trip back home to Naz'a·reth. They think that Jesus is with others traveling along. But when they stop at the end of the day, they can't find Jesus. They look for him among their relatives and friends, but he's not with them! So they return to Jerusalem to look for him there.

At last they find Jesus here with the teachers. He is listening to them and asking questions. And all the people are amazed at how wise Jesus is. But Mary says: 'Child, why have you done this to us? Your father and I have been very worried trying to find you.'

'Why did you have to look for me?' Jesus answers. 'Didn't you know that I had to be in the house of my Father?'

Yes, Jesus loves to be where he can learn about God. Isn't that the way we should feel too? Back home in Naz'a·reth, Jesus would go to meetings for worship every week. Because he always paid attention, he learned many things from the Bible. Let's be like Jesus and follow his example.　　Luke 2:41-52; Matthew 13:53-56.

SEE the dove coming down on the man's head. The man is Jesus. He is about 30 years old now. And the man with him is John. We already learned something about him. Do you remember when Mary went to visit her relative Elizabeth, and the baby inside Elizabeth jumped for joy? That unborn baby was John. But what are John and Jesus doing now?

John has just dipped Jesus into the waters of the Jordan River. This is how a person is baptized. First, he is dipped under water, and then brought up again. Because this is what John does to people, he is called John the Baptizer. But why has John baptized Jesus?

Well, John did it because Jesus came and asked John to baptize him. John baptizes people who want to show that they are sorry for the bad things they have done. But did Jesus ever do anything bad to be sorry about? No, Jesus never did, because he is God's own Son from heaven. So he asked John to baptize him for a different reason. Let's see what that reason was.

Before Jesus came here to John, he was a carpenter. A carpenter is a person who makes things out of wood, such as tables and chairs and benches. Mary's husband Joseph was a carpenter, and he taught Jesus to be one too. But Jehovah did not send his Son to earth to be a carpenter. He has special work for him to do, and the time has come for Jesus to begin doing it. So to show that he has now come to do his Father's will, Jesus asks John to baptize him. Is God pleased with this?

Yes, he is, because, after Jesus comes up from the water, a voice from heaven says: 'This is my Son, with whom I am pleased.' Also, it seems that the heavens open up and this dove comes down on Jesus. But it is not a real dove. It only looks like one. It is really God's holy spirit.

Now Jesus has a lot to think about, so he goes away to a lonely place for 40 days. There Satan comes to him. Three times Satan tries to get Jesus to do something against God's laws. But Jesus won't do it.

After that, Jesus returns and meets some men who become his first followers, or disciples. Some of their names are Andrew, Peter (also called Simon), Philip and Na·than'a·el (also called Bar·thol'o·mew). Jesus and these new disciples leave for the district of Gal'i·lee. In Gal'i·lee they stop at Na·than'a·el's hometown of Ca'na. There Jesus goes to a big wedding feast, and does his first miracle. Do you know what it is? He turns water into wine.

Matthew 3:13-17; 4:1-11; 13:55; Mark 6:3; John 1:29-51; 2:1-12.

JESUS really looks angry here, doesn't he? Do you know why he is so angry? It is because these men at God's temple in

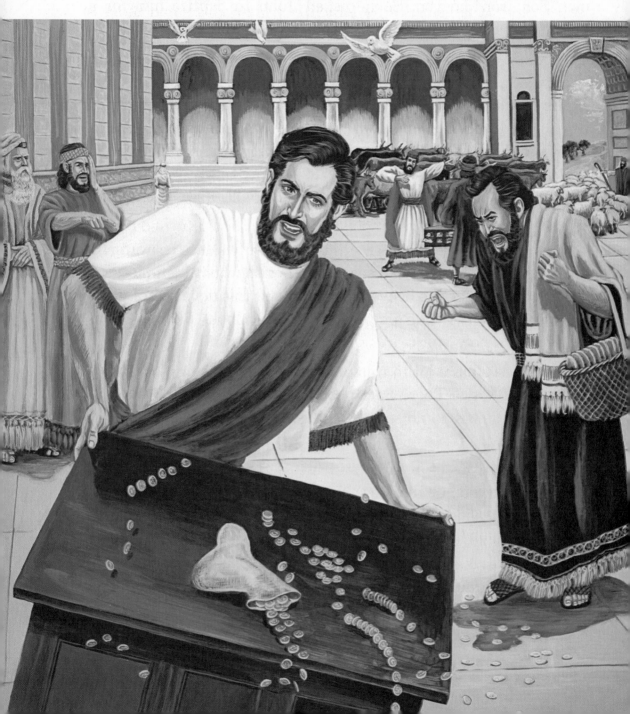

Jerusalem are very greedy. They are trying to make a lot of money from the people who have come here to worship God.

Do you see all those young bulls and sheep and doves? Well, the men are selling these animals right here at the temple. Do you know why? It is because the Israelites need animals and birds to sacrifice to God.

God's law said that when an Israelite did wrong, he should make an offering to God. And there were other times, too, when Israelites had to make offerings. But where could an Israelite get birds and animals to offer to God?

Some Israelites owned birds and animals. So they could offer these. But many Israelites didn't own any animals or birds. And others lived so far away from Jerusalem they couldn't bring one of their animals to the temple. So the people came here and bought the animals or birds they needed. But these men were charging the people too much money. They were cheating the people. Besides that, they should not be selling right here in God's temple.

This is what makes Jesus angry. So he turns over the tables of the men with the money and scatters their coins. Also, he makes a whip from ropes and drives all the animals out of the temple. He commands the men who are selling the doves: 'Take them out of here! Stop making my Father's house a place for making a lot of money.'

Some of Jesus' followers are with him here at the temple in Jerusalem. They are surprised at what they see Jesus doing. Then they remember the place in the Bible where it says about God's Son: 'Love for God's house will burn in him like a fire.'

While Jesus is here in Jerusalem attending the Passover, he does many miracles. Afterward, Jesus leaves Ju·de′a and begins his trip back to Gal′i·lee. But on his way, he goes through the district of Sa·mar′i·a. Let's see what happens there.   John 2:13-25; 4:3, 4.

WITH THE WOMAN AT THE WELL

JESUS has stopped to rest by a well in Sa·mar'i·a. His disciples have gone into town to buy food. The woman Jesus is speaking to has come to get some water. He says to her: 'Give me a drink.'

This surprises the woman very much. Do you know why? It is because Jesus is a Jew, and she is a Sa·mar'i·tan. And most Jews do not like Sa·mar'i·tans. They won't even talk to them! But Jesus loves all kinds of people. So he says: 'If you knew who was asking you for a drink, you would ask him and he would give you life-giving water.'

'Sir,' the woman says, 'the well is deep, and you don't even have a bucket. Where would you get this life-giving water?'

'If you drink water from this well you will get thirsty again,' Jesus explains. 'But the water I will give can make a person live forever.'

'Sir,' the woman says, 'give me this water! Then I will never be thirsty again. And I won't have to come here to get water anymore.'

The woman thinks Jesus is talking about real water. But he is talking about the truth concerning God and his kingdom. This truth is like life-giving water. It can give a person everlasting life.

Jesus now tells the woman: 'Go and call your husband and come back.'

'I don't have a husband,' she answers.

'You answered right,' Jesus says. 'But you have had five husbands, and the man you are living with now is not your husband.'

The woman is amazed, because all of this is true. How did Jesus know these things? Yes, it is because Jesus is the Promised

One sent by God, and God gives him this information. At this moment Jesus' disciples come back, and they are surprised that he is talking to a Sa·mar'i·tan woman.

What do we learn from all of this? It shows that Jesus is kind to people of all races. And we should be too. We should not think some people are bad just because they are of a certain race. Jesus wants all people to know the truth that leads to everlasting life. And we too should want to help people learn the truth.

John 4:5-43; 17:3.

SEE Jesus sitting here. He is teaching all these people on a mountain in Gal'i·lee. Those sitting closest to him are his disciples. He has chosen 12 of them to be apostles. The apostles are Jesus' special disciples. Do you know their names?

There is Simon Peter and his brother Andrew. Then there are James and John, who are brothers too. Another apostle is also named James, and another one is also called Simon. Two apostles are named Judas. One is Judas Is·car'i·ot, and the other Judas is also called by the name Thad·dae'us. Then there are Philip and Na·than'a·el (also called Bar·thol'o·mew), and Matthew and Thomas.

After coming back from Sa·mar'i·a, Jesus began to preach for the first time: 'The kingdom of the heavens is near.' Do you know what

that kingdom is? It is a real government of God. Jesus is its king. He will rule from heaven and bring peace to the earth. The whole earth will be made into a beautiful paradise by God's kingdom.

Jesus is here teaching the people about the kingdom. 'This is how you should pray,' he is explaining. 'Our Father in heaven, let your name be honored. Let your kingdom come. Let your will be done on earth, as it is in heaven.' Many people call this 'The Lord's Prayer.' Others call it the 'Our Father.' Can you say the whole prayer?

Jesus also is teaching the people how they should treat one another. 'Do for others what you want them to do for you,' he says. Don't you like it when others treat you in a kind way? So, Jesus is saying, we should treat other people kindly. Won't it be wonderful in the paradise earth when everybody will do this?

Matthew chapters 5 to 7; 10:1-4.

THE girl you see here is 12 years old. Jesus is holding her hand, and her mother and father are standing close by. Do you know why they look so happy? Let's find out.

The girl's father is an important man named Ja'i·rus. One day his daughter becomes sick, and she is put to bed. But she does not get any better. She only gets sicker and sicker. Ja'i·rus and his wife are very worried, because it looks like their little girl is

going to die. She is their only daughter. So Ja'i·rus goes to look for Jesus. He has heard about the miracles Jesus is doing.

When Ja'i·rus finds Jesus, there is a big crowd around him. But Ja'i·rus gets through the crowd and falls at Jesus' feet. 'My daughter is very, very sick,' he says. 'Please, come and make her well,' he begs. Jesus says that he will come.

As they walk along, the crowd keeps pushing to get closer. Suddenly Jesus stops. 'Who touched me?' he asks. Jesus felt power go out from him, so he knows that someone touched him. But who? It is a woman who has been very sick for 12 years. She had come up and touched Jesus' clothes, and was healed!

This makes Ja'i·rus feel better, because he can see how easy it is for Jesus to heal someone. But then a messenger comes. 'Don't bother Jesus anymore,' he tells Ja'i·rus. 'Your daughter has died.' Jesus overhears this and says to Ja'i·rus: 'Don't worry, she will be all right.'

When they finally get to Ja'i·rus' house, the people are crying with great grief. But Jesus says: 'Don't cry. The child did not die. She is only sleeping.' But they laugh and make fun of Jesus, because they know she is dead.

Jesus then takes the girl's father and mother and three of his apostles into the room where the child is lying. He takes her by the hand and says: 'Get up!' And she comes to life, just as you see here. And she gets up and walks about! That is why her mother and father are so very, very happy.

This is not the first person Jesus raised from the dead. The first one the Bible tells about is the son of a widow who lives in the city of Na'in. Later, Jesus also raises Laz'a·rus, the brother of Mary and Martha, from the dead. When Jesus rules as God's king, he will bring many, many dead people back to life. Can't we be glad about that?   Luke 8:40-56; 7:11-17; John 11:17-44.

JESUS FEEDS MANY PEOPLE

93

SOMETHING terrible has happened. John the Baptizer has just been killed. He·ro′di·as, the wife of the king, did not like him. And she was able to get the king to have John's head cut off.

When Jesus hears about this, he is very sad. He goes into a lonely place by himself. But the people follow him. When Jesus sees the crowds, he feels sorry for them. So he talks to them about the kingdom of God, and he heals their sick ones.

That evening his disciples come to him and say: 'It is already late, and this is a lonely place. Send the people away so they can buy some food for themselves in the nearby villages.'

'They don't have to leave,' Jesus answers. 'You give them something to eat.' Turning to Philip, Jesus asks: 'Where can we buy enough food to feed all these people?'

'It will cost lots and lots of money to buy enough so everyone can have only a little bit,' Philip answers. Andrew speaks up: 'This boy, who is carrying our food, has five loaves of bread and two fishes. But it won't be nearly enough for all these people.'

'Tell the people to sit down on the grass,' Jesus says. Then he thanks God for the food, and starts breaking it into pieces. Next, the disciples give the bread and fish to all the people. There are 5,000 men, and many more thousands of women and children. They all eat until they are full. And when the disciples gather up what is left over, there are 12 baskets full!

Jesus now has his disciples get into a boat to go across the Sea of Gal′i·lee. During the night a big storm comes up, and waves toss the boat this way and that way. The disciples are very much afraid. Then, in the middle of the night, they see someone walking toward them across the water. They cry out in fear, because they do not know what they are seeing.

'Don't be afraid,' Jesus says. 'It is I!' They still can't believe it. So Peter says: 'If it really is you, Lord, tell me to walk across the water to you.' Jesus answers: 'Come!' And Peter gets out and walks on the water! Then he becomes afraid and begins to sink, but Jesus saves him.

Later, Jesus again feeds thousands of people. This time he does so with seven loaves of bread and a few small fishes. And again there is plenty for all. Isn't it wonderful how Jesus takes care of people? When he rules as God's king we will never have to worry about anything! Matthew 14:1-32; 15:29-38; John 6:1-21.

HE LOVES LITTLE CHILDREN

94

LOOK at Jesus here with his arms around the little boy. You can tell that Jesus really cares for little ones. The men watching are his apostles. What is Jesus saying to them? Let's find out.

Jesus and his apostles have just come back from a long trip. Along the way the apostles had an argument among themselves. So after the trip Jesus asks them: 'What were you arguing about on the road?' Really, Jesus knows what the argument was about. But he asks the question to see if the apostles will tell him.

The apostles don't answer, because on the road they were arguing about which one of them is the greatest. Some apostles want to be more important than the others. How will Jesus tell them it is not right to want to be the greatest?

He calls the little boy, and stands him in front of them all. Then he says to his disciples: 'I want you to know this for certain, Unless you change and become like young children, you will never get into God's kingdom. The greatest person in the kingdom is the one who becomes like this child.' Do you know why Jesus said this?

Well, very little children do not worry about being greater or more important than others are. So the apostles should learn to be like children in this way and not quarrel about being great or important.

There are other times, too, when Jesus shows how much he cares for little children. A few months later some people bring their children to see Jesus. The apostles try to keep them away. But Jesus tells his apostles: 'Let the children come to me, and do not stop them, because the kingdom of God belongs to persons like them.' Then Jesus takes the children in his arms, and blesses them. Isn't it good to know that Jesus loves little children?

Matthew 18:1-4; 19:13-15; Mark 9:33-37; 10:13-16.

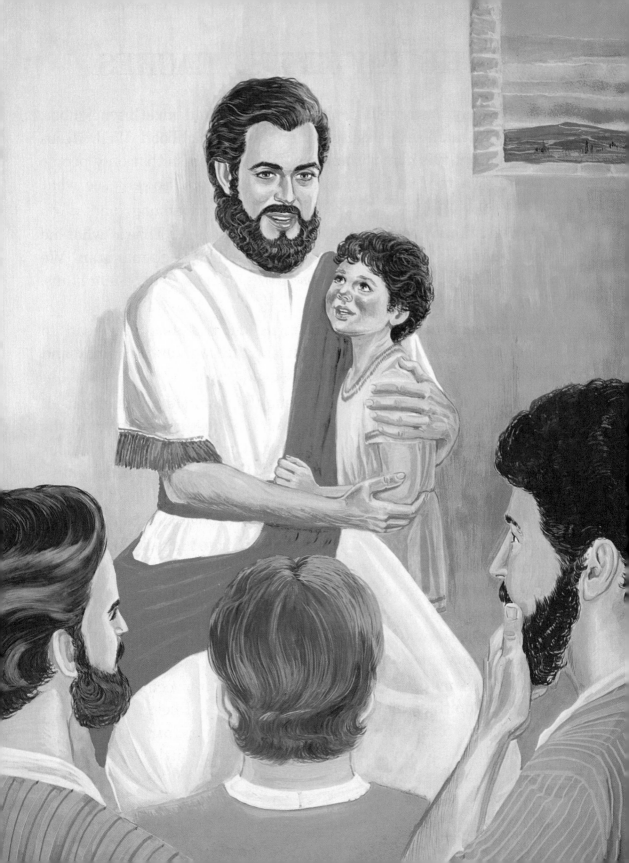

THE WAY JESUS TEACHES

95

ONE day Jesus tells a man that he should love his neighbor. The man asks Jesus: 'Who is my neighbor?' Well, Jesus knows what this man is thinking. The man thinks that only people of his own race and religion are his neighbors. So let's see what Jesus says to him.

Sometimes Jesus teaches by telling a story. This is what he does now. He tells a story about a Jew and a Sa·mar′i·tan. We have already learned that most Jews do not like Sa·mar′i·tans. Well, this is Jesus' story:

One day there was a Jew going down a mountain road to Jer′i·cho. But robbers jumped on him. They took his money and beat him up until he was almost dead.

Later, a Jewish priest came along the road. He saw the beat-up man. What do you think he did? Why, he just crossed over to the other side of the road and kept going. Then another very religious person came along. He was a Levite. Did he stop? No, he didn't stop to help the beat-up man either. You can see the priest and the Levite in the distance going down the road.

But see who is here with the beat-up man. He is a Sa·mar′i·tan. And he is helping the Jew. He is putting some medicine on his wounds. Afterward, he takes the Jew to a place where he can rest and get well.

After finishing his story, Jesus says to the man who asked him the question: 'Which one of these three do you think acted like a neighbor to the beat-up man? Was it the priest, the Levite or the Sa·mar'i·tan?'

The man answers: 'The Sa·mar'i·tan man. He was kind to the man who was beat up.'

Jesus says: 'You are right. So go and treat others the same way as he did.'

Don't you like the way Jesus teaches? We can learn many, many important things if we listen to what Jesus says in the Bible, can't we?   Luke 10:25-37.

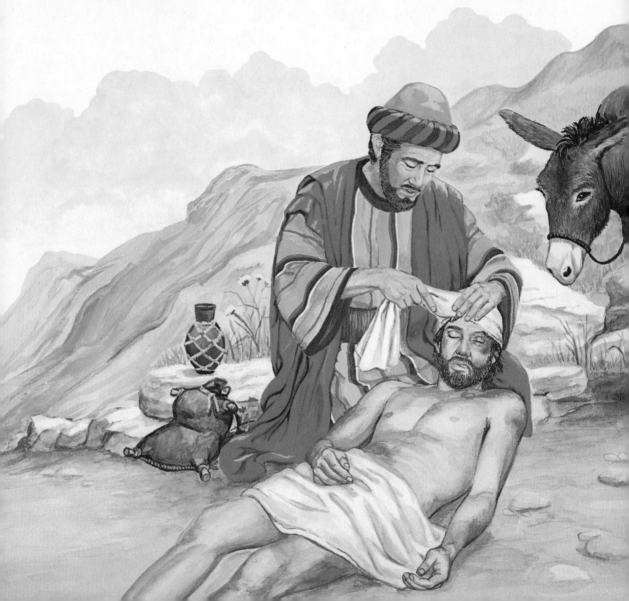

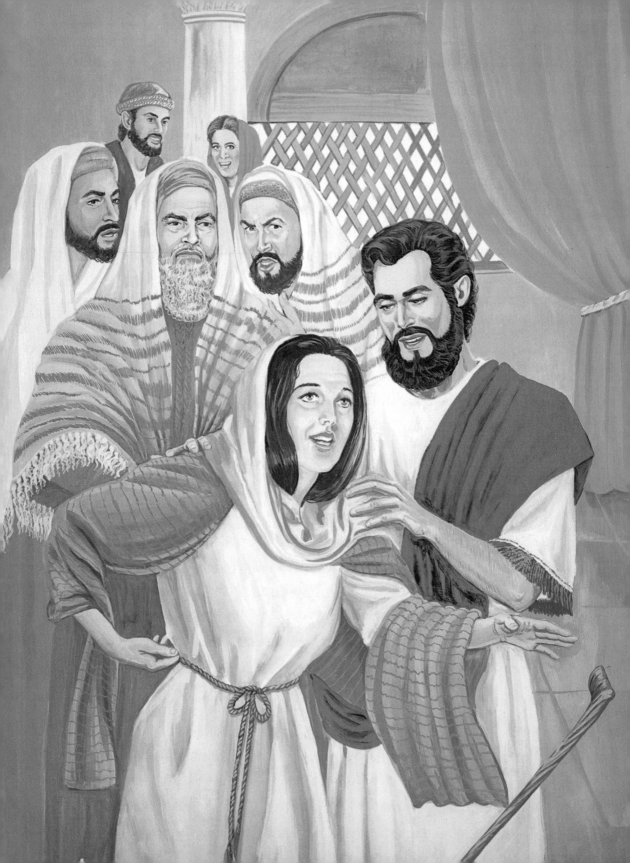

A S JESUS travels throughout the land, he heals the sick. The news of these miracles is told about in the villages and towns all around. So people bring to him those who are crippled and blind and deaf, and many others who are sick. And Jesus heals them all.

Over three years have now passed since John baptized Jesus. And Jesus tells his apostles that soon he will go up to Jerusalem, where he will be killed, and then rise from the dead. In the meantime, Jesus keeps on healing the sick.

One day Jesus is teaching on a Sabbath. The Sabbath is a day of rest for the Jews. The woman you see here has been very sick. For 18 years she was bent over, and couldn't stand up straight. So Jesus puts his hands on her, and she begins to stand up. She is healed!

This makes the religious leaders angry. 'There are six days in which we should work,' one of them shouts to the crowd. 'Those are the days to come for healing, not on the Sabbath!'

But Jesus answers: 'You bad men. Any one of you would untie your donkey and take it out for a drink on the Sabbath. So shouldn't this poor woman, who has been sick for 18 years, be healed on the Sabbath?' Jesus' answer makes these bad men ashamed.

Later Jesus and his apostles travel on toward Jerusalem. When they are just outside the town of Jer'i·cho, two blind beggars hear that Jesus is passing by. So they shout: 'Jesus, help us!'

Jesus calls the blind men over, and asks: 'What do you want me to do for you?' They say: 'Lord, let our eyes be opened.' Jesus touches their eyes, and right away they can see! Do you know why Jesus does all these wonderful miracles? Because he loves people and wants them to have faith in him. And so we can be sure that when he rules as King nobody on earth will be sick again.

Matthew 15:30, 31; Luke 13:10-17; Matthew 20:29-34.

JESUS COMES AS KING

A SHORT time after healing the two blind beggars, Jesus comes to a small village near Jerusalem. He tells two of his disciples: 'Go into the village and you will find a young donkey. Untie it and bring it to me.'

When the donkey is brought to him, Jesus sits on it. Then he rides to Jerusalem a short distance away. When he gets near the city, a large crowd of people comes out to meet him. Most of them take off their coats and put them on the road. Others cut off branches from palm trees. They put these on the road too, and they shout: 'God bless the king who comes in Jehovah's name!'

Long ago in Israel new kings would ride into Jerusalem on a young donkey to show themselves to the people. This is what Jesus

is doing. And these people are showing that they want Jesus to be their king. But not all the people want him. We can see this by what happens when Jesus goes to the temple.

At the temple Jesus heals persons who are blind and crippled. When the young children see this, they shout praises to Jesus. But this makes the priests angry, and they tell Jesus: 'Do you hear what the children are saying?'

'Yes, I do,' Jesus answers. 'Did you never read in the Bible where it says: "Out of the mouths of little children God will bring forth praise?"' So the children keep on praising God's king.

We want to be like those children, don't we? Some people may try to stop us from talking about God's kingdom. But we will keep right on telling others about the wonderful things Jesus will do for people.

It was not time for Jesus to begin ruling as king when he was on earth. When will this time come? Jesus' disciples want to know. We will read about this next.   Matthew 21:1-17; John 12:12-16.

THIS is Jesus on the Mount of Olives. The four men with him are his apostles. They are the brothers Andrew and Peter, and also the brothers James and John. That is God's temple in Jerusalem you can see over there in the distance.

It has been two days since Jesus rode into Jerusalem on the young donkey. It is Tuesday. Earlier in the day Jesus was at the temple. There the priests tried to grab Jesus to kill him. But they were afraid to do this because the people like Jesus.

'You snakes and sons of snakes!' Jesus called those religious leaders. Then Jesus said that God would punish them because of all the bad things they had done. After that Jesus came up to the Mount of Olives, and then these four apostles started asking him questions. Do you know what they are asking Jesus?

The apostles are asking about things in the future. They know that Jesus will put an end to all badness on earth. But they want to know *when* this will happen. When will Jesus come again to rule as King?

Jesus knows that his followers on earth will not be able to see him when he comes again. This is because he will be in heaven, and they will not be able to see him there. So Jesus tells his apostles some of the things that will be happening on earth when he is ruling as King in heaven. What are some of these things?

Jesus says that there will be great wars, many people will be sick and hungry, crime will be very bad, and there will be big earthquakes. Jesus also says that the good news about God's kingdom will be preached everywhere in the earth. Have we seen these things happening in our time? Yes! And so we can be sure that Jesus is now ruling in heaven. Soon he will put an end to all badness on earth. Matthew 21:46; 23:1-39; 24:1-14; Mark 13:3-10.

IT IS Thursday night now, two days later. Jesus and his 12 apostles have come to this large upstairs room to eat the Passover meal. The man you see leaving is Judas Is·car′i·ot. He is going to tell the priests how they can get Jesus.

Just the day before, Judas went to them and asked: 'What will you give me if I help you catch Jesus?' They said: 'Thirty silver coins.' So Judas is now going to meet these men so that he can lead them to Jesus. Isn't that terrible?

The Passover meal is finished. But Jesus now begins another special meal. He hands his apostles a loaf of bread and says: 'Eat it, because this means my body which is to be given for you.' Then

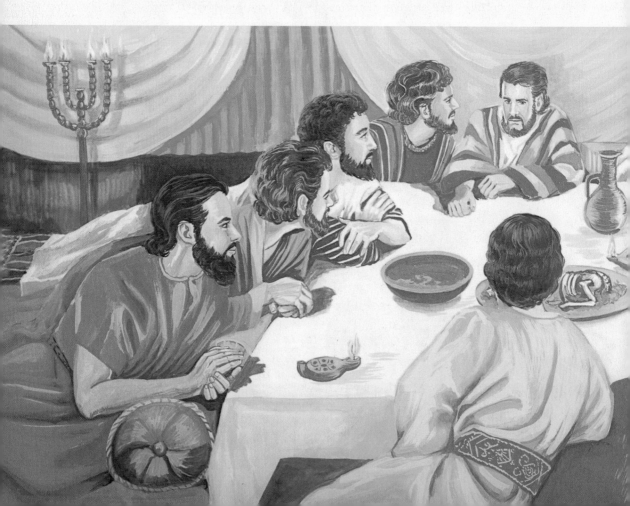

he hands them a glass of wine and says: 'Drink it, because this means my blood, which is to be poured out for you.' The Bible calls this 'the Lord's evening meal,' or the 'Lord's supper.'

The Israelites ate the Passover to remind them of when God's angel 'passed over' their houses in Egypt, but killed the firstborn in the houses of the Egyptians. But now Jesus wants his followers to remember him, and how he gave his life for them. And that is why he tells them to celebrate this special meal each year.

After eating the Lord's Evening Meal, Jesus tells his apostles to be brave and strong in faith. Finally, they sing songs to God and then leave. It is very late now, probably past midnight. Let's see where they go.

Matthew 26:14-30; Luke 22:1-39; John chapters 13 to 17; 1 Corinthians 11:20.

JESUS IN THE GARDEN

100

AFTER leaving the upstairs room, Jesus and his apostles go out to the garden of Geth·sem′a·ne. They have come here many times before. Jesus now tells them to keep awake and to pray. Then he goes a little distance away, and gets face down on the ground to pray.

Later Jesus comes back to where his apostles are. What do you think they are doing? They are asleep! Three times Jesus tells them they should keep awake, but each time he returns he finds them sleeping. 'How can you sleep at a time like this?' Jesus says the last time he comes back. 'The hour has come for me to be handed over to my enemies.'

Just at that moment the noise of a large crowd can be heard. Look! The men are coming with swords and clubs! And they are carrying torches to give them light. When they get closer, someone steps out from the crowd and comes right up to Jesus. He kisses him, as you can see here. The man is Judas Is·car′i·ot! Why does he kiss Jesus?

Jesus asks: 'Judas, do you betray me with a kiss?' Yes, the kiss is a sign. It lets the men with Judas know that this is Jesus, the man they want. So Jesus' enemies step forward to grab him. But Peter is not going to let them take Jesus without a fight. He pulls out the sword that he has brought along and strikes at the man near him. The sword just misses the man's head and chops off his right ear. But Jesus touches the man's ear and heals it.

Jesus tells Peter: 'Return your sword to its place. Don't you think that I can ask my Father for thousands of angels to save me?' Yes, he can! But Jesus doesn't ask God to send any angels, because he knows that the time has come for his enemies to take him. So he lets them lead him away. Let's see what happens to Jesus now.

Matthew 26:36-56; Luke 22:39-53; John 18:1-12.

JESUS IS KILLED

101

LOOK at the terrible thing that is happening! Jesus is being killed. They have put him on a stake. Nails are driven into his hands and feet. Why would anybody want to do this to Jesus?

It is because some persons hate Jesus. Do you know who they are? One of them is the wicked angel Satan the Devil. He is the one who was able to get Adam and Eve to disobey Jehovah. And Satan is the one who got the enemies of Jesus to commit this terrible crime.

Even before Jesus is nailed here on the stake, his enemies do mean things to him. Remember how they came to the garden of Geth·sem′a·ne and took him away? Who were those enemies? Yes, they were the religious leaders. Well, let's see what happens next.

When Jesus is taken by the religious leaders, his apostles run away. They leave Jesus alone with his enemies, because they become afraid. But the apostles Peter and John do not go very far away. They follow along to see what happens to Jesus.

The priests take Jesus to the old man An′nas, who used to be the high priest. The crowd does not stay here long. They next take Jesus to the house of Ca′ia·phas, who is now the high priest. Many religious leaders have gathered at his house.

Here at the house of Ca′ia·phas they have a trial. People are brought in to tell lies about Jesus. The religious leaders all say: 'Jesus should be put to death.' Then they spit in his face, and hit him with their fists.

While all of this is going on, Peter is outside in the yard. It is a cold night, and so the people make a fire. While they are warming themselves around the fire, a servant girl looks at Peter, and says: 'This man also was with Jesus.'

'No, I wasn't!' Peter answers.

Three times people say to Peter that he was with Jesus. But each time Peter says it is not true. The third time Peter says this, Jesus turns and looks at him. Peter feels very sorry for telling these lies, and he goes away and weeps.

As the sun starts to come up on Friday morning, the priests take Jesus to their big meeting place, the San'he·drin hall. Here they talk over what they are going to do with him. They take him to Pontius Pilate, the ruler of the district of Ju·de'a.

'This is a bad man,' the priests tell Pilate. 'He should be killed.' After asking Jesus questions, Pilate says: 'I can't see that he has done anything wrong.' Then Pilate sends Jesus to Herod An'ti·pas. Herod is the ruler of Gal'i·lee, but he is staying in Jerusalem. Herod can't see that Jesus has done anything wrong either, so he sends him back to Pilate.

Pilate wants to let Jesus go. But Jesus' enemies want another prisoner to be let go instead. This man is the robber Bar·ab'bas. It is now about noon when Pilate brings Jesus outside. He says to the people: 'See! Your king!' But the' chief priests yell: 'Take him away! Kill him! Kill him!' So Pilate lets Bar·ab'bas go free, and they take Jesus away to be killed.

Early Friday afternoon Jesus is nailed to a stake. You can't see them in the picture, but on each side of Jesus a criminal is also being put to death on a stake. Shortly before Jesus dies, one of the criminals says to him: 'Remember me when you get into your kingdom.' And Jesus answers: 'I promise you that you will be with me in Paradise.'

Isn't that a wonderful promise? Do you know what paradise Jesus is talking about? Where was the paradise that God made at the beginning? Yes, on earth. And when Jesus rules as king in heaven, he will bring this man back to life to enjoy the new Paradise on earth. Can't we be happy about that?

Matthew 26:57-75; 27:1-50; Luke 22:54-71; 23:1-49; John 18:12-40; 19:1-30.

PART 7

Jesus' Resurrection to Paul's Imprisonment

On the third day after his death, Jesus was resurrected. On that day he appeared to his followers five different times. Jesus continued to appear to them for 40 days. Then, while some of his disciples watched, Jesus ascended to heaven. Ten days later God poured holy spirit on Jesus' followers waiting in Jerusalem.

Later, enemies of God had the apostles thrown into prison, but an angel freed them. The disciple Stephen was stoned to death by opposers. But we learn how Jesus chose one of these opposers to be his special servant, and he became the apostle Paul. Then, three and a half years after Jesus' death, God sent the apostle Peter to preach to the non-Jew Cornelius and his household.

About 13 years later Paul began his first preaching trip. On his second trip Timothy joined Paul. We learn how Paul and his traveling companions had many exciting times in serving God. At last, Paul was put in prison in Rome. Two years later he was set free, but then he was put in prison again and killed. The events of PART 7 happened over a period of about 32 years.

DO YOU know who the woman and the two men are? The woman is Mary Mag'da·lene, a friend of Jesus. And the men in white clothing are angels. This little room that Mary is looking

into is the place where Jesus' body was put after he died. It is called a tomb. But now the body is gone! Who took it? Let's see.

After Jesus dies, the priests say to Pilate: 'When Jesus was alive he said that he would be raised up after three days. So command that the tomb be guarded. Then his disciples can't steal his body and say that he has been raised from the dead!' Pilate tells the priests to send soldiers to guard the tomb.

But very early on the third day after Jesus had died an angel of Jehovah suddenly comes. He rolls the stone away from the tomb. The soldiers are so afraid that they can't move. Finally, when they look inside the tomb, the body is gone! Some of the soldiers go into the city and tell the priests. Do you know what the bad priests do? They pay the soldiers to lie. 'Say that his disciples came in the night, while we were asleep, and stole the body,' the priests tell the soldiers.

Meanwhile, some women friends of Jesus visit the tomb. How surprised they are to find it empty! Suddenly two angels in bright clothing appear. 'Why are you looking for Jesus here?' they ask. 'He has been raised up. Go quickly and tell his disciples.' How fast the women run! But on the way a man stops them. Do you know who it is? It is Jesus! 'Go tell my disciples,' he says.

When the women tell the disciples that Jesus is alive and they have seen him, the disciples find this hard to believe. Peter and John run to the tomb to look for themselves, but the tomb is empty! When Peter and John leave, Mary Mag'da·lene stays behind. That is when she looks in and sees the two angels.

Do you know what happened to Jesus' body? God caused it to disappear. God did not raise Jesus to life in the fleshly body in which he died. He gave Jesus a new spirit body, as the angels in heaven have. But to show his disciples he is alive, Jesus can take on a body that people can see, as we will learn.

Matthew 27:62-66; 28:1-15; Luke 24:1-12; John 20:1-12.

AFTER Peter and John leave the tomb where Jesus' body had been, Mary is left there alone. She begins to cry. Then she bends over and looks inside the tomb, as we saw in the last picture. There she sees two angels! They ask her: 'Why are you crying?'

Mary answers: 'They have taken my Lord away, and I do not know where they have put him.' Then Mary turns around and sees a man. He asks her: 'Who is it that you are looking for?'

Mary thinks the man is the gardener, and that he may have taken Jesus' body. So she says: 'If you have taken him away, tell me where you have put him.' But, really, this man is Jesus. He has taken on a body that Mary does not recognize. But when he calls her by her name, Mary knows this is Jesus. She runs and tells the disciples: 'I have seen the Lord!'

Later in the day, while two disciples are walking to the village of Em·ma'us, a man joins them. The disciples are very sad because Jesus has been killed. But as they walk along, the man explains many things from the Bible that make them feel better. Finally, when they stop for a meal, the disciples recognize that this man is Jesus. Then Jesus disappears, and these two disciples quickly go all the way back to Jerusalem to tell the apostles about him.

While that is going on, Jesus appears also to Peter. The others get excited when they hear this. Then these two disciples go to Jerusalem and find the apostles. They tell them how Jesus also appeared to them on the road. And just when they are telling about this, do you know the amazing thing that happens?

Look at the picture. Jesus appears right there in the room, even though the door is locked. How happy the disciples are! Isn't that an exciting day? Can you count the number of times that Jesus has appeared by now to his followers? Do you count five times?

The apostle Thomas is not with them when Jesus appears. So the disciples tell him: 'We have seen the Lord!' But Thomas says he will have to see Jesus himself before he believes it. Well, eight days later the disciples are together again in a locked room, and this time Thomas is with them. Suddenly, Jesus appears right there in the room. Now Thomas believes. John 20:11-29; Luke 24:13-43.

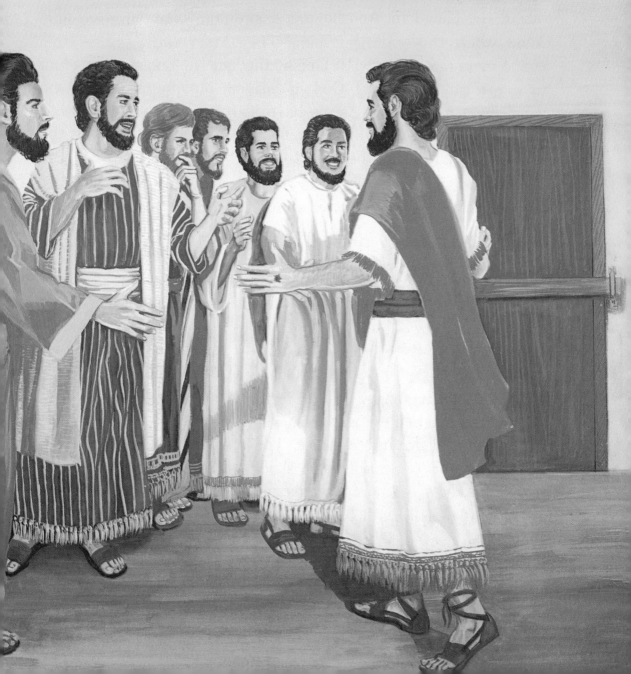

A S THE days pass, Jesus shows himself to his followers many times. Once about 500 of the disciples see him. When he appears to them, do you know what Jesus talks to them about? The kingdom of God. Jehovah sent Jesus to the earth to teach about the Kingdom. And he keeps on doing this even after he is raised up from the dead.

Do you remember what God's kingdom is? Yes, the Kingdom is a real government of God in heaven, and Jesus is the One God chose to be king. As we have learned, Jesus showed what a wonderful king he will be by feeding the hungry, healing the sick, and even raising the dead to life!

So when Jesus rules as king in heaven for a thousand years, what will it be like on the earth? Yes, the whole earth will be made into a beautiful paradise. There will be no more wars, or crime, or sickness, or even death. We know this is true because God made the earth to be a paradise for people to enjoy. That is why he made the garden of Eden in the beginning. And Jesus will see to it that what God wants done is finally carried out.

The time now comes for Jesus to go back to heaven. For 40 days Jesus has been showing himself to his disciples. So they are certain that he is alive again. But before he leaves his disciples he tells them: 'Stay in Jerusalem until you receive holy spirit.' The holy spirit is God's active force, like blowing wind, that will help his followers to do God's will. Finally, Jesus says: 'You are to preach about me to the most distant parts of the earth.'

After Jesus says this, an amazing thing happens. He begins going up into heaven, as you can see here. Then a cloud hides him from sight, and the disciples don't see Jesus again. Jesus goes to heaven, and he begins to rule over his followers on earth from there.

1 Corinthians 15:3-8; Revelation 21:3, 4; Acts 1:1-11.

THESE people here are Jesus' followers. They have obeyed him and stayed in Jerusalem. And while they are all waiting together, a loud noise fills the whole house. It sounds like a rushing strong wind. And then tongues of fire begin to appear over the heads of each one of the disciples. Can you see the fire over each one of them? What does it all mean?

It is a miracle! Jesus is back in heaven with his Father, and he is pouring out God's holy spirit on his followers. Do you know what this spirit causes them to do? They all begin to speak in different languages.

Many people in Jerusalem hear the noise that sounds like a strong wind, and they come to see what is happening. Some of the people are from other nations who have come here for the Israelite feast of Pentecost. What a surprise these visitors receive! They hear the disciples speaking in their own languages about the wonderful things that God has done.

'These people are all from Gal'i·lee,' the visitors say. 'How is it, then, that they are able to speak in these different languages that belong to the countries where we come from?'

Peter now stands up to explain to them. He raises his voice and tells the people how Jesus was killed and that Jehovah raised him from the dead. 'Now Jesus is in heaven at the right hand of God,' Peter says. 'And he has poured out the promised holy spirit. That is why you have seen and heard these miracles.'

Well, when Peter says these things, many of the people feel very sorry about what was done to Jesus. 'What should we do?' they ask. Peter tells them: 'You need to change your lives and be baptized.' So on that very day about 3,000 people get baptized and become followers of Jesus.

Acts 2:1-47.

L OOK at the angel here holding open the door of the prison. The men he is setting free are Jesus' apostles. Let's find out what led to their being put in prison.

It has been only a short time since the holy spirit was poured out on Jesus' disciples. And this is what happens: Peter and John are going into the temple in Jerusalem one afternoon. There, near the door, is a man who has been crippled all his life. People carry him here every day so that he can beg for money from those going into the temple. When he sees Peter and John, he begs them to give him something. What will the apostles do?

They stop and look at the poor man. 'I have no money,' Peter says, 'but I will give you what I have. In the name of Jesus, get up and walk!' Peter then takes the man by the right hand, and

at once he jumps up and begins walking. When the people see this, they are amazed and very happy for this wonderful miracle.

'It is by the power of God, who raised Jesus from the dead, that we did this miracle,' Peter says. While he and John are speaking, some religious leaders come along. They are angry because Peter and John are telling the people about Jesus' being raised from the dead. So they grab them and put them into prison.

The next day the religious leaders have a big meeting. Peter and John, along with the man they healed, are brought in. 'By what power did you do this miracle?' the religious leaders ask.

Peter tells them that it is by the power of God, who raised Jesus from the dead. The priests do not know what to do, for they cannot deny that this wonderful miracle really happened. So they warn the apostles not to talk about Jesus anymore, and then let them go.

As the days go by the apostles keep on preaching about Jesus and healing the sick. News about these miracles spreads. And so even crowds from the towns around Jerusalem bring sick ones for the apostles to heal. This makes the religious leaders jealous, so they grab the apostles and put them into prison. But they don't stay there long.

During the night God's angel opens the prison door, as you can see here. The angel says: 'Go and stand in the temple, and keep on speaking to the people.' The next morning, when the religious leaders send men to the prison to get the apostles, they are gone. Later the men find them teaching in the temple and bring them to the San'he·drin hall.

'We gave you strict orders not to teach about Jesus anymore,' the religious leaders say. 'But you have filled Jerusalem with your teaching.' Then the apostles answer: 'We must obey God as ruler rather than men.' So they keep right on teaching the "good news." Isn't that a fine example for us to follow?   Acts chapters 3 to 5.

THE man kneeling here is Stephen. He is a faithful disciple of Jesus. But look at what's happening to him now! These men are throwing big stones at him. Why do they hate Stephen so much that they are doing this terrible thing? Let's see.

God has been helping Stephen to do wonderful miracles. These men don't like this, and so they get into an argument with him about his teaching the people the truth. But God gives Stephen great wisdom, and Stephen shows that these men have been teaching false things. This makes them even angrier. So they grab him, and call in people to tell lies about him.

The high priest asks Stephen: 'Are these things true?' Stephen answers by giving a fine talk from the Bible. At the end of it, he tells how bad men hated Jehovah's prophets long ago. Then he says: 'You are just like those men. You killed God's servant Jesus, and you have not obeyed God's laws.'

This makes these religious leaders very angry! They grind their teeth in rage. But then Stephen lifts his head up, and says: 'Look! I see Jesus standing at the right side of God in heaven.' At this, these men put their hands over their ears and rush at Stephen. They grab him and drag him outside the city.

Here they take their coats off and give them to the young man Saul to take care of. Do you see Saul? Then some of the men begin throwing stones at Stephen. Stephen kneels down, as you can see, and he prays to God: 'Jehovah, do not punish them for this bad thing.' He knows some of them have been fooled by the religious leaders. After that Stephen dies.

When someone does something bad to you, do you try to hurt them back, or ask God to hurt them? That's not what Stephen or Jesus did. They were kind even to those who were unkind to them. Let's try to copy their example.   Acts 6:8-15; 7:1-60.

ON THE ROAD TO DAMASCUS 108

DO YOU know who that is lying on the ground? It is Saul. Remember, he's the one who watched the coats for the men who stoned Stephen. Look at that bright light! What's happening?

After Stephen is killed, Saul takes the lead in hunting for Jesus' followers to hurt them. He goes into one house after another and drags them out and throws them into prison. Many of the disciples flee to other cities and begin to declare the "good news" there. But Saul goes to other cities to find Jesus' followers. He is now on his way to Damascus. But, on the way, this is the amazing thing that happens:

Suddenly a light from the sky flashes around Saul. He falls to the ground, as we see here. Then a voice says: 'Saul, Saul! Why are you hurting me?' The men with Saul see the light and hear the sound of the voice, but they can't understand what is being said.

'Who are you, Lord?' Saul asks.

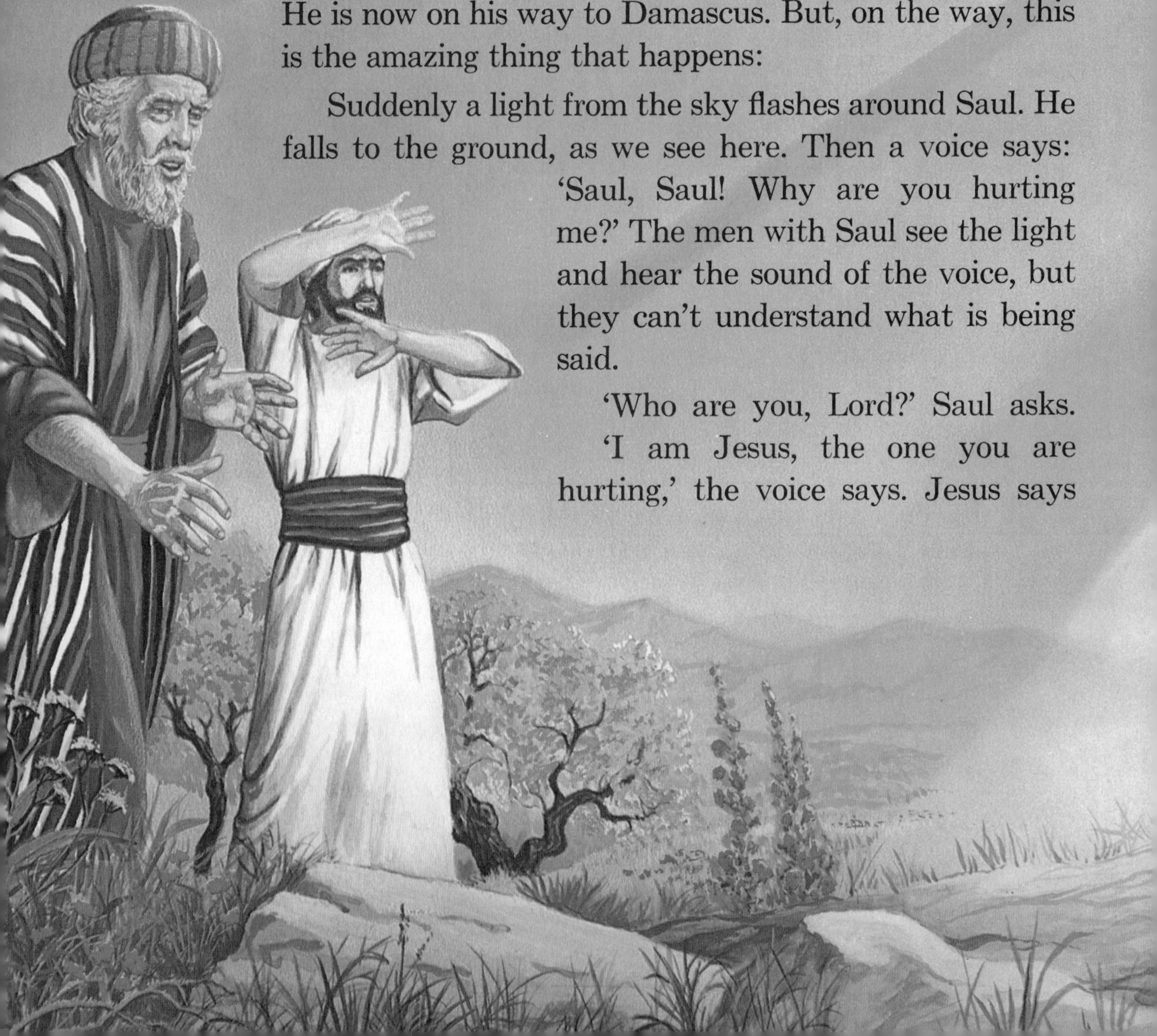

'I am Jesus, the one you are hurting,' the voice says. Jesus says this because when Saul hurts Jesus' followers, Jesus feels as if he is being hurt himself.

Saul now asks: 'What shall I do, Lord?'

'Get up and go into Damascus,' Jesus says. 'There you will be told what you must do.' When Saul gets up and opens his eyes, he can't see a thing. He is blind! So the men with him take him by the hand and lead him into Damascus.

Jesus now speaks to one of his disciples in Damascus, saying: 'Get up, An·a·ni'as. Go to the street called Straight. At the house of Judas ask for a man named Saul. I have chosen him to be a special servant of mine.'

An·a·ni'as obeys. When he meets Saul, he lays his hands on him and says: 'The Lord has sent me that you might see again and be filled with holy spirit.' At once something that looks like scales falls from Saul's eyes, and he is able to see again.

Saul is used in a mighty way to preach to people of many nations. He becomes known as the apostle Paul, whom we will learn a lot more about. But first, let's see what God sends Peter to do. Acts 8:1-4; 9:1-20; 22:6-16; 26:8-20.

THAT is the apostle Peter standing there, and those are some of his friends behind him. But why is the man bowing down to Peter? Should he do that? Do you know who he is?

The man is Cornelius. He is a Roman army officer. Cornelius doesn't know Peter, but he was told to invite him to his house. Let's find out how this came about.

The first followers of Jesus were Jews, but Cornelius is not a Jew. Yet he loves God, he prays to him, and he does many kind things for people. Well, one afternoon an angel appears to him and says: 'God is pleased with you, and he is going to answer your

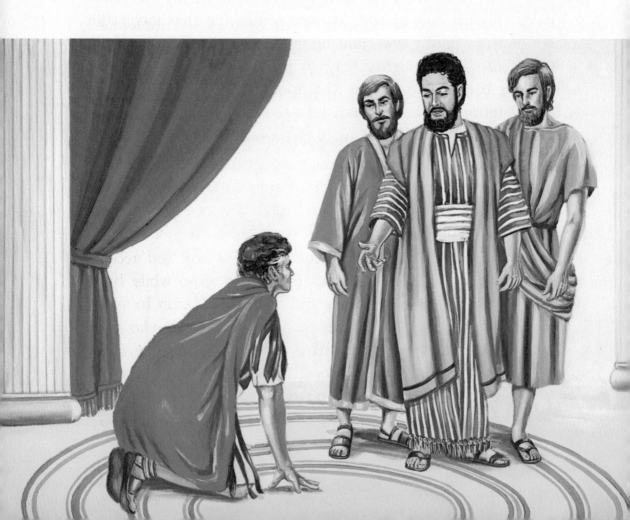

prayers. Send some men to get a certain man named Peter. He is staying in Jop'pa at the house of Simon, who lives by the sea.'

Well, right away Cornelius sends some men to find Peter. The next day, when the men are getting near to Jop'pa, Peter is on the flat roof of Simon's house. There God makes Peter think that he sees a large cloth coming down from heaven. In the cloth are all kinds of animals. According to God's law, these animals were unclean for food, and yet a voice says: 'Get up, Peter. Kill and eat.'

'No!' Peter answers. 'I have never eaten what is not clean.' But the voice tells Peter: 'Stop calling unclean what God now says is clean.' Three times this happens. While Peter is wondering what it all means, the men sent by Cornelius arrive at the house and ask for Peter.

Peter goes downstairs and says: 'I am the man you are looking for. Why have you come?' When the men explain that an angel told Cornelius to invite Peter to his house, Peter agrees to go with them. The next day Peter and friends leave to visit Cornelius in Caes·a·re'a.

Cornelius has gathered together his relatives and close friends. When Peter comes, Cornelius meets him. He falls down and bows at Peter's feet, as you see here. But Peter says: 'Rise; I myself am only a man.' Yes, the Bible shows that it is not right to bow down and worship a man. We should worship only Jehovah.

Peter now preaches to those gathered. 'I see that God accepts all people who want to serve him,' Peter says. And while he is talking, God sends his holy spirit, and the people begin to speak in different languages. This amazes the Jewish disciples who came with Peter, because they thought that God favors only the Jews. So this teaches them that God does not view people of any one race as better or more important to God than people of any other race. Isn't that something good for all of us to remember?

Acts 10:1-48; 11:1-18; Revelation 19:10.

THE young man you see here with the apostle Paul is Timothy. Timothy lives with his family in Lys'tra. His mother is named Eu'nice and his grandmother Lo'is.

This is the third time that Paul has visited Lys'tra. About a year or so before, Paul and Bar'na·bas first came here on a preaching trip. And now Paul has returned again with his friend Silas.

Do you know what Paul is saying to Timothy? 'Would you like to join Silas and me?' he is asking. 'We could use your help in preaching to people in faraway places.'

'Yes,' Timothy answers, 'I would like to go.' So soon afterward Timothy leaves his family and goes with Paul and Silas. But before we learn about their trip, let's find out what's been happening to Paul. It's been about 17 years since Jesus appeared to him on the road to Damascus.

Remember, Paul came to Damascus to hurt Jesus' disciples, but now he is a disciple himself! Later some enemies plan to kill Paul because they don't like his teaching about Jesus. But the disciples help Paul to escape. They put him in a basket and let him down outside the city wall.

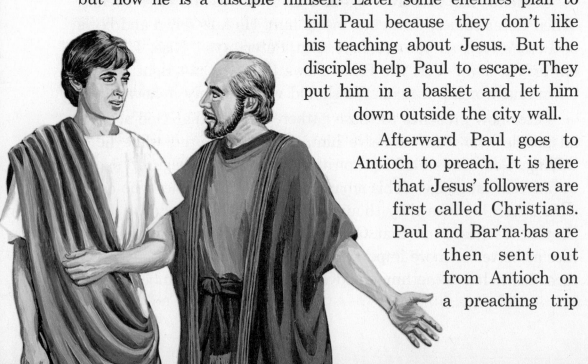

Afterward Paul goes to Antioch to preach. It is here that Jesus' followers are first called Christians. Paul and Bar'na·bas are then sent out from Antioch on a preaching trip

The map shows locations including Rome, Thessalonica, Philippi, Beroea, Troas, Antioch, Iconium, Corinth, Athens, Ephesus, Colossae, Lystra, Miletus, Malta, Crete, Antioch, Cyprus, Damascus, Caesarea, Joppa, Jerusalem, and THE GREAT SEA (MEDITERRANEAN).

to far-off countries. One of the cities they visit is Lys'tra, the home of Timothy.

Now, about a year later, Paul is back in Lys'tra on a second trip. When Timothy leaves with Paul and Silas, do you know where they go? Look at the map, and let's learn some of the places.

First, they go to nearby I·co'ni·um, then to a second city named Antioch. After that they travel up to Tro'as, then over to Phi·lip'pi, Thes·sa·lo·ni'ca and Be·roe'a. Do you see Athens on the map? Paul preaches there. After that they spend a year and a half preaching in Corinth. Finally they make a short stop in Eph'e·sus. Then they come back by boat to Caes·a·re'a, and travel up to Antioch, where Paul stays.

So Timothy travels hundreds and hundreds of miles helping Paul to preach the "good news" and to start many Christian congregations. When you grow older, will you be a faithful servant of God like Timothy? Acts 9:19-30; 11:19-26; chapters 13 to 17; 18:1-22.

OH! OH! What's happening here? Is the boy who is lying on the ground hurt very bad? Look! one of the men coming out of the house is Paul! Can you see Timothy there too? Did the boy fall out the window?

Yes, that's just what happened. Paul was giving a talk to the disciples here in Tro'as. He knew that he would not see them again for a long time because he had to leave on a boat the next day. So he kept talking until midnight.

Well, this boy named Eu'ty·chus was sitting at the window, and he fell asleep. He fell over, and right out the window, three stories to the ground below! So you can see why the people look so worried. When the men pick up the boy, it's just as they fear. He is dead!

When Paul sees that the boy is dead, he lies on top of him and hugs him. Then he says: 'Don't worry. He's all right!' And he is! It's a miracle! Paul has brought him back to life! A wave of joy sweeps over the crowd.

They all go upstairs again and have a meal. Paul keeps on talking until it is daylight. But you can be sure that Eu'ty·chus doesn't go to sleep again! Then Paul, Timothy and those traveling with them get onto the boat. Do you know where they are going?

Paul is just finishing his third preaching trip, and he is on his way home. On this trip Paul had stayed three years in the city of Eph'e·sus alone. So this is an even longer trip than his second one.

After leaving Tro'as, the boat stops at Mi·le'tus for a while. Since Eph'e·sus is just a few miles away, Paul sends for the older men in the congregation to come over to Mi·le'tus so he can talk to them for the last time. Afterward, when it is time for the boat to leave, how sad they are to see Paul go!

At last the boat comes back to Caes·a·re′a. While Paul is staying here at the house of the disciple Philip, the prophet Ag′a·bus warns Paul. He says that Paul will be made a prisoner when he comes to Jerusalem. And sure enough, this is what happens. Then, after being in prison for two years in Caes·a·re′a, Paul is sent to Rome to stand trial before the Roman ruler Caesar. Let's see what happens on the trip to Rome.   Acts chapters 19 to 26.

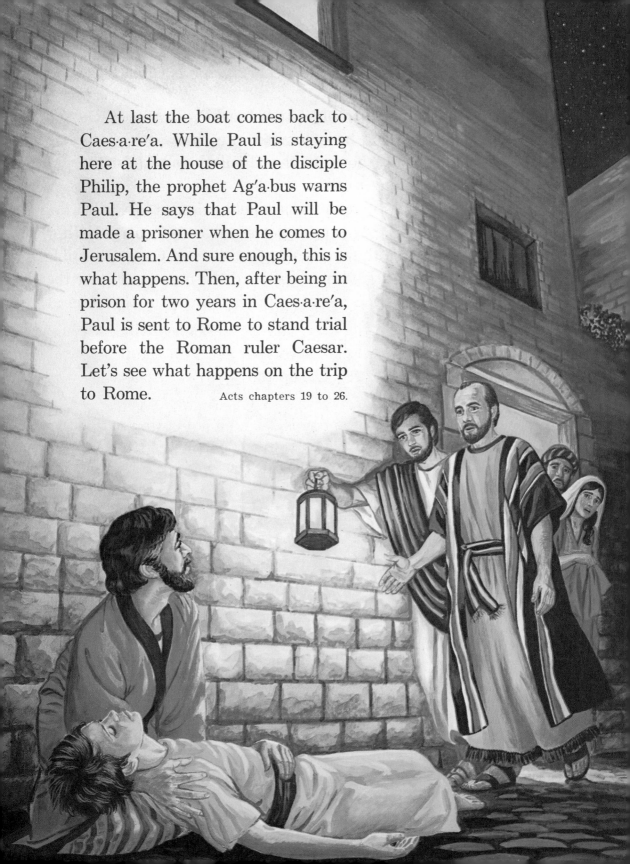

LOOK! the boat is in trouble! It is breaking to pieces! Do you see the people who have jumped into the water? Some are already making it to shore. Is that Paul there? Let's find out what's been happening to him.

Remember, for two years Paul is held prisoner in Caes·a·re'a. Then he and some other prisoners are put on a boat, and they start for Rome. When they pass near the island of Crete, a terrible storm hits them. The wind blows so hard the men can't steer the boat. And they can't see the sun during the day or the stars at

night. Finally, after many days, those on board give up all hope of being saved.

Then Paul stands up and says: 'Not one of you will lose his life; only the boat will be lost. For last night an angel of God came to me and said, "Don't be afraid, Paul! You must stand before the Roman ruler Caesar. And God will save all those who are sailing with you."'

About midnight on the 14th day after the storm began, the sailors notice that the water is becoming less deep! Because of fear of smashing into some rocks in the dark, they drop their anchors. The next morning they see a bay. They decide to try to sail the boat right up onto the beach there.

Well, when they get closer to shore, the boat hits a sandbank and gets stuck. Then the waves begin to smash it, and the boat starts to break in pieces. The army officer in charge says: 'All of you who can swim jump into the sea first and swim ashore. The rest of you jump in after them, and grab some pieces from the boat to hold onto.' And that's what they do. In this way all 276 persons who were on the boat get to shore safely, just as the angel promised.

The island is called Malta. The people are very kind, and they take care of those from the boat. When the weather gets better, Paul is put on another boat and taken to Rome. Acts 27:1-44; 28:1-14.

PAUL IN ROME

113

SEE the chains on Paul, and look at the Roman soldier guarding him. Paul is a prisoner in Rome. He is waiting until the Roman Caesar decides what to do with him. While he is a prisoner, people are allowed to visit him.

Three days after Paul gets to Rome he sends word for some Jewish leaders to come to see him. As a result, many Jews in Rome come. Paul preaches to them about Jesus and the kingdom of God. Some believe and become Christians, but others do not believe.

Paul also preaches to the different soldiers that have the job of guarding him. For the two years he is kept here as a prisoner Paul preaches to everyone he can. As a result, even the household of Caesar hears about the good news of the Kingdom, and some of them become Christians.

But who is this visitor at the table writing? Can you guess? Yes, it is Timothy. Timothy had also been in prison for preaching about the Kingdom, but he is free again. And he has come here to help Paul. Do you know what Timothy is writing? Let's see.

Do you remember the cities of Phi·lip′pi and Eph′e·sus in Story 110? Paul helped to start Christian congregations in those cities. Now, while he is in prison, Paul writes letters to these Christians. The letters are in the Bible, and they are called E·phe′sians and Phi·lip′pi·ans. Paul is now telling Timothy what to write to their Christian friends in Phi·lip′pi.

The Phi·lip′pi·ans have been very kind to Paul. They sent a gift to him here in prison, and so Paul is thanking them for it. E·paph·ro·di′tus is the man who brought the gift. But he got very sick and almost died. Now he is well again and ready to go home. He will carry this letter from Paul and Timothy with him when he returns to Phi·lip′pi.

While he is in prison Paul writes two more letters that we have in the Bible. One is to the Christians in the city of Co·los'sae. Do you know what it is called? Co·los'sians. The other is a personal letter to a close friend named Phi·le'mon who also lives in Co·los'sae. The letter is about Phi·le'mon's servant O·nes'i·mus.

O·nes'i·mus ran away from Phi·le'mon and came to Rome. In some way O·nes'i·mus learned about Paul's being in prison here. He came to visit, and Paul preached to O·nes'i·mus. Soon O·nes'i·mus also became a Christian. Now O·nes'i·mus is sorry that he ran away. So do you know what Paul writes in this letter to Phi·le'mon?

Paul asks Phi·le'mon to forgive O·nes'i·mus. 'I am sending him back to you,' Paul writes. 'But now he is not just your servant. He is also a fine Christian brother.' When O·nes'i·mus goes back to Co·los'sae he carries with him these two letters, one to the Co·los'sians and the other to Phi·le'mon. We can just imagine how happy Phi·le'mon is when he learns that his servant has become a Christian.

When Paul writes to the Phi·lip'pians and to Phi·le'mon, he has some really good news. 'I am sending Timothy to you,' Paul tells the Phi·lip'pi·ans. 'But I also will visit you shortly.' And, to Phi·le'mon, he writes: 'Get a place ready for me to stay there.'

When Paul is set free he visits his Christian brothers and sisters in many places. But later Paul is made a prisoner in Rome again. This time he knows he is going to be killed. So he writes to Timothy and asks him to come quickly. 'I have been faithful to God,' Paul writes, 'and God will reward me.' A few years after Paul is put to death, Jerusalem is destroyed again, this time by the Romans.

But there is more in the Bible. Jehovah God has the apostle John write its last books, including the book of Revelation. This Bible book tells about the future. Let's learn now what the future holds. Acts 28:16-31; Philippians 1:13; 2:19-30; 4:18-23; Hebrews 13:23; Philemon 1-25; Colossians 4:7-9; 2 Timothy 4:7-9.

PART 8

What the Bible Foretells Comes True

The Bible not only gives the true story of what happened in the past but also tells what will happen in the future. Humans cannot tell the future. That is why we know that the Bible is from God. What does the Bible say about the future?

It tells about a great war of God. In this war God will clean the earth of all badness and bad people, but he will protect those who serve him. God's king, Jesus Christ, will see to it that God's servants enjoy peace and happiness, and that they will never get sick again or die.

We can be glad that God will make a new paradise on earth, can't we? But we must do something if we are to live in this paradise. In the last story of the book we learn what we must do to enjoy the wonderful things God has in store for those who serve him. So read PART 8 and find out what the Bible foretells for the future.

THE END OF ALL BADNESS

114

WHAT do you see here? Yes, an army on white horses. But notice where they are coming from. The horses are galloping down from heaven on the clouds! Are there really horses in heaven?

No, these are not real horses. We know this because horses can't run on the clouds, can they? But the Bible does speak about horses in heaven. Do you know why it does?

It is because once horses were used a lot in fighting wars. So the Bible tells of persons riding horses down from heaven to show that God has a war to fight with people on earth. Do you know what the place of this war is called? Armageddon. That war is to destroy all badness on earth.

Jesus is the One who will take the lead in fighting this war at Armageddon. Remember, Jesus is the one Jehovah chose to be king of His government. That is why Jesus wears a king's headpiece. And the sword shows that he will kill all of God's enemies. Should we be surprised that God would destroy all bad people?

Look back to Story 10. What do you see there? Yes, the great Flood that destroyed bad people. Who caused that Flood? Jehovah God. Now look at Story 15. What's happening there? Sod'om and Go·mor'rah are being destroyed by fire that Jehovah sent.

Turn to Story 33. See what's happening to the horses and war chariots of the Egyptians. Who caused the water to come crashing down on them? Jehovah. He did it to protect his people. Look at Story 76. You will see there that Jehovah even let his people, the Israelites, be destroyed because of their badness.

So, then, we should not be surprised that Jehovah will send his heavenly armies to put an end to all badness on earth. But just think what that will mean! Turn the page and let's see.

Revelation 16:16; 19:11-16.

LOOK at those tall trees, pretty flowers and high mountains. Isn't it beautiful here? See how the deer is eating out of the little boy's hand. And look at the lions and the horses standing over there in the meadow. Wouldn't you like to live in a house in a place like this?

God wants you to live forever on earth in a paradise. And he doesn't want you to have any of the aches and pains that people suffer today. This is the Bible's promise to those who will live in the new paradise: 'God will be with them. There will be no more death or crying or pain. The old things have passed away.'

Jesus will see to it that this wonderful change takes place. Do you know when? Yes, after he cleans the earth of all badness

and bad people. Remember, when Jesus was on earth he healed people of all kinds of sicknesses, and he even raised people from the dead. Jesus did this to show what he would do all over the earth when he became King of God's kingdom.

Just think how wonderful it will be in the new paradise on earth! Jesus, along with some of those whom he chooses, will be ruling in heaven. These rulers will take care of everyone on earth and see that they are happy. Let's see what we need to do to make sure that God will give us everlasting life in his new paradise.
Revelation 21:3, 4; 5:9, 10; 14:1-3.

CAN you tell what the little girl and her friends are reading? Yes, it is this very book that you are reading—*My Book of Bible Stories*. And they are reading the very story that you are —"How We Can Live Forever."

Do you know what they are learning? First, that we need to know about Jehovah and his Son Jesus if we are to live forever. The Bible says: 'This is the way to live forever. Learn about the only true God, and the Son he sent to earth, Jesus Christ.'

How can we learn about Jehovah God and his Son Jesus? One way is by reading *My Book of Bible Stories* from beginning to end. It tells a lot about Jehovah and Jesus, doesn't it? And it tells a lot about the things that they have done and the things that they will yet do. But we need to do more than just read this book.

Do you see the other book lying on the floor? It's the Bible. Have someone read to you the parts from the Bible on which the stories of this book are based. The Bible gives us the full information we need so that we can all serve Jehovah in the right way and get everlasting life. So we should make it a habit to study the Bible often.

But just learning about Jehovah God and Jesus Christ is not enough. We could have lots and lots of knowledge about them and their teachings, and yet not gain everlasting life. Do you know what else is needed?

We also need to live in harmony with the things we learn. Do you remember Judas Is·car'i·ot? He was one of the 12 that Jesus chose to be his apostles. Judas had a lot of knowledge about Jehovah and Jesus. But what happened to him? After a while he became selfish, and he betrayed Jesus to his enemies for 30 pieces of silver. So Judas will not receive everlasting life.

Do you remember Ge·ha′zi, the man we learned about in Story 69? He wanted to have some clothes and money that did not belong to him. So he told a lie to get these things. But Jehovah punished him. And he will punish us too if we do not obey his laws.

But there are many good people who always served Jehovah faithfully. We want to be like them, don't we? Little Samuel is a good example to follow. Remember, as we saw in Story 55, he was only four or five years old when he started serving Jehovah at his tabernacle. So no matter how young you are, you are not too young to serve Jehovah.

Of course, the person we all want to follow is Jesus Christ. Even when he was a boy, as shown in Story 87, he was there in the temple talking to others about his heavenly Father. Let's follow his example. Let's tell as many people as we can about our wonderful God Jehovah and his Son, Jesus Christ. If we do these things, then we will be able to live forever in God's new paradise on earth. John 17:3; Psalm 145:1-21.

Study Questions for *My Book of Bible Stories*

Story 1

God Begins to Make Things

1. Where have all good things come from, and can you give an example?
2. What was the first thing God created?
3. Why was the first angel special?
4. Describe what the earth was like in the beginning. (See picture.)
5. How did God start getting the earth ready for animals and people?

Additional questions:

1. *Read Jeremiah 10:12.*
What qualities of God are shown through his creation? (Isa. 40:26; Rom. 11:33)
2. *Read Colossians 1:15-17.*
What part did Jesus play in creation, and how should this affect our view of him? (Col. 1:15-17)
3. *Read Genesis 1:1-10.*
(a) What is the origin of the earth? (Gen. 1:1)
(b) What happened on the first creative day? (Gen. 1:3-5)
(c) Describe what happened during the second creative day. (Gen. 1:7, 8)

Story 2

A Beautiful Garden

1. How did God prepare the earth to be our home?
2. Describe the great variety of animals that God made. (See picture.)
3. Why was the garden of Eden special?
4. What did God want the whole earth to become?

Additional questions:

1. *Read Genesis 1:11-25.*
(a) What did God create during the third creative day? (Gen. 1:12)
(b) What occurred during the fourth creative day? (Gen. 1:16)
(c) What kinds of animals did God make on the fifth and sixth days? (Gen. 1:20, 21, 25)
2. *Read Genesis 2:8, 9.*
What two special trees did God place in the garden, and what did they symbolize?

Story 3

The First Man and Woman

1. How is the picture in Story 3 different from the picture in Story 2?
2. Who made the first man, and what was the man's name?
3. What work did God give Adam to do?
4. Why did God make Adam fall into a deep sleep?
5. How long could Adam and Eve live, and what work did Jehovah want them to do?

Additional questions:

1. *Read Psalm 83:18.*
What is God's name, and what is his unique position over the earth? (Jer. 16:21; Dan. 4:17)
2. *Read Genesis 1:26-31.*
(a) What was the climax of God's creation on the sixth day, and how was this creation different from the animals? (Gen. 1:26)
(b) What provision did Jehovah make for both man and animals? (Gen. 1:30)
3. *Read Genesis 2:7-25.*
(a) What was involved in Adam's assignment to name the animals? (Gen. 2:19)
(b) How does Genesis 2:24 help us to understand Jehovah's view of marriage, separation, and divorce? (Matt. 19:4-6, 9)

Story 4

Why They Lost Their Home

1. In the picture, what is happening to Adam and Eve?
2. Why did Jehovah punish them?
3. What did a snake tell Eve?
4. Who made the snake speak to Eve?
5. Why did Adam and Eve lose their Paradise home?

Additional questions:

1. *Read Genesis 2:16, 17 and 3:1-13, 24.*
(a) How did the serpent's question to Eve misrepresent Jehovah? (Gen. 3:1-5; 1 John 5:3)
(b) How does Eve serve as a warning example to us? (Phil. 4:8; Jas. 1:14, 15; 1 John 2:16)

(c) In what way did Adam and Eve fail to accept responsibility for their actions? (Gen. 3:12, 13)

(d) How did the cherubs posted at the east of the garden of Eden uphold Jehovah's sovereignty? (Gen. 3:24)

2. *Read Revelation 12:9.*

How successful has Satan been at turning humankind against God's rulership? (1 John 5:19)

Story 5

A Hard Life Begins

1. What was life like for Adam and Eve outside the garden of Eden?

2. What started to happen to Adam and Eve, and why?

3. Why would Adam and Eve's children grow old and die?

4. If Adam and Eve had obeyed Jehovah, what would life have been like for them and their children?

5. How did Eve's disobedience cause her pain?

6. What were the names of Adam and Eve's first two sons?

7. Who are the other children in the picture?

Additional questions:

1. *Read Genesis 3:16-23 and 4:1, 2.*

(a) How was Adam's life affected by the curse on the ground? (Gen. 3:17-19; Rom. 8:20, 22)

(b) Why was the name Eve, meaning "Living One," appropriate? (Gen. 3:20)

(c) How did Jehovah show consideration for Adam and Eve even after they sinned? (Gen. 3:7, 21)

2. *Read Revelation 21:3, 4.*

What "former things" do you look forward to seeing eliminated?

Story 6

A Good Son, and a Bad One

1. What occupations do Cain and Abel take up?

2. What gifts do Cain and Abel bring to Jehovah?

3. Why is Jehovah pleased with Abel's gift, and why is he not pleased with Cain's?

4. What kind of person is Cain, and how does Jehovah try to correct him?

5. What does Cain do when he is alone with his brother in the field?

6. Explain what happened to Cain after he killed his brother.

Additional questions:

1. *Read Genesis 4:2-26.*

(a) How did Jehovah describe the dangerous position that Cain was in? (Gen. 4:7)

(b) How did Cain reveal his heart attitude? (Gen. 4:9)

(c) What is Jehovah's view of shedding innocent blood? (Gen. 4:10; Isa. 26:21)

2. *Read 1 John 3:11, 12.*

(a) Why did Cain grow hot with anger, and how does this serve as a warning to us today? (Gen. 4: 4, 5; Prov. 14:30; 28:22)

(b) How does the Bible show that even when all our family members oppose Jehovah, we can still maintain our integrity? (Ps. 27:10; Matt. 10:21, 22)

3. *Read John 11:25.*

What assurance does Jehovah give regarding all who die for righteousness' sake? (John 5:24)

Story 7

A Brave Man

1. How was Enoch different?

2. Why did people in Enoch's day do so many bad things?

3. What bad things were people doing? (See picture.)

4. Why did Enoch need to be brave?

5. How long did men live back then, but how long did Enoch live?

6. What happened after Enoch died?

Additional questions:

1. *Read Genesis 5:21-24, 27.*

(a) What kind of relationship did Enoch have with Jehovah? (Gen. 5:24)

(b) According to the Bible, who is the oldest man who ever lived, and how old was he when he died? (Gen. 5:27)

2. *Read Genesis 6:5.*

How bad did conditions on the earth become after Enoch's death, and how does this compare with our day? (2 Tim. 3:13)

3. *Read Hebrews 11:5.*

What quality of Enoch "pleased God well," and with what result? (Gen. 5:22)

4. *Read Jude 14, 15.*

How can Christians today imitate Enoch's courage when warning people about the coming battle of Armageddon? (2 Tim. 4:2; Heb. 13:6)

Story 8

Giants in the Earth

1. What happened when some of God's angels listened to Satan?

2. Why did some angels stop their work in heaven and come down to the earth?

3. Why was it wrong for the angels to come down to the earth and make human bodies for themselves?

4. What was different about the children of the angels?

5. As you can see in the picture, what did the children of the angels do when they became giants?

6. After Enoch, what good man lived on earth, and why did God like him?

Additional questions:

1. *Read Genesis 6:1-8.*

What does Genesis 6:6 reveal about how our conduct can affect Jehovah's feelings? (Ps. 78:40, 41; Prov. 27:11)

2. *Read Jude 6.*

How do the angels that "did not keep their original position" in Noah's day serve as a reminder to us today? (1 Cor. 3:5-9; 2 Pet. 2:4, 9, 10)

Story 9

Noah Builds an Ark

1. How many were in Noah's family, and what were the names of his three sons?

2. What unusual thing did God ask Noah to do, and why?

3. How did Noah's neighbors react when he told them about the ark?

4. What did God tell Noah to do with the animals?

5. After God shut the door of the ark, what did Noah and his family have to do?

Additional questions:

1. *Read Genesis 6:9-22.*

(a) What made Noah an outstanding worshiper of the true God? (Gen. 6:9, 22)

(b) How does Jehovah feel about violence, and how should this affect our choice of entertainment? (Gen. 6:11, 12; Ps. 11:5)

(c) How can we imitate Noah when we receive direction through Jehovah's organization? (Gen. 6:22; 1 John 5:3)

2. *Read Genesis 7:1-9.*

How does the fact that Jehovah viewed the imperfect man Noah as being righteous encourage us today? (Gen. 7:1; Prov. 10:16; Isa. 26:7)

Story 10

The Great Flood

1. Why could no one get inside the ark once the rain started?

2. For how many days and nights did Jehovah make it rain, and how deep did the water get?

3. What happened to the ark as the water started to cover the earth?

4. Did the giants survive the Flood, and what became of the giants' fathers?

5. What happened to the ark after five months?

6. Why did Noah let a raven out of the ark?

7. How did Noah know that the waters on the earth had gone down?

8. What did God say to Noah after he and his family had been in the ark more than one year?

Additional questions:

1. *Read Genesis 7:10-24.*

(a) How complete was the destruction of life on the earth? (Gen. 7:23)

(b) How long did it take for the Flood waters to go down? (Gen. 7:24)

2. *Read Genesis 8:1-17.*

How does Genesis 8:17 show that Jehovah's original purpose for the earth did not change? (Gen. 1:22)

3. *Read 1 Peter 3:19, 20.*

(a) When the rebellious angels returned to heaven, what judgment did they receive? (Jude 6)

(b) How does the account of Noah and his family strengthen our confidence in Jehovah's ability to deliver his people? (2 Pet. 2:9)

Story 11

The First Rainbow

1. As shown in the picture, what did Noah do when he first came out of the ark?

2. What command did God give Noah and his family after the Flood?

3. What promise did God make?

4. When we see a rainbow, of what should it remind us?

Additional questions:

1. *Read Genesis 8:18-22.*

(a) How can we today provide "a restful odor" to Jehovah? (Gen. 8:21; Heb. 13:15, 16)

(b) What observation did Jehovah make about man's heart condition, and what caution should we therefore exercise? (Gen. 8:21; Matt. 15:18, 19)

2. *Read Genesis 9:9-17.*

(a) What covenant did Jehovah make with all of earth's creatures? (Gen. 9:10, 11)

(b) How long will the rainbow covenant remain in effect? (Gen. 9:16)

Story 12

Men Build a Big Tower

1. Who was Nimrod, and how did God feel about him?

2. In the picture, why were people making bricks?

3. Why was Jehovah not pleased with the building work?

4. How did God stop the building of the tower?
5. What was the city called, and what did that name mean?
6. What happened to the people after God confused their languages?

Additional questions:
1. *Read Genesis 10:1, 8-10.*
What characteristics did Nimrod display, and what warning does this provide for us? (Prov. 3:31)
2. *Read Genesis 11:1-9.*
What was the motive behind the building of the tower, and why was the project doomed to failure? (Gen. 11:4; Prov. 16:18; John 5:44)

Story 13

Abraham—A Friend of God

1. What kind of people lived in the city of Ur?
2. Who is the man in the picture, when was he born, and where did he live?
3. What did God tell Abraham to do?
4. Why was Abraham called God's friend?
5. Who went with Abraham when he left Ur?
6. What did God tell Abraham when he got to the land of Canaan?
7. What promise did God make to Abraham when he was 99 years old?

Additional questions:
1. *Read Genesis 11:27-32.*
(a) How were Abraham and Lot related? (Gen. 11:27)
(b) Although Terah was credited with moving his family toward Canaan, how do we know that it was actually Abraham who initiated this move, and why did he do so? (Gen. 11:31; Acts 7:2-4)
2. *Read Genesis 12:1-7.*
What enlargement of the Abrahamic covenant did Jehovah make after Abraham reached the land of Canaan? (Gen. 12:7)
3. *Read Genesis 17:1-8, 15-17.*
(a) What change in name did Abram receive when he was 99 years old, and why? (Gen. 17:5)
(b) What future blessings did Jehovah promise to Sarah? (Gen. 17:15, 16)
4. *Read Genesis 18:9-19.*
(a) At Genesis 18:19, what responsibilities are set out for fathers? (Deut. 6:6, 7; Eph. 6:4)
(b) What experience of Sarah shows that we cannot hide anything from Jehovah? (Gen. 18:12, 15; Ps. 44:21)

Story 14

God Tests Abraham's Faith

1. What promise did God make to Abraham, and how did God keep his promise?

2. As shown in the picture, how did God test Abraham's faith?
3. What did Abraham do, even though he did not understand the reason for God's command?
4. What happened when Abraham took out the knife to kill his son?
5. How strong was Abraham's faith in God?
6. What did God provide for Abraham to sacrifice, and how?

Additional questions:
1. *Read Genesis 21:1-7.*
Why did Abraham circumcise his son on the eighth day? (Gen. 17:10-12; 21:4)
2. *Read Genesis 22:1-18.*
How did Isaac show submission to his father, Abraham, and how did this prefigure a future event of greater significance? (Gen. 22:7-9; 1 Cor. 5:7; Phil. 2:8, 9)

Story 15

Lot's Wife Looked Back

1. Why did Abraham and Lot separate?
2. Why did Lot choose to live in Sodom?
3. What were the people of Sodom like?
4. What warning did two angels give Lot?
5. Why did Lot's wife become a pillar of salt?
6. What lesson can we learn from the case of Lot's wife?

Additional questions:
1. *Read Genesis 13:5-13.*
In regard to resolving problems between individuals, what lesson can we learn from Abraham? (Gen. 13:8, 9; Rom. 12:10; Phil. 2:3, 4)
2. *Read Genesis 18:20-33.*
How do Jehovah's dealings with Abraham give us confidence that Jehovah and Jesus will judge righteously? (Gen. 18:25, 26; Matt. 25:31-33)
3. *Read Genesis 19:1-29.*
(a) What does this Bible account show regarding God's view of homosexuality? (Gen. 19:5, 13; Lev. 20:13)
(b) What difference do we find in the ways that Lot and Abraham responded to God's direction, and what can we learn from this? (Gen. 19:15, 16, 19, 20; 22:3)
4. *Read Luke 17:28-32.*
What heart attitude did Lot's wife have toward material things, and how does this serve as a warning to us? (Luke 12:15; 17:31, 32; Matt. 6:19-21, 25)
5. *Read 2 Peter 2:6-8.*
In imitation of Lot, what should be our attitude toward the ungodly world around us? (Ezek. 9:4; 1 John 2:15-17)

Story 16

Isaac Gets a Good Wife

1. Who are the man and the woman in the picture?
2. What did Abraham do to get a wife for his son, and why?
3. How was the prayer of Abraham's servant answered?
4. What answer did Rebekah give when she was asked if she wanted to marry Isaac?
5. What made Isaac happy again?

Additional questions:

1. *Read Genesis 24:1-67.*
(a) What fine qualities did Rebekah display when she met Abraham's servant at the well? (Gen. 24:17-20; Prov. 31:17, 31)
(b) Abraham's arrangement for Isaac provides what fine example for Christians today? (Gen. 24: 37, 38; 1 Cor. 7:39; 2 Cor. 6:14)
(c) Why should we find time for meditation, just as Isaac did? (Gen. 24:63; Ps. 77:12; Phil. 4:8)

Story 17

Twins Who Were Different

1. Who were Esau and Jacob, and how were they different?
2. How old were Esau and Jacob when their grandfather Abraham died?
3. What did Esau do that made his mother and father very sad?
4. Why did Esau get very angry with his brother, Jacob?
5. What instruction did Isaac give to his son Jacob?

Additional questions:

1. *Read Genesis 25:5-11, 20-34.*
(a) What did Jehovah prophesy regarding Rebekah's two sons? (Gen. 25:23)
(b) What contrast was there between Jacob's and Esau's attitude toward the birthright? (Gen. 25:31-34)
2. *Read Genesis 26:34, 35; 27:1-46; and 28:1-5.*
(a) How was Esau's lack of appreciation for spiritual things evident? (Gen. 26:34, 35; 27:46)
(b) In order for Jacob to receive God's blessing, what did Isaac tell him to do? (Gen. 28:1-4)
3. *Read Hebrews 12:16, 17.*
What does Esau's example demonstrate as to the outcome of those who despise sacred things?

Story 18

Jacob Goes to Haran

1. Who is the young woman in the picture, and what did Jacob do for her?

2. What was Jacob willing to do in order to marry Rachel?
3. What did Laban do when the time came for Jacob's marriage to Rachel?
4. What did Jacob agree to do to get Rachel as his wife?

Additional questions:

1. *Read Genesis 29:1-30.*
(a) Even when Laban tricked him, how did Jacob show himself to be honorable, and what can we learn from this? (Gen. 25:27; 29:26-28; Matt. 5:37)
(b) How does Jacob's example show the difference between love and infatuation? (Gen. 29:18, 20, 30; Song of Sol. 8:6)
(c) What four women became part of Jacob's household and later bore him sons? (Gen. 29:23, 24, 28, 29)

Story 19

Jacob Has a Big Family

1. What were the names of the six sons Jacob had by his first wife, Leah?
2. What two sons did Leah's maidservant Zilpah bear to Jacob?
3. What were the names of the two sons Rachel's maidservant Bilhah bore to Jacob?
4. What two sons did Rachel bear, but what happened when the second son was born?
5. According to the picture, how many sons did Jacob have, and what came from them?

Additional questions:

1. *Read Genesis 29:32-35; 30:1-26; and 35:16-19.*
As indicated in the case of Jacob's 12 sons, how were Hebrew boys often named in ancient times?
2. *Read Genesis 37:35.*
Although only Dinah is named in the Bible, how do we know that Jacob had more than one daughter? (Gen. 37:34, 35)

Story 20

Dinah Gets Into Trouble

1. Why did Abraham and Isaac not want their children to marry people from the land of Canaan?
2. Did Jacob approve of his daughter's making friends with Canaanite girls?
3. Who is the man looking at Dinah in the picture, and what bad thing did he do?
4. What did Dinah's brothers Simeon and Levi do when they heard about what had happened?
5. Did Jacob agree with what Simeon and Levi had done?
6. How did all the family trouble get started?

Additional questions:

1. *Read Genesis 34:1-31.*

(a) Was Dinah's association with the daughters of the land of Canaan an isolated incident? Explain. (Gen. 34:1)

(b) Why did Dinah bear a measure of responsibility for losing her virginity? (Gal. 6:7)

(c) How can young ones today show that they have taken to heart the warning example of Dinah? (Prov. 13:20; 1 Cor. 15:33; 1 John 5:19)

Story 21

Joseph's Brothers Hate Him

1. Why were Joseph's brothers jealous of him, and what did they do?

2. What do Joseph's brothers want to do to him, but what does Reuben say?

3. What happens when Ishmaelite traders come along?

4. What do Joseph's brothers do to make their father think that Joseph is dead?

Additional questions:

1. *Read Genesis 37:1-35.*

(a) How can Christians imitate Joseph's example by reporting wrongdoing in the congregation? (Gen. 37:2; Lev. 5:1; 1 Cor. 1:11)

(b) What led Joseph's brothers to deal treacherously with him? (Gen. 37:11, 18; Prov. 27:4; Jas. 3:14-16)

(c) What action by Jacob is a normal part of grieving? (Gen. 37:35)

Story 22

Joseph Is Put Into Prison

1. How old is Joseph when he is taken to Egypt, and what happens when he gets there?

2. How does Joseph end up in prison?

3. What responsibility is Joseph given in the prison?

4. In prison, what does Joseph do for Pharaoh's cupbearer and baker?

5. What happens after the cupbearer is released from prison?

Additional questions:

1. *Read Genesis 39:1-23.*

Since there was no written law from God that condemned adultery in Joseph's day, what compelled him to flee from Potiphar's wife? (Gen. 2:24; 20:3; 39:9)

2. *Read Genesis 40:1-23.*

(a) Briefly describe the cupbearer's dream and the interpretation that Jehovah gave to Joseph. (Gen. 40:9-13)

(b) What dream did the baker have, and what did it mean? (Gen. 40:16-19)

(c) How has the faithful and discreet slave class today imitated Joseph's attitude? (Gen. 40:8; Ps. 36:9; John 17:17; Acts 17:2, 3)

(d) How does Genesis 40:20 shed light on the Christian view of birthday celebrations? (Eccl. 7:1; Mark 6:21-28)

Story 23

Pharaoh's Dreams

1. What happens to Pharaoh one night?

2. Why does the cupbearer finally remember Joseph?

3. As shown in the picture, what two dreams does Pharaoh have?

4. What does Joseph say the dreams mean?

5. How does Joseph become the most important man in Egypt next to Pharaoh?

6. Why do Joseph's brothers come to Egypt, and why do they not recognize him?

7. What dream does Joseph remember, and what does it help him to understand?

Additional questions:

1. *Read Genesis 41:1-57.*

(a) How did Joseph direct attention to Jehovah, and in what way can Christians today imitate his example? (Gen. 41:16, 25, 28; Matt. 5:16; 1 Pet. 2:12)

(b) How do the years of plenty in Egypt followed by the years of famine accurately contrast the spiritual condition of Jehovah's people today with that of Christendom? (Gen. 41:29, 30; Amos 8:11, 12)

2. *Read Genesis 42:1-8 and 50:20.*

Is it wrong for worshipers of Jehovah to bow before a man out of honor and respect for his position if that is the custom of the land? (Gen. 42:6)

Story 24

Joseph Tests His Brothers

1. Why does Joseph accuse his brothers of being spies?

2. Why does Jacob let his youngest son, Benjamin, go to Egypt?

3. How does Joseph's silver cup get into Benjamin's bag?

4. What does Judah offer to do to gain Benjamin's release?

5. How have Joseph's brothers changed?

Additional questions:

1. *Read Genesis 42:9-38.*
How is Joseph's expression at Genesis 42:18 a fine reminder to those with responsibility in Jehovah's organization today? (Neh. 5:15; 2 Cor. 7:1, 2)

2. *Read Genesis 43:1-34.*
(a) Although Reuben was the firstborn, how is it evident that Judah became the spokesman for his brothers? (Gen. 43:3, 8, 9; 44:14, 18; 1 Chron. 5:2)
(b) How did Joseph evidently test his brothers, and why? (Gen. 43:33, 34)

3. *Read Genesis 44:1-34.*
(a) As part of the ruse to hide his identity from his brothers, how did Joseph represent himself? (Gen. 44:5, 15; Lev. 19:26)
(b) How did Joseph's brothers show that the envious spirit they formerly had toward their brother was now gone? (Gen. 44:13, 33, 34)

Story 25

The Family Moves to Egypt

1. What happens when Joseph tells his brothers who he is?
2. What does Joseph kindly explain to his brothers?
3. What does Pharaoh say when he hears about Joseph's brothers?
4. How big was Jacob's family when they moved to Egypt?
5. What did Jacob's family come to be called, and why?

Additional questions:

1. *Read Genesis 45:1-28.*
How does the Bible account of Joseph show that Jehovah can turn what is intended to harm his servants into a good result? (Gen. 45:5-8; Isa. 8:10; Phil. 1:12-14)

2. *Read Genesis 46:1-27.*
What reassurance did Jehovah give Jacob on his way to Egypt? (Gen. 46:1-4, ftn.)

Story 26

Job Is Faithful to God

1. Who was Job?
2. What did Satan try to do, but did he succeed?
3. What did Jehovah give Satan permission to do, and why?
4. Why did Job's wife tell him to "curse God and die"? (See picture.)
5. As you can see from the second picture, how did Jehovah bless Job, and why?
6. If we, like Job, are faithful to Jehovah, what blessings will we receive?

Additional questions:

1. *Read Job 1:1-22.*
How can Christians today imitate Job? (Job 1:1; Phil. 2:15; 2 Pet. 3:14)

2. *Read Job 2:1-13.*
In what two contrasting ways did Job and his wife respond to Satan's persecution? (Job 2:9, 10; Prov. 19:3; Mic. 7:7; Mal. 3:14)

3. *Read Job 42:10-17.*
(a) What similarities are there between the reward that Job received and what Jesus received for a faithful life course? (Job 42:12; Phil. 2:9-11)
(b) How are we encouraged by the blessings that Job received for maintaining his integrity to God? (Job 42:10, 12; Heb. 6:10; Jas. 1:2-4, 12; 5:11)

Story 27

A Bad King Rules Egypt

1. In the picture, who is the man with the whip, and who is he beating?
2. After Joseph died, what happened to the Israelites?
3. Why did the Egyptians become afraid of the Israelites?
4. What command did Pharaoh give to the women who helped the Israelite women give birth?

Additional questions:

1. *Read Exodus 1:6-22.*
(a) In what way did Jehovah begin to fulfill his promise to Abraham? (Ex. 1:7; Gen. 12:2; Acts 7:17)
(b) How did the Hebrew midwives show respect for the sanctity of life? (Ex. 1:17; Gen. 9:6)
(c) How were the midwives rewarded for their faithfulness to Jehovah? (Ex. 1:20, 21; Prov. 19:17)
(d) How did Satan attempt to thwart Jehovah's purpose regarding the promised Seed of Abraham? (Ex. 1:22; Matt. 2:16)

Story 28

How Baby Moses Was Saved

1. Who is the baby in the picture, and whose finger is he holding?
2. What did Moses' mother do to save him from being killed?
3. Who is the little girl in the picture, and what did she do?
4. When Pharaoh's daughter found the baby, what did Miriam suggest?
5. What did the princess say to Moses' mother?

Additional question:

1. *Read Exodus 2:1-10.*
What opportunity did Moses' mother have to train and teach Moses during infancy, and what example does this provide for parents today? (Ex. 2:9, 10; Deut. 6:6-9; Prov. 22:6; Eph. 6:4; 2 Tim. 3:15)

Story 29

Why Moses Ran Away

1. Where did Moses grow up, but what did he know about his parents?
2. What did Moses do when he was 40 years old?
3. What did Moses say to an Israelite man who was fighting, and what answer did the man give?
4. Why did Moses run away from Egypt?
5. Where did Moses run away to, and whom did he meet there?
6. What did Moses do during the 40 years after he fled Egypt?

Additional questions:

1. *Read Exodus 2:11-25.*
Despite years of education in the wisdom of the Egyptians, how did Moses show his loyalty to Jehovah and to his people? (Ex. 2:11, 12; Heb. 11:24)
2. *Read Acts 7:22-29.*
What lesson can we learn from Moses' trying to rescue Israel from Egyptian bondage by himself? (Acts 7:23-25; 1 Pet. 5:6, 10)

Story 30

The Burning Bush

1. What is the name of the mountain in the picture?
2. Describe the unusual thing that Moses saw when he went to the mountain with his sheep.
3. What did a voice say from the burning bush, and whose voice was it?
4. How did Moses answer when God told him that he would lead God's people out of Egypt?
5. What did God tell Moses to say if the people asked who sent him?
6. How would Moses be able to prove that God had sent him?

Additional questions:

1. *Read Exodus 3:1-22.*
How does Moses' experience give us confidence that even if we feel unqualified to fulfill a theocratic assignment, Jehovah will back us up? (Ex. 3:11, 13; 2 Cor. 3:5, 6)
2. *Read Exodus 4:1-20.*
(a) What change in Moses' attitude occurred during the 40 years he spent in Midian, and what les-

son can those reaching out for congregation privileges learn from this? (Ex. 2:11, 12; 4:10, 13; Mic. 6:8; 1 Tim. 3:1, 6, 10)
(b) Even if we are disciplined by Jehovah through his organization, what confidence can Moses' example give us? (Ex. 4:12-14; Ps. 103:14; Heb. 12: 4-11)

Story 31

Moses and Aaron See Pharaoh

1. What effect did the miracles that Moses and Aaron performed have on the Israelites?
2. What did Moses and Aaron tell Pharaoh, and what was Pharaoh's answer?
3. As shown in the picture, what happened when Aaron threw down his stick?
4. How did Jehovah teach Pharaoh a lesson, and how did Pharaoh respond?
5. What happened after the tenth plague?

Additional questions:

1. *Read Exodus 4:27-31 and 5:1-23.*
What did Pharaoh mean when he said: "I do not know Jehovah at all"? (Ex. 5:2; 1 Sam. 2:12; Rom. 1:21)
2. *Read Exodus 6:1-13, 26-30.*
(a) In what sense did Jehovah not make himself known to Abraham, Isaac, and Jacob? (Ex. 3:13, 14; 6:3; Gen. 12:8)
(b) How does it make us feel to know that Jehovah still used Moses, even though Moses felt unqualified for his assigned task? (Ex. 6:12, 30; Luke 21:13-15)
3. *Read Exodus 7:1-13.*
(a) When Moses and Aaron courageously delivered Jehovah's judgments to Pharaoh, what pattern did they set for God's servants today? (Ex. 7:2, 3, 6; Acts 4:29-31)
(b) How did Jehovah show his supremacy over Egypt's gods? (Ex. 7:12; 1 Chron. 29:12)

Story 32

The Ten Plagues

1. Using the pictures shown here, describe the first three plagues that Jehovah brought on Egypt.
2. What was the difference between the first three plagues and the rest of the plagues?
3. What were the fourth, fifth, and sixth plagues?
4. Describe plagues seven, eight, and nine.
5. What did Jehovah tell the Israelites to do before the tenth plague?
6. What was the tenth plague, and what happened after it?

Additional questions:

1. *Read Exodus 7:19–8:23.*

(a) Even though Egypt's magic-practicing priests were able to duplicate Jehovah's first two plagues, what were they forced to admit after the third plague? (Ex. 8:18, 19; Matt. 12:24-28)

(b) How did the fourth plague demonstrate Jehovah's ability to protect his people, and how does knowing this make God's people feel as they face the foretold "great tribulation"? (Ex. 8:22, 23; Rev. 7:13, 14; 2 Chron. 16:9)

2. *Read Exodus 8:24; 9:3, 6, 10, 11, 14, 16, 23-25; and 10:13-15, 21-23.*

(a) What two groups were exposed by the Ten Plagues, and how does this affect our view of those groups today? (Ex. 8:10, 18, 19; 9:14)

(b) How does Exodus 9:16 help us to understand why Jehovah has allowed Satan to remain until now? (Rom. 9:21, 22)

3. *Read Exodus 12:21-32.*

How did the Passover make salvation possible for many, and to what did the Passover point? (Ex. 12:21-23; John 1:29; Rom. 5:18, 19, 21; 1 Cor. 5:7)

Crossing the Red Sea

1. How many Israelite men, along with women and children, left Egypt, and who left with them?
2. How did Pharaoh feel after he let the Israelites go, and what did he do?
3. What did Jehovah do to stop the Egyptians from attacking his people?
4. What happened when Moses stretched out his stick over the Red Sea, and what did the Israelites do?
5. What happened when the Egyptians rushed into the sea after the Israelites?
6. How did the Israelites show that they were happy and thankful to Jehovah that they had been saved?

Additional questions:

1. *Read Exodus 12:33-36.*

How did Jehovah see to it that his people were repaid for all their years of slavery under the Egyptians? (Ex. 3:21, 22; 12:35, 36)

2. *Read Exodus 14:1-31.*

How do Moses' words recorded at Exodus 14:13, 14 affect Jehovah's servants today as they face the coming battle of Armageddon? (2 Chron. 20:17; Ps. 91:8)

3. *Read Exodus 15:1-8, 20, 21.*

(a) Why should Jehovah's servants sing praises to him? (Ex. 15:1, 2; Ps. 105:2, 3; Rev. 15:3, 4)

(b) What example in praising Jehovah did Miriam and the women at the Red Sea set for Christian women today? (Ex. 15:20, 21; Ps. 68:11)

A New Kind of Food

1. In the picture, what are the people picking up off the ground, and what is it called?
2. What instruction does Moses give the people about picking up the manna?
3. What does Jehovah tell the people to do on the sixth day, and why?
4. What miracle does Jehovah perform when the manna is kept over to the seventh day?
5. For how long does Jehovah feed the people manna?

Additional questions:

1. *Read Exodus 16:1-36 and Numbers 11:7-9.*

(a) What does Exodus 16:8 show regarding the need for us to respect theocratic appointments in the Christian congregation? (Heb. 13:17)

(b) In the wilderness, how were the Israelites reminded daily of their dependence on Jehovah? (Ex. 16:14-16, 35; Deut. 8:2, 3)

(c) What symbolic meaning did Jesus give to the manna, and how do we benefit from this "bread from heaven"? (John 6:31-35, 40)

2. *Read Joshua 5:10-12.*

For how many years did the Israelites eat manna, how did this test them, and what can we learn from this account? (Ex. 16:35; Num. 11:4-6; 1 Cor. 10:10, 11)

Jehovah Gives His Laws

1. About two months after leaving Egypt, where do the Israelites camp?
2. What does Jehovah say he wants the people to do, and what is their answer?
3. Why does Jehovah give Moses two flat stones?
4. Besides the Ten Commandments, what other laws did Jehovah give the Israelites?
5. What two laws did Jesus Christ say are the greatest?

Additional questions:

1. *Read Exodus 19:1-25; 20:1-21; 24:12-18; and 31:18.*

How do the words recorded at Exodus 19:8 help us to understand what is involved in making a Christian dedication? (Matt. 16:24; 1 Pet. 4:1-3)

2. *Read Deuteronomy 6:4-6; Leviticus 19:18; and Matthew 22:36-40.*

How do Christians demonstrate their love for God and neighbor? (Mark 6:34; Acts 4:20; Rom. 15:2)

Story 36

The Golden Calf

1. In the picture, what are the people doing, and why?
2. Why is Jehovah angry, and what does Moses do when he sees what the people are doing?
3. What does Moses tell some of the men to do?
4. What lesson should this story teach us?

Additional questions:

1. *Read Exodus 32:1-35.*

(a) How does this account show Jehovah's attitude toward mixing false religion with true worship? (Ex. 32:4-6, 10; 1 Cor. 10:7, 11)

(b) What caution should Christians exercise in their choice of entertainment, such as singing and dancing? (Ex. 32:18, 19; Eph. 5:15, 16; 1 John 2: 15-17)

(c) How did the tribe of Levi provide a fine example in standing up for righteousness? (Ex. 32:25-28; Ps. 18:25)

Story 37

A Tent for Worship

1. What is the building in the picture called, and what is it used for?
2. Why did Jehovah tell Moses to make the tent so that it could be taken apart easily?
3. What is the box in the small room at the end of the tent, and what does the box contain?
4. Whom does Jehovah choose to be high priest, and what does the high priest do?
5. Name the three things in the larger room of the tent.
6. What two things are in the courtyard of the tabernacle, and what are they used for?

Additional questions:

1. *Read Exodus 25:8-40; 26:1-37; 27:1-8; and 28:1.* What did the cherubs on "the ark of the testimony" represent? (Ex. 25:20, 22; Num. 7:89; 2 Ki. 19:15)

2. *Read Exodus 30:1-10, 17-21; 34:1, 2; and Hebrews 9:1-5.*

(a) Why did Jehovah emphasize the importance of maintaining physical cleanness to the priests serving at the tabernacle, and how should this affect us today? (Ex. 30:18-21; 40:30, 31; Heb. 10:22)

(b) How does the apostle Paul show that the tabernacle and the Law covenant were obsolete at the time he wrote his letter to Hebrew Christians? (Heb. 9:1, 9; 10:1)

Story 38

The 12 Spies

1. What do you notice about the bunch of grapes in the picture, and where did it come from?
2. Why does Moses send 12 spies into the land of Canaan?
3. What do ten spies say when they report back to Moses?
4. How do two spies show trust in Jehovah, and what are their names?
5. Why is Jehovah angry, and what does he tell Moses?

Additional questions:

1. *Read Numbers 13:1-33.*

(a) Who were chosen to spy out the land, and what grand opportunity did they have? (Num. 13:2, 3, 18-20)

(b) Why did Joshua and Caleb's view differ from that of the other spies, and what does this teach us? (Num. 13:28-30; Matt. 17:20; 2 Cor. 5:7)

2. *Read Numbers 14:1-38.*

(a) What warning about murmuring against Jehovah's earthly representatives should we heed? (Num. 14:2, 3, 27; Matt. 25:40, 45; 1 Cor. 10:10)

(b) How does Numbers 14:24 show that Jehovah takes a personal interest in each one of his servants? (1 Ki. 19:18; Prov. 15:3)

Story 39

Aaron's Rod Grows Flowers

1. Who rebel against the authority of Moses and Aaron, and what do they say to Moses?
2. What does Moses tell Korah and his 250 followers to do?
3. What does Moses say to the people, and what happens as soon as he stops talking?
4. What happens to Korah and his 250 followers?
5. What does Eleazar, Aaron's son, do with the dead men's fire holders, and why?
6. Why does Jehovah make Aaron's rod grow flowers? (See picture.)

Additional questions:

1. *Read Numbers 16:1-49.*

(a) What did Korah and his followers do, and why was it an act of rebellion against Jehovah? (Num. 16:9, 10, 18; Lev. 10:1, 2; Prov. 11:2)

(b) What wrong viewpoint did Korah and the 250 "chieftains of the assembly" cultivate? (Num. 16: 1-3; Prov. 15:33; Isa. 49:7)

2. *Read Numbers 17:1-11 and 26:10.*

(a) What did the sprouting of Aaron's rod indicate, and why did Jehovah direct that it be kept in the ark? (Num. 17:5, 8, 10)

(b) What vital lesson can we learn from the sign of Aaron's rod? (Num. 17:10; Acts 20:28; Phil. 2:14; Heb. 13:17)

Moses Strikes the Rock

1. How does Jehovah take care of the Israelites while they are in the wilderness?
2. What complaint do the Israelites make when they camp at Kadesh?
3. How does Jehovah provide water for the people and their animals?
4. In the picture, who is the man pointing to himself, and why is he doing that?
5. Why is Jehovah angry with Moses and Aaron, and how are they punished?
6. What happens at Mount Hor, and who becomes Israel's high priest?

Additional questions:

1. *Read Numbers 20:1-13, 22-29 and Deuteronomy 29:5.*

(a) What do we learn from the way Jehovah cared for the Israelites in the wilderness? (Deut. 29:5; Matt. 6:31; Heb. 13:5; Jas. 1:17)

(b) How did Jehovah view the failure of Moses and Aaron to sanctify him before Israel? (Num. 20:12; 1 Cor. 10:12; Rev. 4:11)

(c) What can we learn from the way Moses reacted to the discipline he received from Jehovah? (Num. 12:3; 20:12, 27, 28; Deut. 32:4; Heb. 12:7-11)

The Copper Serpent

1. In the picture, what is wrapped around the pole, and why did Jehovah tell Moses to put it there?
2. How are the people unthankful for all that God has done for them?
3. What do the people ask Moses to do after Jehovah sends poisonous snakes to punish them?
4. Why does Jehovah tell Moses to make a copper snake?
5. What lesson can we learn from this story?

Additional questions:

1. *Read Numbers 21:4-9.*

(a) What warning is provided for us by Israel's complaining about the provisions from Jehovah? (Num. 21:5, 6; Rom. 2:4)

(b) In later centuries, how did the Israelites use the copper serpent, and what action did King Hezekiah take? (Num. 21:9; 2 Ki. 18:1-4)

2. *Read John 3:14, 15.*

How did the placing of the copper serpent on a signal pole well picture the impaling of Jesus Christ? (Gal. 3:13; 1 Pet. 2:24)

A Donkey Talks

1. Who is Balak, and why does he send for Balaam?
2. Why does Balaam's donkey lie down in the road?
3. What does Balaam hear the donkey saying?
4. What does an angel say to Balaam?
5. What happens when Balaam tries to curse Israel?

Additional questions:

1. *Read Numbers 21:21-35.*

Why did Israel defeat King Sihon of the Amorites and King Og of Bashan? (Num. 21:21, 23, 33, 34)

2. *Read Numbers 22:1-40.*

What was Balaam's motive in trying to curse Israel, and what lessons can we draw from this? (Num. 22:16, 17; Prov. 6:16, 18; 2 Pet. 2:15; Jude 11)

3. *Read Numbers 23:1-30.*

Although Balaam talked as though he was a worshiper of Jehovah, how did his actions demonstrate otherwise? (Num. 23:3, 11-14; 1 Sam. 15:22)

4. *Read Numbers 24:1-25.*

How does this Bible account strengthen our faith in the outworking of Jehovah's purpose? (Num. 24: 10; Isa. 54:17)

Joshua Becomes Leader

1. In the picture, who are the two men standing with Moses?
2. What does Jehovah tell Joshua?
3. Why does Moses climb to the top of Mount Nebo, and what does Jehovah say to him?
4. How old is Moses when he dies?
5. Why are the people sad, but what reason do they have to be happy?

Additional questions:

1. *Read Numbers 27:12-23.*

What weighty assignment did Joshua receive from Jehovah, and how is Jehovah's care for His people shown today? (Num. 27:15-19; Acts 20:28; Heb. 13:7)

2. *Read Deuteronomy 3:23-29.*

Why did Jehovah not allow Moses and Aaron to cross over to the land of promise, and what lesson can we learn from this? (Deut. 3:25-27; Num. 20: 12, 13)

3. *Read Deuteronomy 31:1-8, 14-23.*

How do Moses' parting words to Israel show that he humbly accepted the discipline from Jehovah? (Deut. 31:6-8, 23)

4. *Read Deuteronomy 32:45-52.*

How should God's Word touch our lives? (Deut. 32: 47; Lev. 18:5; Heb. 4:12)

5. *Read Deuteronomy 34:1-12.*

Although Moses never literally saw the very person of Jehovah, what does Deuteronomy 34:10 indicate regarding his relationship with Jehovah? (Ex. 33:11, 20; Num. 12:8)

Story 44

Rahab Hides the Spies

1. Where does Rahab live?
2. Who are the two men in the picture, and why are they in Jericho?
3. What does the king of Jericho command Rahab to do, and what answer does she give?
4. How does Rahab help the two men, and what favor does she ask?
5. What promise do the two spies make to Rahab?

Additional questions:

1. *Read Joshua 2:1-24.*

How was Jehovah's promise recorded at Exodus 23:28 fulfilled when the Israelites came against Jericho? (Josh. 2:9-11)

2. *Read Hebrews 11:31.*

How does Rahab's example highlight the importance of faith? (Rom. 1:17; Heb. 10:39; Jas. 2:25)

Story 45

Crossing the Jordan River

1. What miracle does Jehovah perform so that the Israelites can cross the Jordan River?
2. What act of faith must the Israelites perform in order to cross the Jordan River?
3. Why does Jehovah tell Joshua to gather 12 large stones from the riverbed?
4. What happens as soon as the priests go up out of the Jordan?

Additional questions:

1. *Read Joshua 3:1-17.*

(a) As illustrated by this account, what do we need to do in order to receive Jehovah's help and blessing? (Josh. 3:13, 15; Prov. 3:5; Jas. 2:22, 26)

(b) What was the condition of the Jordan River when the Israelites crossed over into the Promised Land, and how did this magnify Jehovah's name? (Josh. 3:15; 4:18; Ps. 66:5-7)

2. *Read Joshua 4:1-18.*

The 12 stones that were taken from the Jordan and set up at Gilgal served what purpose? (Josh. 4:4-7)

Story 46

The Walls of Jericho

1. What does Jehovah tell the fighting men and the priests to do for six days?
2. What are the men to do on the seventh day?
3. As you see in the picture, what is happening to the walls of Jericho?
4. Why is there a red cord hanging from the window?
5. What does Joshua tell the fighting men to do to the people and the city, but what about the silver, gold, copper, and iron?
6. What are the two spies told to do?

Additional questions:

1. *Read Joshua 6:1-25.*

(a) How is the Israelites' marching around Jericho on the seventh day similar to the preaching activities of Jehovah's Witnesses in these last days? (Josh. 6:15, 16; Isa. 60:22; Matt. 24:14; 1 Cor. 9:16)

(b) How was the prophecy recorded at Joshua 6: 26 fulfilled some 500 years later, and what does this teach us about Jehovah's word? (1 Ki. 16:34; Isa. 55:11)

Story 47

A Thief in Israel

1. In the picture, who is the man burying riches taken from Jericho, and who are the ones helping him?
2. Why is the action of Achan and his family so serious?
3. What does Jehovah say when Joshua asks why the Israelites were defeated in the battle at Ai?
4. After Achan and his family are brought to Joshua, what happens to them?
5. What important lesson does the judgment of Achan teach us?

Additional questions:

1. *Read Joshua 7:1-26.*

(a) What did Joshua's prayers reveal about his relationship with his Creator? (Josh. 7:7-9; Ps. 119: 145; 1 John 5:14)

(b) What does the example of Achan show, and how is this a warning to us? (Josh. 7:11, 14, 15; Prov. 15:3; 1 Tim. 5:24; Heb. 4:13)

2. *Read Joshua 8:1-29.*

What personal responsibility do we have toward the Christian congregation today? (Josh. 7:13; Lev. 5:1; Prov. 28:13)

Story 48

The Wise Gibeonites

1. How are the people of Gibeon different from the Canaanites in nearby cities?
2. As illustrated in the picture, what do the Gibeonites do, and why?
3. What promise do Joshua and the Israelite leaders make to the Gibeonites, but what do they find out three days later?
4. What happens when kings in other cities hear that the Gibeonites have made peace with Israel?

Additional questions:

1. *Read Joshua 9:1-27.*

(a) Since Jehovah had instructed the nation of Israel "to annihilate all the inhabitants of the land," what qualities did his sparing of the Gibeonites highlight? (Josh. 9:22, 24; Matt. 9:13; Acts 10:34, 35; 2 Pet. 3:9)

(b) By sticking to the covenant he made with the Gibeonites, how did Joshua set a fine example for Christians today? (Josh. 9:18, 19; Matt. 5:37; Eph. 4:25)

2. *Read Joshua 10:1-5.*

How does the great crowd today imitate the Gibeonites, thus becoming targets for what? (Josh. 10:4; Zech. 8:23; Matt. 25:35-40; Rev. 12:17)

Story 49

The Sun Stands Still

1. In the picture, what is Joshua saying, and why?
2. How does Jehovah help Joshua and his fighting men?
3. How many enemy kings does Joshua defeat, and how long does it take?
4. Why does Joshua divide the land of Canaan?
5. How old is Joshua when he dies, and what happens to the people afterward?

Additional questions:

1. *Read Joshua 10:6-15.*

Knowing that Jehovah made the sun and the moon stand still for Israel, we have what confidence today? (Josh. 10:8, 10, 12, 13; Ps. 18:3; Prov. 18:10)

2. *Read Joshua 12:7-24.*

Who was really responsible for defeating 31 kings in Canaan, and why is this important for us today? (Josh. 12:7; 24:11-13; Deut. 31:8; Luke 21:9, 25-28)

3. *Read Joshua 14:1-5.*

How was the land divided among Israel's tribes, and what does this indicate regarding inheritances in Paradise? (Josh. 14:2; Isa. 65:21; Ezek. 47:21-23; 1 Cor. 14:33)

4. *Read Judges 2:8-13.*

Like Joshua in Israel, who today act as a restraint against apostasy? (Judg. 2:8, 10, 11; Matt. 24:45-47; 2 Thess. 2:3-6; Titus 1:7-9; Rev. 1:1; 2:1, 2)

Story 50

Two Brave Women

1. Who are the judges, and what are the names of some of them?
2. What special privilege does Deborah have, and what does this involve?
3. When Israel is threatened by King Jabin and his army chief, Sisera, what message from Jehovah does Deborah give Judge Barak, and who does she say will get the credit?
4. How does Jael show that she is a courageous woman?
5. What happens after King Jabin's death?

Additional questions:

1. *Read Judges 2:14-22.*

How did the Israelites bring Jehovah's anger upon themselves, and what lesson can we learn from this? (Judg. 2:20; Prov. 3:1, 2; Ezek. 18:21-23)

2. *Read Judges 4:1-24.*

What lessons regarding faith and courage can Christian women today learn from the examples of Deborah and Jael? (Judg. 4:4, 8, 9, 14, 21, 22; Prov. 31:30; 1 Cor. 16:13)

3. *Read Judges 5:1-31.*

How can the victory song of Barak and Deborah be applied as a prayer regarding the coming war at Har–Magedon? (Judg. 5:3, 31; 1 Chron. 16:8-10; Rev. 7:9, 10; 16:16; 19:19-21)

Story 51

Ruth and Naomi

1. How does Naomi come to be in the land of Moab?
2. Who are Ruth and Orpah?
3. How do Ruth and Orpah each respond when Naomi tells them to go back to their people?
4. Who is Boaz, and how does he help Ruth and Naomi?

5. What is the name of the child born to Boaz and Ruth, and why should we remember him?

Additional questions:

1. *Read Ruth 1:1-17.*
(a) What beautiful expression of loyal love does Ruth make? (Ruth 1:16, 17)
(b) How does Ruth's mental disposition well express the attitude of the "other sheep" toward the anointed ones on earth today? (John 10:16; Zech. 8:23)
2. *Read Ruth 2:1-23.*
How does Ruth provide a fine example for young women today? (Ruth 2:17, 18; Prov. 23:22; 31:15)
3. *Read Ruth 3:5-13.*
(a) How did Boaz view Ruth's willingness to marry him rather than a younger man?
(b) What does Ruth's attitude teach us about loyal love? (Ruth 3:10; 1 Cor. 13:4, 5)
4. *Read Ruth 4:7-17.*
How can Christian men today be like Boaz? (Ruth 4:9, 10; 1 Tim. 3:1, 12, 13; 5:8)

Story 52
Gideon and His 300 Men

1. How and why are the Israelites in a lot of trouble?
2. Why does Jehovah tell Gideon that he has too many men in his army?
3. How many men remain after Gideon tells the fearful men to go back home?
4. From the picture, explain how Jehovah reduces the number of Gideon's army to just 300 men.
5. How does Gideon organize his 300 men, and how does Israel win the battle?

Additional questions:

1. *Read Judges 6:36-40.*
(a) How did Gideon make sure of Jehovah's will?
(b) How do we today find out what Jehovah's will is? (Prov. 2:3-6; Matt. 7:7-11; 2 Tim. 3:16, 17)
2. *Read Judges 7:1-25.*
(a) What lesson can we learn from the 300 who remained alert in contrast with those who showed carelessness? (Judg. 7:3, 6; Rom. 13:11, 12; Eph. 5:15-17)
(b) Just as the 300 learned by watching Gideon, how do we learn by watching the Greater Gideon, Jesus Christ? (Judg. 7:17; Matt. 11:29, 30; 28:19, 20; 1 Pet. 2:21)
(c) How does Judges 7:21 help us be content to serve wherever we are assigned in Jehovah's organization? (1 Cor. 4:2; 12:14-18; Jas. 4:10)
3. *Read Judges 8:1-3.*
When it comes to handling personal differences with a brother or a sister, what can we learn from the way Gideon solved the dispute with the Ephraimites? (Prov. 15:1; Matt. 5:23, 24; Luke 9:48)

Story 53
Jephthah's Promise

1. Who is Jephthah, and during what time did he live?
2. What promise does Jephthah make to Jehovah?
3. Why does Jephthah become sad when he returns home from the victory over the Ammonites?
4. What does Jephthah's daughter say when she learns of her father's promise?
5. Why do the people love Jephthah's daughter?

Additional questions:

1. *Read Judges 10:6-18.*
What warning should we heed from Israel's record of unfaithfulness to Jehovah? (Judg. 10:6, 15, 16; Rom. 15:4; Rev. 2:10)
2. *Read Judges 11:1-11, 29-40.*
(a) How do we know that Jephthah's giving his daughter as "a burnt offering" did not mean offering her by fire as a human sacrifice? (Judg. 11:31; Lev. 16:24; Deut. 18:10, 12)
(b) In what way did Jephthah offer up his daughter as a sacrifice?
(c) What can we learn from Jephthah's attitude toward his vow to Jehovah? (Judg. 11:35, 39; Eccl. 5:4, 5; Matt. 16:24)
(d) How is Jephthah's daughter a fine example for young Christians in pursuing a career in full-time service? (Judg. 11:36; Matt. 6:33; Phil. 3:8)

Story 54
The Strongest Man

1. What is the name of the strongest man who ever lived, and who gave him his strength?
2. On one occasion, what does Samson do to a big lion, as you can see in the picture?
3. What secret is Samson telling Delilah in the picture, and how does this lead to his capture by the Philistines?
4. How does Samson bring about the death of 3,000 enemy Philistines on the day that he died?

Additional questions:

1. *Read Judges 13:1-14.*
How do Manoah and his wife provide a good example for parents in rearing their children? (Judg. 13:8; Ps. 127:3; Eph. 6:4)
2. *Read Judges 14:5-9 and 15:9-16.*
(a) What do the accounts of Samson's killing the lion, breaking new ropes that bound him, and using the jawbone of a male ass to kill 1,000 men reveal about the operation of Jehovah's holy spirit?

(b) How does holy spirit help us today? (Judg. 14:6; 15:14; Zech. 4:6; Acts 4:31)

3. *Read Judges 16:18-31.*
How was Samson affected by bad associations, and what can we learn from this? (Judg. 16:18, 19; 1 Cor. 15:33)

Story 55
A Little Boy Serves God

1. What is the name of the little boy in the picture, and who are the others?
2. What prayer does Hannah say one day when she is visiting Jehovah's tabernacle, and how does Jehovah answer her?
3. How old is Samuel when he is taken to serve at Jehovah's tent, and what does his mother do for him each year?
4. What are the names of Eli's sons, and what kind of men are they?
5. How does Jehovah call Samuel, and what message does He give him?
6. What does Samuel become when he grows up, and what happens when he grows old?

Additional questions:

1. *Read 1 Samuel 1:1-28.*
(a) What fine example for family heads does Elkanah provide in taking the lead in true worship? (1 Sam. 1:3, 21; Matt. 6:33; Phil. 1:10)
(b) What lesson can we learn from Hannah's example in dealing with a perplexing problem? (1 Sam. 1:10, 11; Ps. 55:22; Rom. 12:12)

2. *Read 1 Samuel 2:11-36.*
How did Eli honor his sons more than Jehovah, and how can this serve as a warning to us? (1 Sam. 2:22-24, 27, 29; Deut. 21:18-21; Matt. 10:36, 37)

3. *Read 1 Samuel 4:16-18.*
What fourfold message of woe comes from the battle line, and what effect does it have on Eli?

4. *Read 1 Samuel 8:4-9.*
How did Israel greatly offend Jehovah, and how can we loyally support his Kingdom today? (1 Sam. 8:5, 7; John 17:16; Jas. 4:4)

Story 56
Saul—Israel's First King

1. In the picture, what is Samuel doing, and why?
2. Why does Jehovah like Saul, and what kind of man is he?
3. What is the name of Saul's son, and what does the son do?
4. Why does Saul offer a sacrifice instead of waiting for Samuel to do it?
5. What lessons can we learn from the account about Saul?

Additional questions:

1. *Read 1 Samuel 9:15-21 and 10:17-27.*
How did Saul's modest attitude help him to avoid rash action when certain men talked disrespectfully about him? (1 Sam. 9:21; 10:21, 22, 27; Prov. 17:27)

2. *Read 1 Samuel 13:5-14.*
What was the sin that Saul committed at Gilgal? (1 Sam. 10:8; 13:8, 9, 13)

3. *Read 1 Samuel 15:1-35.*
(a) What serious sin did Saul commit in connection with Agag, the king of Amalek? (1 Sam. 15:2, 3, 8, 9, 22)
(b) How did Saul try to justify his actions and shift the blame? (1 Sam. 15:24)
(c) What warning should we heed today when we are given counsel? (1 Sam. 15:19-21; Ps. 141:5; Prov. 9:8, 9; 11:2)

Story 57
God Chooses David

1. What is the name of the boy in the picture, and how do we know that he is brave?
2. Where does David live, and what are the names of his father and grandfather?
3. Why does Jehovah tell Samuel to go to Jesse's house in Bethlehem?
4. What happens when Jesse brings seven of his sons to Samuel?
5. When David is brought in, what does Jehovah tell Samuel?

Additional questions:

1. *Read 1 Samuel 17:34, 35.*
How do these events emphasize David's courage and reliance on Jehovah? (1 Sam. 17:37)

2. *Read 1 Samuel 16:1-14.*
(a) How do Jehovah's words at 1 Samuel 16:7 help us to be impartial and to avoid being prejudiced by outward appearances? (Acts 10:34, 35; 1 Tim. 2:4)
(b) How does Saul's example show that when Jehovah removes his holy spirit from a person, the vacancy can be filled by a bad spirit, or an inward urge to do wrong? (1 Sam. 16:14; Matt. 12:43-45; Gal. 5:16)

Story 58
David and Goliath

1. What challenge does Goliath make to the Israelite army?
2. How big is Goliath, and what reward does King Saul promise to the man who kills Goliath?

3. What does David say when Saul tells him that he cannot fight Goliath because David is just a boy?

4. In his reply to Goliath, how does David show his trust in Jehovah?

5. As you can see in the picture, what does David use to kill Goliath, and what happens to the Philistines after this?

Additional questions:

1. *Read 1 Samuel 17:1-54.*

(a) What was the secret of David's fearlessness, and how can we imitate his courage? (1 Sam. 17: 37, 45; Eph. 6:10, 11)

(b) Why should Christians avoid a competitive spirit like that of Goliath when engaging in games or recreation? (1 Sam. 17:8; Gal. 5:26; 1 Tim. 4:8)

(c) How do David's words indicate that he had faith in God's backing? (1 Sam. 17:45-47; 2 Chron. 20:15)

(d) Rather than describing just a contest between two opposing armies, how does this account show that the battle was really between false gods and the true God, Jehovah? (1 Sam. 17:43, 46, 47)

(e) How do the anointed remnant imitate David's example of trusting in Jehovah? (1 Sam. 17:37; Jer. 1:17-19; Rev. 12:17)

Story 59

Why David Must Run Away

1. Why is Saul jealous of David, but how is Saul's son Jonathan different?

2. What happens one day when David is playing the harp for Saul?

3. What does Saul say that David must do before he can take Saul's daughter Michal as a wife, and why does Saul say this?

4. When David plays the harp for Saul, what happens for the third time, as the picture shows?

5. How does Michal help save David's life, and what does David then have to do for seven years?

Additional questions:

1. *Read 1 Samuel 18:1-30.*

(a) How did the unbreakable love of Jonathan for David foreshadow the mutual love between the "other sheep" and the "little flock"? (1 Sam. 18:1; John 10:16; Luke 12:32; Zech. 8:23)

(b) In view of the fact that Jonathan would normally have been Saul's heir, how does 1 Samuel 18:4 show Jonathan's outstanding submission to the one chosen to be king?

(c) How does Saul's example show that jealousy can lead to grave sin, and what warning does this provide for us? (1 Sam. 18:7-9, 25; Jas. 3:14-16)

2. *Read 1 Samuel 19:1-17.*

How did Jonathan put his own life at risk when he spoke the words recorded at 1 Samuel 19:4, 5? (1 Sam. 19:1, 6)

Story 60

Abigail and David

1. What is the name of the woman coming to meet David in the picture, and what kind of person is she?

2. Who is Nabal?

3. Why does David send some of his men to ask Nabal for a favor?

4. What does Nabal say to David's men, and how does David respond?

5. How does Abigail show that she is a wise woman?

Additional questions:

1. *Read 1 Samuel 22:1-4.*

How did David's family provide a fine example of how we should support one another in the Christian brotherhood? (Prov. 17:17; 1 Thess. 5:14)

2. *Read 1 Samuel 25:1-43.*

(a) Why is Nabal described so contemptuously? (1 Sam. 25:2-5, 10, 14, 21, 25)

(b) What can Christian wives today learn from Abigail's example? (1 Sam. 25:32, 33; Prov. 31:26; Eph. 5:24)

(c) Abigail restrained David from doing what two bad things? (1 Sam. 25:31, 33; Rom. 12:19; Eph. 4:26)

(d) How does David's reaction to Abigail's words help men today to have Jehovah's view of women? (Acts 21:8, 9; Rom. 2:11; 1 Pet. 3:7)

Story 61

David Is Made King

1. What did David and Abishai do while Saul was sleeping in his camp?

2. What questions does David ask Saul?

3. After leaving Saul, where does David go?

4. What makes David very sad, so that he writes a beautiful song?

5. How old is David when he is made king in Hebron, and what are the names of some of his sons?

6. Where does David later rule as king?

Additional questions:

1. *Read 1 Samuel 26:1-25.*

(a) David's expression recorded at 1 Samuel 26: 11 reveals what attitude toward theocratic order? (Ps. 37:7; Rom. 13:2)

(b) When we put forth an earnest effort to express loving-kindness but meet with an unappreciative response, how can David's words found at 1 Samuel 26:23 help us maintain a proper viewpoint? (1 Ki. 8:32; Ps. 18:20)

2. *Read 2 Samuel 1:26.*
How can Christians today develop the same kind of "intense love for one another" that David and Jonathan had? (1 Pet. 4:8; Col. 3:14; 1 John 4:12)

3. *Read 2 Samuel 5:1-10.*
(a) For how many years did David reign as king, and how was this period divided up? (2 Sam. 5: 4, 5)
(b) To what is David's greatness attributed, and how does it serve as a reminder for us today? (2 Sam. 5:10; 1 Sam. 16:13; 1 Cor. 1:31; Phil. 4:13)

Story 62

Trouble in David's House

1. With Jehovah's help, what finally happens to the land of Canaan?
2. What happens one evening when David is on the roof of his palace?
3. Why is Jehovah very angry with David?
4. In the picture, whom does Jehovah send to tell David about his sins, and what does that man say will happen to David?
5. What trouble does David have?
6. After David, who becomes the king of Israel?

Additional questions:

1. *Read 2 Samuel 11:1-27.*
(a) How is keeping busy in Jehovah's service a protection for us?
(b) How was David drawn into sin, and what warning does this provide for Jehovah's servants today? (2 Sam. 11:2; Matt. 5:27-29; 1 Cor. 10:12; Jas. 1:14, 15)

2. *Read 2 Samuel 12:1-18.*
(a) What lesson can elders and parents learn from the way that Nathan approached David to offer counsel? (2 Sam. 12:1-4; Prov. 12:18; Matt. 13:34)
(b) Why did Jehovah act mercifully toward David? (2 Sam. 12:13; Ps. 32:5; 2 Cor. 7:9, 10)

Story 63

Wise King Solomon

1. What does Jehovah ask Solomon, and how does he answer?
2. Because he is pleased with Solomon's request, what does Jehovah promise to give him?
3. What hard problem do two women present to Solomon?
4. As you can see in the picture, how does Solomon solve the problem?

5. What is Solomon's rule like, and why?

Additional questions:

1. *Read 1 Kings 3:3-28.*
(a) What can men who are given responsibilities in God's organization today learn from Solomon's heartfelt expression at 1 Kings 3:7? (Ps. 119:105; Prov. 3:5, 6)
(b) How is Solomon's request a fine example of the proper things for which to pray? (1 Ki. 3:9, 11; Prov. 30:8, 9; 1 John 5:14)
(c) What confidence does Solomon's handling of the dispute between the two women give us regarding the future rulership of the Greater Solomon, Jesus Christ? (1 Ki. 3:28; Isa. 9:6, 7; 11:2-4)

2. *Read 1 Kings 4:29-34.*
(a) How did Jehovah answer Solomon's request for an obedient heart? (1 Ki. 4:29)
(b) In view of the efforts made by people to hear Solomon's wisdom, what should be our attitude toward the study of God's Word? (1 Ki. 4:29, 34; John 17:3; 2 Tim. 3:16)

Story 64

Solomon Builds the Temple

1. How long does it take Solomon to complete the building of Jehovah's temple, and why does it cost so much money?
2. How many main rooms are there in the temple, and what is put in the inside room?
3. What does Solomon say in his prayer when the temple is finished?
4. How does Jehovah show that he is pleased with Solomon's prayer?
5. What do Solomon's wives get him to do, and what happens to Solomon?
6. Why is Jehovah angry with Solomon, and what does Jehovah say to him?

Additional questions:

1. *Read 1 Chronicles 28:9, 10.*
In view of David's words recorded at 1 Chronicles 28:9, 10, what should we strive to do in our daily lives? (Ps. 19:14; Phil. 4:8, 9)

2. *Read 2 Chronicles 6:12-21, 32-42.*
(a) How did Solomon show that no man-made building can hold the Most High God? (2 Chron. 6:18; Acts 17:24, 25)
(b) What do Solomon's words found at 2 Chronicles 6:32, 33 show about Jehovah? (Acts 10:34, 35; Gal. 2:6)

3. *Read 2 Chronicles 7:1-5.*
Just as the sons of Israel were moved to make an expression of praise to Jehovah at seeing his glory, how should we today be affected when we contemplate Jehovah's blessing on his people? (2 Chron. 7:3; Ps. 22:22; 34:1; 96:2)

4. *Read 1 Kings 11:9-13.*
How does Solomon's life course show the importance of remaining faithful to the end? (1 Ki. 11:4, 9; Matt. 10:22; Rev. 2:10)

Story 65

The Kingdom Is Divided

1. What are the names of the two men in the picture, and who are they?
2. What does Ahijah do with the robe he is wearing, and what does that act mean?
3. What does Solomon try to do to Jeroboam?
4. Why do the people make Jeroboam king over ten tribes?
5. Why does Jeroboam make two golden calves, and what happens to the land soon afterward?
6. What happens to the two-tribe kingdom and Jehovah's temple in Jerusalem?

Additional questions:

1. *Read 1 Kings 11:26-43.*
What kind of person was Jeroboam, and what did Jehovah promise him if he kept God's laws? (1 Ki. 11:28, 38)
2. *Read 1 Kings 12:1-33.*
(a) From Rehoboam's bad example, what can parents and elders learn regarding abuse of authority? (1 Ki. 12:13; Eccl. 7:7; 1 Pet. 5:2, 3)
(b) To whom should youths today turn for reliable guidance when making serious decisions in life? (1 Ki. 12:6, 7; Prov. 1:8, 9; 2 Tim. 3:16, 17; Heb. 13:7)
(c) What moved Jeroboam to set up two centers for calf worship, and how did this show a great lack of faith in Jehovah? (1 Ki. 11:37; 12:26-28)
(d) Who led the people of the ten-tribe kingdom in a rebellion against true worship? (1 Ki. 12:32, 33)

Story 66

Jezebel—A Wicked Queen

1. Who is Jezebel?
2. Why is King Ahab sad one day?
3. What does Jezebel do to get Naboth's vineyard for her husband, Ahab?
4. Who does Jehovah send to punish Jezebel?
5. As you can see in the picture, what happens when Jehu arrives at Jezebel's palace?

Additional questions:

1. *Read 1 Kings 16:29-33 and 18:3, 4.*
How bad were conditions in Israel during the time of King Ahab? (1 Ki. 14:9)

2. *Read 1 Kings 21:1-16.*
(a) How did Naboth show courage and loyalty to Jehovah? (1 Ki. 21:1-3; Lev. 25:23-28)
(b) From Ahab's example, what can we learn about coping with disappointment? (1 Ki. 21:4; Rom. 5:3-5)
3. *Read 2 Kings 9:30-37.*
What can we learn from Jehu's zeal in doing Jehovah's will? (2 Ki. 9:4-10; 2 Cor. 9:1, 2; 2 Tim. 4:2)

Story 67

Jehoshaphat Trusts Jehovah

1. Who is Jehoshaphat, and at what time does he live?
2. Why are the Israelites afraid, and what do many of them do?
3. What answer does Jehovah give to Jehoshaphat's prayer?
4. What does Jehovah cause to happen before the battle?
5. What lesson can we learn from Jehoshaphat?

Additional questions:

1. *Read 2 Chronicles 20:1-30.*
(a) How did Jehoshaphat demonstrate what faithful servants of God should do when faced with threatening circumstances? (2 Chron. 20:12; Ps. 25:15; 62:1)
(b) Since Jehovah has always used a channel of communication when dealing with his people, what channel does he use today? (2 Chron. 20:14, 15; Matt. 24:45-47; John 15:15)
(c) When God launches the "war of the great day of God the Almighty," how will our situation be similar to that of Jehoshaphat? (2 Chron. 20:15, 17; 32:8; Rev. 16:14, 16)
(d) Imitating the Levites, pioneers and missionaries make what kind of contribution to the worldwide preaching work today? (2 Chron. 20:19; Rom. 10:13-15; 2 Tim. 4:2)

Story 68

Two Boys Who Live Again

1. Who are the three people in the picture, and what happens to the little boy?
2. What does Elijah pray regarding the boy, and what happens next?
3. What is the name of Elijah's helper?
4. Why is Elisha called to the home of a woman in Shunem?
5. What does Elisha do, and what happens to the dead child?
6. What power does Jehovah have, as shown through Elijah and Elisha?

Additional questions:

1. *Read 1 Kings 17:8-24.*
(a) How was Elijah's obedience and faith tested? (1 Ki. 17:9; 19:1-4, 10)
(b) Why was the faith of the widow of Zarephath outstanding? (1 Ki. 17:12-16; Luke 4:25, 26)
(c) How does the experience of the widow of Zarephath bear out the truthfulness of Jesus' words recorded at Matthew 10:41, 42? (1 Ki. 17:10-12, 17, 23, 24)

2. *Read 2 Kings 4:8-37.*
(a) What does the woman of Shunem teach us about hospitality? (2 Ki. 4:8; Luke 6:38; Rom. 12: 13; 1 John 3:17)
(b) In what ways can we show acts of kindness toward God's servants today? (Acts 20:35; 28:1, 2; Gal. 6:9, 10; Heb. 6:10)

Story 69

A Girl Helps a Mighty Man

1. In the picture, what is the little girl telling the lady?
2. Who is the lady in the picture, and what is the little girl doing at the lady's house?
3. What does Elisha instruct his servant to tell Naaman, and why does Naaman get angry?
4. What happens when Naaman listens to his servants?
5. Why does Elisha refuse Naaman's gift, but what does Gehazi do?
6. What happens to Gehazi, and what can we learn from this?

Additional questions:

1. *Read 2 Kings 5:1-27.*
(a) How can the example set by the little Israelite girl encourage young ones today? (2 Ki. 5:3; Ps. 8:2; 148:12, 13)
(b) Why is it good to keep Naaman's example in mind when we receive Scriptural counsel? (2 Ki. 5:15; Heb. 12:5, 6; Jas. 4:6)
(c) What lessons can we learn by contrasting Elisha's example with that of Gehazi? (2 Ki. 5:9, 10, 14-16, 20; Matt. 10:8; Acts 5:1-5; 2 Cor. 2:17)

Story 70

Jonah and the Big Fish

1. Who is Jonah, and what does Jehovah tell him to do?
2. Because he does not want to go where Jehovah tells him, what does Jonah do?
3. What does Jonah tell the sailors to do in order to stop the storm?
4. As you can see in the picture, what happens when Jonah sinks down into the water?

5. How long is Jonah inside the big fish, and what does he do there?
6. Where does Jonah go after he gets out of the big fish, and what does this teach us?

Additional questions:

1. *Read Jonah 1:1-17.*
Evidently, how did Jonah feel about his assignment to preach to the Ninevites? (Jonah 1:2, 3; Prov. 3:7; Eccl. 8:12)
2. *Read Jonah 2:1, 2, 10.*
How does Jonah's experience give us confidence that Jehovah will answer our prayers? (Ps. 22:24; 34:6; 1 John 5:14)
3. *Read Jonah 3:1-10.*
(a) What encouragement do we get from the fact that Jehovah continued to use Jonah despite his initial failure to fulfill his assignment? (Ps. 103: 14; 1 Pet. 5:10)
(b) What does Jonah's experience with the Ninevites teach us about prejudging people in our territory? (Jonah 3:6-9; Eccl. 11:6; Acts 13:48)

Story 71

God Promises a Paradise

1. Who was Isaiah, when did he live, and what did Jehovah show him?
2. What does the word "paradise" mean, and of what does it remind you?
3. What did Jehovah tell Isaiah to write about the new Paradise?
4. Why did Adam and Eve lose their beautiful home?
5. What does Jehovah promise for those who love him?

Additional questions:

1. *Read Isaiah 11:6-9.*
(a) How does God's Word portray the peace that will exist between animals and humans in the new world? (Ps. 148:10, 13; Isa. 65:25; Ezek. 34:25)
(b) What spiritual fulfillment of Isaiah's words is taking place among Jehovah's people today? (Rom. 12:2; Eph. 4:23, 24)
(c) Who deserves the credit for the transformation in human personalities both now and in the new world? (Isa. 48:17, 18; Gal. 5:22, 23; Phil. 4:7)
2. *Read Revelation 21:3, 4.*
(a) How do the Scriptures indicate that God's dwelling with mankind means that he is figuratively present, not physically present, on earth? (Lev. 26:11, 12; 2 Chron. 6:18; Isa. 66:1; Rev. 21: 2, 3, 22-24)
(b) What kind of tears and pain will be done away with? (Luke 8:49-52; Rom. 8:21, 22; Rev. 21:4)

Story 72

God Helps King Hezekiah

1. Who is the man in the picture, and why is he in a lot of trouble?
2. What are the letters that Hezekiah has put before God, and what does Hezekiah pray?
3. What kind of a king is Hezekiah, and what message does Jehovah send to him through the prophet Isaiah?
4. What does Jehovah's angel do to the Assyrians, as shown in the picture?
5. Although the two-tribe kingdom has peace for a while, what happens after Hezekiah dies?

Additional questions:

1. *Read 2 Kings 18:1-36.*
(a) How did the Assyrian spokesman Rabshakeh seek to weaken the faith of the Israelites? (2 Ki. 18:19, 21; Ex. 5:2; Ps. 64:3)
(b) When dealing with opposers, how do Jehovah's Witnesses heed the example of Hezekiah? (2 Ki. 18:36; Ps. 39:1; Prov. 26:4; 2 Tim. 2:24)
2. *Read 2 Kings 19:1-37.*
(a) How do Jehovah's people today imitate Hezekiah in times of distress? (2 Ki. 19:1, 2; Prov. 3:5, 6; Heb. 10:24, 25; Jas. 5:14, 15)
(b) What threefold defeat did King Sennacherib experience, and whom does he prophetically picture? (2 Ki. 19:32, 35, 37; Rev. 20:2, 3)
3. *Read 2 Kings 21:1-6, 16.*
Why can it be said that Manasseh was one of the wickedest kings ever to rule in Jerusalem? (2 Chron. 33:4-6, 9)

Story 73

Israel's Last Good King

1. How old is Josiah when he becomes king, and what does he start to do when he has been king for seven years?
2. What do you see Josiah doing in the first picture?
3. What does the high priest find when the men are repairing the temple?
4. Why does Josiah tear his clothes apart?
5. What message from Jehovah does the prophetess Huldah give Josiah?

Additional questions:

1. *Read 2 Chronicles 34:1-28.*
(a) What example does Josiah provide for those who may have had to endure a difficult childhood? (2 Chron. 33:21-25; 34:1, 2; Ps. 27:10)

(b) What significant steps did Josiah take to advance true worship during the 8th, 12th, and 18th years of his reign? (2 Chron. 34:3, 8)
(c) What lessons in maintaining our places of worship can we learn from the examples set by King Josiah and High Priest Hilkiah? (2 Chron. 34:9-13; Prov. 11:14; 1 Cor. 10:31)

Story 74

A Man Who Is Not Afraid

1. Who is the young man in the picture?
2. What does Jeremiah think about his becoming a prophet, but what does Jehovah tell him?
3. What message does Jeremiah keep telling the people?
4. How do the priests try to stop Jeremiah, but how does he show that he is not afraid?
5. What happens when the Israelites do not change their bad ways?

Additional questions:

1. *Read Jeremiah 1:1-8.*
(a) As Jeremiah's example demonstrates, what qualifies a person for Jehovah's service? (2 Cor. 3:5, 6)
(b) What encouragement does Jeremiah's example provide for Christian youths today? (Eccl. 12:1; 1 Tim. 4:12)
2. *Read Jeremiah 10:1-5.*
What powerful illustration does Jeremiah use to show the futility of trusting in idols? (Jer. 10:5; Isa. 46:7; Hab. 2:19)
3. *Read Jeremiah 26:1-16.*
(a) When sounding the warning message today, how has the anointed remnant taken to heart Jehovah's command to Jeremiah 'not to take away a word'? (Jer. 26:2; Deut. 4:2; Acts 20:27)
(b) What fine example did Jeremiah provide for Jehovah's Witnesses today in declaring Jehovah's warning to the nations? (Jer. 26:8, 12, 14, 15; 2 Tim. 4:1-5)
4. *Read 2 Kings 24:1-17.*
What sad consequences resulted from Judah's unfaithfulness to Jehovah? (2 Ki. 24:2-4, 14)

Story 75

Four Boys in Babylon

1. Who are the four boys in the picture, and why are they in Babylon?
2. What plans does Nebuchadnezzar have for the four boys, and what orders does he give his servants?
3. What request does Daniel make regarding food and drink for himself and his three friends?

4. After eating vegetables for ten days, how do Daniel and his three friends compare with the other young men?

5. How do Daniel and his three friends come to be in the king's palace, and in what way are they better than the priests and wise men?

Additional questions:

1. *Read Daniel 1:1-21.*

(a) What kind of effort is needed if we hope to resist temptations and overcome weaknesses? (Dan. 1:8; Gen. 39:7, 10; Gal. 6:9)

(b) In what ways might youths today be tempted or pressured to indulge in what some consider to be "delicacies"? (Dan. 1:8; Prov. 20:1; 2 Cor. 6:17–7:1)

(c) What does the Bible account of the four Hebrew youths help us to appreciate regarding taking in secular knowledge? (Dan. 1:20; Isa. 54:13; 1 Cor. 3:18-20)

Story 76

Jerusalem Is Destroyed

1. What is happening to Jerusalem and to the Israelites shown in the picture?

2. Who is Ezekiel, and what shocking things does Jehovah show him?

3. Because the Israelites have no respect for Jehovah, what does he promise?

4. What does King Nebuchadnezzar do after the Israelites rebel against him?

5. Why does Jehovah let this terrible destruction happen to the Israelites?

6. How is the land of Israel left without any people, and for how long?

Additional questions:

1. *Read 2 Kings 25:1-26.*

(a) Who was Zedekiah, what happened to him, and how did this fulfill Bible prophecy? (2 Ki. 25:5-7; Ezek. 12:13-15)

(b) Whom did Jehovah hold accountable for all the unfaithfulness that Israel committed? (2 Ki. 25:9, 11, 12, 18, 19; 2 Chron. 36:14, 17)

2. *Read Ezekiel 8:1-18.*

How has Christendom imitated apostate Israelite sun worshipers? (Ezek. 8:16; Isa. 5:20, 21; John 3:19-21; 2 Tim. 4:3)

Story 77

They Would Not Bow Down

1. What command has Nebuchadnezzar, the king of Babylon, given to the people?

2. Why are Daniel's three friends not bowing down to the image of gold?

3. When Nebuchadnezzar gives the three Hebrews another chance to bow down, how do they show their trust in Jehovah?

4. What does Nebuchadnezzar have his men do to Shadrach, Meshach, and Abednego?

5. What does Nebuchadnezzar see when he looks into the furnace?

6. Why does the king praise the God of Shadrach, Meshach, and Abednego, and what example do they provide for us?

Additional questions:

1. *Read Daniel 3:1-30.*

(a) What attitude displayed by the three young Hebrews should all of God's servants imitate when faced with tests of integrity? (Dan. 3:17, 18; Matt. 10:28; Rom. 14:7, 8)

(b) What important lesson did Jehovah God teach Nebuchadnezzar? (Dan. 3:28, 29; 4:34, 35)

Story 78

Handwriting on the Wall

1. What happens when the king of Babylon has a big feast and uses the cups and bowls taken from Jehovah's temple in Jerusalem?

2. What does Belshazzar say to his wise men, but what are they unable to do?

3. What does the king's mother tell him to do?

4. According to what Daniel tells the king, why has God sent the hand to write on the wall?

5. How does Daniel explain the meaning of the words on the wall?

6. What happens while Daniel is yet speaking?

Additional questions:

1. *Read Daniel 5:1-31.*

(a) Contrast godly fear with the fear that Belshazzar felt when he saw the writing on the wall. (Dan. 5:6, 7; Ps. 19:9; Rom. 8:35-39)

(b) How did Daniel show great courage when speaking to Belshazzar and his grandees? (Dan. 5:17, 18, 22, 26-28; Acts 4:29)

(c) In what way does Daniel chapter 5 underscore Jehovah's universal sovereignty? (Dan. 4:17, 25; 5:21)

Story 79

Daniel in the Lions' Pit

1. Who is Darius, and how does he view Daniel?

2. What do some jealous men get Darius to do?

3. What does Daniel do when he learns about the new law?

4. Why is Darius so upset that he cannot sleep, and what does he do the next morning?

5. How does Daniel answer Darius?

6. What happens to the bad men who tried to kill Daniel, and what does Darius write to all the people in his kingdom?

Additional questions:

1. *Read Daniel 6:1-28.*

(a) How does the conspiracy against Daniel remind us of what opposers have done to try to suppress the work of Jehovah's Witnesses in modern times? (Dan. 6:7; Ps. 94:20; Isa. 10:1; Rom. 8:31)

(b) How can servants of God today imitate Daniel in remaining subject to "the superior authorities"? (Dan. 6:5, 10; Rom. 13:1; Acts 5:29)

(c) How can we imitate Daniel's example of serving Jehovah "with constancy"? (Dan. 6:16, 20; Phil. 3:16; Rev. 7:15)

Story 80

God's People Leave Babylon

1. As illustrated in the picture, what are the Israelites doing?

2. How did Cyrus fulfill Jehovah's prophecy through Isaiah?

3. What does Cyrus tell the Israelites who cannot return to Jerusalem?

4. What does Cyrus give the people to take back to Jerusalem?

5. How long does it take the Israelites to get back to Jerusalem?

6. How many years have passed since the land was left completely empty of people?

Additional questions:

1. *Read Isaiah 44:28 and 45:1-4.*

(a) How did Jehovah emphasize the certainty of the fulfillment of the prophecy regarding Cyrus? (Isa. 55:10, 11; Rom. 4:17)

(b) What does Isaiah's prophecy regarding Cyrus show about Jehovah God's ability to foretell the future? (Isa. 42:9; 45:21; 46:10, 11; 2 Pet. 1:20)

2. *Read Ezra 1:1-11.*

Following the example of those who were unable to return to Jerusalem, how can we today 'strengthen the hands' of those who are able to enter full-time service? (Ezra 1:4, 6; Rom. 12:13; Col. 4:12)

Story 81

Trusting in God's Help

1. How many people make the long trip from Babylon to Jerusalem, but what do they find when they arrive?

2. What do the Israelites begin to build after they arrive, but what do their enemies do?

3. Who are Haggai and Zechariah, and what do they tell the people?

4. Why does Tattenai send a letter to Babylon, and what answer does he receive?

5. What does Ezra do when he learns about the need to fix up God's temple?

6. What is Ezra praying for in the picture, how is his prayer answered, and what does this teach us?

Additional questions:

1. *Read Ezra 3:1-13.*

If we ever find ourselves in an area where there is no congregation of God's people, what should we continue to do? (Ezra 3:3, 6; Acts 17:16, 17; Heb. 13:15)

2. *Read Ezra 4:1-7.*

What example did Zerubbabel set for Jehovah's people regarding interfaith? (Ex. 34:12; 1 Cor. 15:33; 2 Cor. 6:14-17)

3. *Read Ezra 5:1-5, 17 and 6:1-22.*

(a) Why were the opposers unable to stop the temple building work? (Ezra 5:5; Isa. 54:17)

(b) How does the action of the older men of the Jews encourage Christian elders to seek Jehovah's guidance when facing opposers? (Ezra 6:14; Ps. 32:8; Rom. 8:31; Jas. 1:5)

4. *Read Ezra 8:21-23, 28-36.*

Before we embark on a certain course of action, what example of Ezra would be good for us to imitate? (Ezra 8:23; Ps. 127:1; Prov. 10:22; Jas. 4:13-15)

Story 82

Mordecai and Esther

1. Who are Mordecai and Esther?

2. Why does King Ahasuerus want a new wife, and whom does he choose?

3. Who is Haman, and what makes him very angry?

4. What law is made, and what does Esther do after receiving a message from Mordecai?

5. What happens to Haman, and what happens to Mordecai?

6. How are the Israelites saved from their enemies?

Additional questions:

1. *Read Esther 2:12-18.*

How did Esther demonstrate the value of cultivating a "quiet and mild spirit"? (Esther 2:15; 1 Pet. 3:1-5)

2. *Read Esther 4:1-17.*

Just as Esther was given an opportunity to act in behalf of true worship, what opportunity are we given today to express our devotion and loyalty to Jehovah? (Esther 4:13, 14; Matt. 5:14-16; 24:14)

3. *Read Esther 7:1-6.*
How have many of God's people today similarly risked persecution, as Esther did? (Esther 7:4; Matt. 10:16-22; 1 Pet. 2:12)

Story 83
The Walls of Jerusalem

1. How did the Israelites feel about not having walls around their city of Jerusalem?
2. Who is Nehemiah?
3. What is Nehemiah's job, and why is it important?
4. What news makes Nehemiah sad, and what does he do?
5. How does King Artaxerxes show kindness to Nehemiah?
6. How does Nehemiah arrange the building work so that the Israelites' enemies cannot stop it?

Additional questions:
1. *Read Nehemiah 1:4-6 and 2:1-20.*
How did Nehemiah seek Jehovah's guidance? (Neh. 2:4, 5; Rom. 12:12; 1 Pet. 4:7)
2. *Read Nehemiah 3:3-5.*
What can elders and ministerial servants learn from the contrast between the Tekoites and their "majestic ones"? (Neh. 3:5, 27; 2 Thess. 3:7-10; 1 Pet. 5:5)
3. *Read Nehemiah 4:1-23.*
(a) What motivated the Israelites to continue building despite fierce opposition? (Neh. 4:6, 8, 9; Ps. 50:15; Isa. 65:13, 14)
(b) In what way does the Israelites' example encourage us today?
4. *Read Nehemiah 6:15.*
What does the fact that Jerusalem's walls were completed within two months demonstrate regarding the power of faith? (Ps. 56:3, 4; Matt. 17:20; 19:26)

Story 84
An Angel Visits Mary

1. Who is the woman in the picture?
2. What does Gabriel tell Mary?
3. How does Gabriel explain to Mary that she will have a baby even though she has not lived with a man?
4. What happens when Mary visits her relative Elizabeth?
5. What does Joseph think when he learns that Mary is going to have a baby, but why does he change his mind?

Additional questions:
1. *Read Luke 1:26-56.*
(a) What does Luke 1:35 indicate regarding any Adamic imperfection in Mary's ovum when the life of God's Son was transferred from the spirit realm? (Hag. 2:11-13; John 6:69; Heb. 7:26; 10:5)
(b) How did Jesus receive honor even before his birth? (Luke 1:41-43)
(c) What fine example did Mary provide for Christians today who receive special privileges of service? (Luke 1:38, 46-49; 17:10; Prov. 11:2)
2. *Read Matthew 1:18-25.*
Although Jesus was not given the personal name Immanuel, how did his role as a human fulfill its meaning? (Matt. 1:22, 23; John 14:8-10; Heb. 1:1-3)

Story 85
Jesus Born in a Stable

1. Who is the little baby in the picture, and where is Mary laying him?
2. Why was Jesus born in a stable with the animals?
3. In the picture, who are the men entering the stable, and what had an angel told them?
4. Why is Jesus special?
5. Why can Jesus be called God's Son?

Additional questions:
1. *Read Luke 2:1-20.*
(a) What part did Caesar Augustus play in the fulfillment of the prophecy concerning Jesus' birth? (Luke 2:1-4; Mic. 5:2)
(b) How may an individual come to be included among those referred to as "men of goodwill"? (Luke 2:14; Matt. 16:24; John 17:3; Acts 3:19; Heb. 11:6)
(c) If those humble Judean shepherds had reason to rejoice over the birth of a Savior, what greater reason for joy do God's servants have today? (Luke 2:10, 11; Eph. 3:8, 9; Rev. 11:15; 14:6)

Story 86
Men Guided by a Star

1. Who are the men in the picture, and why is one of them pointing to a bright star?
2. Why does King Herod get upset, and what does he do?
3. Where does the bright star lead the men, but why do they return to their own country by another road?
4. What command does Herod give, and why?
5. What does Jehovah tell Joseph to do?
6. Who caused the new star to shine, and why?

Additional question:

1. *Read Matthew 2:1-23.*

How old was Jesus and where was he living when the astrologers visited him? (Matt. 2:1, 11, 16)

Young Jesus in the Temple

1. How old is Jesus in the picture, and where is he?
2. What does Joseph do with his family every year?
3. After one day on the journey back home, why do Joseph and Mary return to Jerusalem?
4. Where do Joseph and Mary find Jesus, and why are the people there amazed?
5. What does Jesus say to his mother, Mary?
6. How can we be like Jesus in learning about God?

Additional questions:

1. *Read Luke 2:41-52.*

(a) Even though the Law required that only males attend the annual festivals, what fine example did Joseph and Mary provide for parents today? (Luke 2:41; Deut. 16:16; 31:12; Prov. 22:6)

(b) How did Jesus set a good example for young ones today to be in subjection to their parents? (Luke 2:51; Deut. 5:16; Prov. 23:22; Col. 3:20)

2. *Read Matthew 13:53-56.*

What four natural brothers of Jesus are named in the Bible, and how were two of them later used in the Christian congregation? (Matt. 13:55; Acts 12:17; 15:6, 13; 21:18; Gal. 1:19; Jas. 1:1; Jude 1)

John Baptizes Jesus

1. Who are the two men in the picture?
2. How is a person baptized?
3. Whom does John normally baptize?
4. For what special reason does Jesus ask John to baptize him?
5. How does God show that He is pleased that Jesus got baptized?
6. What happens when Jesus goes away to a lonely place for 40 days?
7. Who are some of Jesus' first followers, or disciples, and what is his first miracle?

Additional questions:

1. *Read Matthew 3:13-17.*

What pattern did Jesus set for the baptism of his disciples? (Ps. 40:7, 8; Matt. 28:19, 20; Luke 3:21, 22)

2. *Read Matthew 4:1-11.*

How does Jesus' skillful use of the Scriptures encourage us to study the Bible regularly? (Matt. 4:5-7; 2 Pet. 3:17, 18; 1 John 4:1)

3. *Read John 1:29-51.*

To whom did John the Baptizer direct his disciples, and how can we imitate him today? (John 1:29, 35, 36; 3:30; Matt. 23:10)

4. *Read John 2:1-12.*

How did Jesus' first miracle show that Jehovah does not withhold anything good from His servants? (John 2:9, 10; Ps. 84:11; Jas. 1:17)

Jesus Cleans Out the Temple

1. Why are animals being sold at the temple?
2. What makes Jesus angry?
3. As you can see in the picture, what does Jesus do, and what command does he give the men who are selling doves?
4. When Jesus' followers see what he is doing, of what are they reminded?
5. Which district does Jesus travel through on his way back to Galilee?

Additional question:

1. *Read John 2:13-25.*

Considering Jesus' outrage over money changers in the temple, what is the proper view of commercial activities in the Kingdom Hall? (John 2:15, 16; 1 Cor. 10:24, 31-33)

With the Woman at the Well

1. Why has Jesus stopped by a well in Samaria, and what is he saying to a woman there?
2. Why is the woman surprised, what does Jesus say to her, and why?
3. What kind of water does the woman think Jesus is talking about, but what water does he actually mean?
4. Why is the woman amazed at what Jesus knows about her, and how did he get this information?
5. What lessons can we learn from the account of the woman at the well?

Additional questions:

1. *Read John 4:5-43.*

(a) Following Jesus' example, what attitude should we display toward people of a different racial or social background? (John 4:9; 1 Cor. 9:22; 1 Tim. 2:3, 4; Titus 2:11)

(b) What spiritual benefits come to a person who becomes Jesus' disciple? (John 4:14; Isa. 58:11; 2 Cor. 4:16)

(c) How can we show appreciation like that of the Samaritan woman, who was eager to share what she had learned? (John 4:7, 28; Matt. 6:33; Luke 10:40-42)

Story 91

Jesus Teaches on a Mountain

1. In the picture, where is Jesus teaching, and who are those sitting closest to him?
2. What are the names of the 12 apostles?
3. What is the Kingdom that Jesus is preaching about?
4. What does Jesus teach the people to pray for?
5. What does Jesus say about how people should treat one another?

Additional questions:
1. *Read Matthew 5:1-12.*
In what ways can we show that we are conscious of our spiritual need? (Matt. 5:3; Rom. 10:13-15; 1 Tim. 4:13, 15, 16)
2. *Read Matthew 5:21-26.*
How does Matthew 5:23, 24 emphasize that our relationship with our brothers affects our relationship with Jehovah? (Matt. 6:14, 15; Ps. 133:1; Col. 3:13; 1 John 4:20)
3. *Read Matthew 6:1-8.*
What are some forms of self-righteousness that Christians are to shun? (Luke 18:11, 12; 1 Cor. 4: 6, 7; 2 Cor. 9:7)
4. *Read Matthew 6:25-34.*
What did Jesus teach regarding the need to trust in Jehovah for our material provisions? (Ex. 16:4; Ps. 37:25; Phil. 4:6)
5. *Read Matthew 7:1-11.*
What does the vivid illustration found at Matthew 7:5 teach us? (Prov. 26:12; Rom. 2:1; 14:10; Jas. 4: 11, 12)

Story 92

Jesus Raises the Dead

1. Who is the father of the girl in the picture, and why are he and his wife very worried?
2. What does Jairus do when he finds Jesus?
3. What happens as Jesus is going to Jairus' home, and what message does Jairus receive on the way?
4. Why do the people in Jairus' house laugh at Jesus?
5. After taking three apostles and the girl's father and mother into the girl's room, what does Jesus do?
6. Who else has Jesus raised from the dead, and what does this show?

Additional questions:
1. *Read Luke 8:40-56.*
How did Jesus show compassion and reasonableness to the woman with the flow of blood, and what can Christian elders today learn from this? (Luke 8:43, 44, 47, 48; Lev. 15:25-27; Matt. 9:12, 13; Col. 3:12-14)
2. *Read Luke 7:11-17.*
Why can those who have lost loved ones in death find great comfort in Jesus' response to the widow from Nain? (Luke 7:13; 2 Cor. 1:3, 4; Heb. 4:15)
3. *Read John 11:17-44.*
How did Jesus demonstrate that it is normal to grieve over the death of a loved one? (John 11:33-36, 38; 2 Sam. 18:33; 19:1-4)

Story 93

Jesus Feeds Many People

1. What terrible thing has happened to John the Baptizer, and how does it make Jesus feel?
2. How does Jesus feed the crowds who have followed him, and how much food is left over?
3. Why are the disciples afraid during the night, and what happens to Peter?
4. How does Jesus feed thousands of people a second time?
5. Why will it be wonderful when Jesus rules the earth as God's King?

Additional questions:
1. *Read Matthew 14:1-32.*
(a) The account at Matthew 14:23-32 provides what insight into Peter's personality?
(b) How does the Scriptural record indicate that Peter matured and overcame his impulsive behavior? (Matt. 14:27-30; John 18:10; 21:7; Acts 2:14, 37-40; 1 Pet. 5:6, 10)
2. *Read Matthew 15:29-38.*
How did Jesus show respect for the material provisions from his Father? (Matt. 15:37; John 6:12; Col. 3:15)
3. *Read John 6:1-21.*
How can Christians today follow Jesus' example with respect to the government? (John 6:15; Matt. 22:21; Rom. 12:2; 13:1-4)

Story 94

He Loves Little Children

1. What are the apostles arguing about on their way back from a long trip?
2. Why does Jesus call a little child and stand it in the midst of the apostles?
3. In what way should the apostles learn to be like children?

4. A few months later, how does Jesus show that he loves children?

Additional questions:

1. *Read Matthew 18:1-4.*

Why did Jesus use illustrations to teach? (Matt. 13:34, 36; Mark 4:33, 34)

2. *Read Matthew 19:13-15.*

What qualities of young children must we imitate if we are to share in Kingdom blessings? (Ps. 25:9; 138:6; 1 Cor. 14:20)

3. *Read Mark 9:33-37.*

What did Jesus teach his disciples about wanting positions of prominence? (Mark 9:35; Matt. 20:25, 26; Gal. 6:3; Phil. 2:5-8)

4. *Read Mark 10:13-16.*

How approachable was Jesus, and what can Christian elders learn from his example? (Mark. 6:30-34; Phil. 2:1-4; 1 Tim. 4:12)

The Way Jesus Teaches

1. What question does a man ask Jesus, and why?
2. What does Jesus sometimes use to teach, and what have we already learned about Jews and Samaritans?
3. In the story Jesus tells, what happens to a Jew traveling on the road to Jericho?
4. What happens when a Jewish priest and a Levite come along the road?
5. In the picture, who is helping the Jew who is hurt?
6. After Jesus finishes the story, what question does he ask, and how does the man answer?

Additional questions:

1. *Read Luke 10:25-37.*

(a) Rather than give a direct answer, how did Jesus help a man versed in the Law to reason on a matter? (Luke 10:26; Matt. 16:13-16)

(b) How did Jesus use illustrations to overcome prejudice on the part of his hearers? (Luke 10:36, 37; 18:9-14; Titus 1:9)

Jesus Heals the Sick

1. What does Jesus do as he travels throughout the land?
2. Some three years after Jesus was baptized, what does he tell his apostles?
3. Who are the people in the picture, and what does Jesus do for the woman?
4. Why does Jesus' response to the objections of the religious leaders make them ashamed?

5. When Jesus and his apostles are near Jericho, what does Jesus do for two blind beggars?
6. Why does Jesus perform miracles?

Additional questions:

1. *Read Matthew 15:30, 31.*

What wonderful display of Jehovah's power is revealed through Jesus, and how should it affect our understanding of what Jehovah has promised for the new world? (Ps. 37:29; Isa. 33:24)

2. *Read Luke 13:10-17.*

How does the fact that Jesus performed some of his most outstanding miracles on the Sabbath show the kind of relief that he will bring to mankind during his Millennial Rule? (Luke 13:10-13; Ps. 46:9; Matt. 12:8; Col. 2:16, 17; Rev. 21:1-4)

3. *Read Matthew 20:29-34.*

How does this account show that Jesus was never too busy to help people, and what can we learn from this? (Deut. 15:7; Jas. 2:15, 16; 1 John 3:17)

Jesus Comes as King

1. When Jesus comes to a small village near Jerusalem, what does he tell his disciples to do?
2. In the picture, what happens when Jesus gets near the city of Jerusalem?
3. What do the young children do when they see Jesus healing people who are blind and crippled?
4. What does Jesus say to the angry priests?
5. How can we be like the children who praise Jesus?
6. What do the disciples want to know?

Additional questions:

1. *Read Matthew 21:1-17.*

(a) How did Jesus' entrance into Jerusalem as King contrast with conquering generals of Roman times? (Matt. 21:4, 5; Zech. 9:9; Phil. 2:5-8; Col. 2:15)

(b) What lesson can young ones learn from the Israelite boys who quoted from Psalm 118 as Jesus entered the temple? (Matt. 21:9, 15; Ps. 118:25, 26; 2 Tim. 3:15; 2 Pet. 3:18)

2. *Read John 12:12-16.*

What does the use of palm branches by the people who hailed Jesus symbolize? (John 12:13; Phil. 2:10; Rev. 7:9, 10)

On the Mount of Olives

1. In the picture, which man is Jesus, and who are with him?
2. What did the priests try to do to Jesus in the temple, and what did he say to them?

3. What do the apostles ask Jesus?

4. Why does Jesus tell his apostles some of the things that will be happening on earth when he is ruling as King in heaven?

5. What does Jesus say will happen before he puts an end to all badness on earth?

Additional questions:

1. *Read Matthew 23:1-39.*

(a) Although the Scriptures indicate that the use of secular titles may be appropriate, what do Jesus' words at Matthew 23:8-11 show regarding the use of flattering titles in the Christian congregation? (Acts 26:25; Rom. 13:7; 1 Pet. 2:13, 14)

(b) What did the Pharisees use to try to prevent people from becoming Christians, and how have religious leaders employed similar tactics in modern times? (Matt. 23:13; Luke 11:52; John 9:22; 12:42; 1 Thess. 2:16)

2. *Read Matthew 24:1-14.*

(a) How is the importance of endurance emphasized at Matthew 24:13?

(b) What does the expression "the end" at Matthew 24:13 mean? (Matt. 16:27; Rom. 14:10-12; 2 Cor. 5:10)

3. *Read Mark 13:3-10.*

What expression at Mark 13:10 shows the urgency of preaching the good news, and how should Jesus' words affect us? (Rom. 13:11, 12; 1 Cor. 7:29-31; 2 Tim. 4:2)

Story 99

In an Upstairs Room

1. As portrayed in the picture, why are Jesus and his 12 apostles in a large upstairs room?

2. Who is the man leaving, and what is he going to do?

3. What special meal does Jesus begin after the Passover meal is finished?

4. The Passover reminded the Israelites of what event, and of what does this special meal remind Jesus' followers?

5. After the Lord's Evening Meal, what does Jesus tell his followers, and what do they do?

Additional questions:

1. *Read Matthew 26:14-30.*

(a) How does Matthew 26:15 show that Judas' betrayal of Jesus was a deliberate act?

(b) What twofold purpose is served by Jesus' shed blood? (Matt. 26:27, 28; Jer. 31:31-33; Eph. 1:7; Heb. 9:19, 20)

2. *Read Luke 22:1-39.*

In what sense did Satan enter into Judas? (Luke 22:3; John 13:2; Acts 1:24, 25)

3. *Read John 13:1-20.*

(a) In view of the account at John 13:2, can Judas be blamed for what he did, and what lesson can God's servants learn from this? (Gen. 4:7; 2 Cor. 2:11; Gal. 6:1; Jas. 1:13, 14)

(b) What powerful object lesson did Jesus provide? (John 13:15; Matt. 23:11; 1 Pet. 2:21)

4. *Read John 17:1-26.*

In what sense did Jesus pray for his followers to "be one"? (John 17:11, 21-23; Rom. 13:8; 14:19; Col. 3:14)

Story 100

Jesus in the Garden

1. Where do Jesus and his apostles go after leaving the upstairs room, and what does he tell them to do?

2. What does Jesus find when he comes back to where the apostles are, and how many times does this happen?

3. Who enters the garden, and what does Judas Iscariot do, as the picture shows?

4. Why does Judas kiss Jesus, and what does Peter do?

5. What does Jesus say to Peter, but why does Jesus not ask God to send any angels?

Additional questions:

1. *Read Matthew 26:36-56.*

(a) How is the way that Jesus counseled his disciples a fine example for Christian elders today? (Matt. 20:25-28; 26:40, 41; Gal. 5:17; Eph. 4:29, 31, 32)

(b) How did Jesus view the use of carnal weapons against one's fellowman? (Matt. 26:52; Luke 6:27, 28; John 18:36)

2. *Read Luke 22:39-53.*

When an angel appeared to Jesus in the garden of Gethsemane to strengthen him, did this indicate that Jesus was wavering in his faith? Explain. (Luke 22:41-43; Isa. 49:8; Matt. 4:10, 11; Heb. 5:7)

3. *Read John 18:1-12.*

How did Jesus protect his disciples from his opposers, and what can we learn from this example? (John 10:11, 12; 18:1, 6-9; Heb. 13:6; Jas. 2:25)

Story 101

Jesus Is Killed

1. Who is primarily responsible for Jesus' death?

2. What do the apostles do when Jesus is taken by the religious leaders?

3. What happens at the house of Caiaphas, the high priest?

4. Why does Peter go away and weep?

5. After Jesus is returned to Pilate, what do the chief priests yell?

6. What happens to Jesus early Friday afternoon, and what promise does he make to an evildoer who hangs on a stake beside him?

7. Where will the Paradise that Jesus spoke of be located?

Additional questions:

1. *Read Matthew 26:57-75.*

In what way did the members of the Jewish high court show that their hearts were wicked? (Matt. 26:59, 67, 68)

2. *Read Matthew 27:1-50.*

Why can we say that the remorse that Judas felt was not genuine? (Matt. 27:3, 4; Mark 3:29; 14:21; 2 Cor. 7:10, 11)

3. *Read Luke 22:54-71.*

What lesson can we learn from Peter's denial of Jesus on the night of his betrayal and arrest? (Luke 22:60-62; Matt. 26:31-35; 1 Cor. 10:12)

4. *Read Luke 23:1-49.*

How did Jesus react to the injustice done to him, and what lesson can we learn from this? (Luke 23: 33, 34; Rom. 12:17-19; 1 Pet. 2:23)

5. *Read John 18:12-40.*

What is shown by the fact that although Peter was momentarily paralyzed by fear of man, he recovered to become an outstanding apostle? (John 18: 25-27; 1 Cor. 4:2; 1 Pet. 3:14, 15; 5:8, 9)

6. *Read John 19:1-30.*

(a) What balanced view of material things did Jesus have? (John 2:1, 2, 9, 10; 19:23, 24; Matt. 6:31, 32; 8:20)

(b) How were Jesus' dying words a triumphant declaration that he had upheld Jehovah's sovereignty? (John 16:33; 19:30; 2 Pet. 3:14; 1 John 5:4)

Story 102

Jesus Is Alive

1. Who is the woman in the picture, who are the two men, and where are they?

2. Why does Pilate tell the priests to send soldiers to guard Jesus' tomb?

3. What does an angel do early on the third day after Jesus died, but what do the priests do?

4. Why are some women surprised when they visit Jesus' tomb?

5. Why do Peter and John run to Jesus' tomb, and what do they find?

6. What happened to Jesus' body, but what does he do to show the disciples that he is alive?

Additional questions:

1. *Read Matthew 27:62-66 and 28:1-15.*

At the time of Jesus' resurrection, how did the chief priests, Pharisees, and older men sin against the holy spirit? (Matt. 12:24, 31, 32; 28:11-15)

2. *Read Luke 24:1-12.*

How does the account of Jesus' resurrection show that Jehovah views women as reliable witnesses? (Luke 24:4, 9, 10; Matt. 28:1-7)

3. *Read John 20:1-12.*

How does John 20:8, 9 help us see the need to be patient if we do not fully understand the fulfillment of a Bible prophecy? (Prov. 4:18; Matt. 17:22, 23; Luke 24:5-8; John 16:12)

Story 103

Into a Locked Room

1. What does Mary say to a man whom she thinks is the gardener, but what makes her realize that he is really Jesus?

2. What happens to two disciples who are walking to the village of Emmaus?

3. What amazing thing happens when two disciples tell the apostles that they saw Jesus?

4. How many times has Jesus appeared to his followers?

5. What does Thomas say when he hears that the disciples have seen the Lord, but what happens eight days later?

Additional questions:

1. *Read John 20:11-29.*

Was Jesus saying at John 20:23 that humans are authorized to forgive sins? Explain. (Ps. 49:2, 7; Isa. 55:7; 1 Tim. 2:5, 6; 1 John 2:1, 2)

2. *Read Luke 24:13-43.*

How can we prepare our heart so that it is receptive to Bible truths? (Luke 24:32, 33; Ezra 7:10; Matt. 5:3; Acts 16:14; Heb. 5:11-14)

Story 104

Jesus Returns to Heaven

1. How many disciples see Jesus on one occasion, and what does he talk to them about?

2. What is the Kingdom of God, and what will life on earth be like when Jesus rules as King for a thousand years?

3. For how many days has Jesus been appearing to his disciples, but what is it now time for him to do?

4. Just before leaving his disciples, what does Jesus tell them to do?

5. What is happening in the picture, and how does Jesus get hidden from sight?

Additional questions:

1. *Read 1 Corinthians 15:3-8.*
Why could the apostle Paul speak so confidently regarding Jesus' resurrection, and about what things can Christians today speak confidently? (1 Cor. 15:4, 7, 8; Isa. 2:2, 3; Matt. 24:14; 2 Tim. 3:1-5)

2. *Read Acts 1:1-11.*
How widely did the preaching work spread, as foretold at Acts 1:8? (Acts 6:7; 9:31; 11:19-21; Col. 1:23)

Story 105

Waiting in Jerusalem

1. As the picture shows, what happens to Jesus' followers who have been waiting in Jerusalem?
2. What surprise do visitors to Jerusalem receive?
3. What does Peter explain to the people?
4. How do the people feel after they listen to Peter, and what does he tell them to do?
5. How many people get baptized on that day of Pentecost, 33 C.E.?

Additional questions:

1. *Read Acts 2:1-47.*
(a) How did Peter's words found at Acts 2:23, 36 show that the entire Jewish nation shared responsibility for Jesus' death? (1 Thess. 2:14, 15)
(b) How did Peter set a good example of reasoning from the Scriptures? (Acts 2:16, 17, 29, 31, 36, 39; Col. 4:6)
(c) How did Peter use the first of "the keys of the kingdom of the heavens," which Jesus had promised to give to him? (Acts 2:14, 22-24, 37, 38; Matt. 16:19)

Story 106

Set Free From Prison

1. What happens to Peter and John one afternoon as they are going into the temple?
2. What does Peter say to a lame man, and what does Peter give him that is more valuable than money?
3. Why are the religious leaders angry, and what do they do to Peter and John?
4. What does Peter say to the religious leaders, and what warning do the apostles receive?
5. Why are the religious leaders jealous, but what happens when the apostles are put into prison the second time?
6. How do the apostles answer when they are brought into the Sanhedrin hall?

Additional questions:

1. *Read Acts 3:1-10.*
Although we are not empowered to perform miracles today, how do Peter's words recorded at Acts 3:6 help us to appreciate the value of the Kingdom message? (John 17:3; 2 Cor. 5:18-20; Phil. 3:8)

2. *Read Acts 4:1-31.*
When we face opposition in the ministry, in what way should we imitate our first-century Christian brothers? (Acts 4:29, 31; Eph. 6:18-20; 1 Thess. 2:2)

3. *Read Acts 5:17-42.*
How have some non-Witnesses, both past and present, shown reasonableness regarding the preaching work? (Acts 5:34-39)

Story 107

Stephen Is Stoned

1. Who is Stephen, and what has God been helping him to do?
2. What does Stephen say that makes the religious leaders very angry?
3. When the men drag Stephen outside the city, what do they do to him?
4. In the picture, who is the young man standing beside the coats?
5. Before he dies, what does Stephen pray to Jehovah?
6. In imitation of Stephen, what should we do when someone does something bad to us?

Additional questions:

1. *Read Acts 6:8-15.*
What deceptive practices have religious leaders used to try to stop the preaching work of Jehovah's Witnesses? (Acts 6:9, 11, 13)

2. *Read Acts 7:1-60.*
(a) What helped Stephen to be effective in defending the good news before the Sanhedrin, and what can we learn from his example? (Acts 7:51-53; Rom. 15:4; 2 Tim. 3:14-17; 1 Pet. 3:15)
(b) What attitude should we cultivate toward opposers of our work? (Acts 7:58-60; Matt. 5:44; Luke 23:33, 34)

Story 108

On the Road to Damascus

1. What does Saul do after Stephen is killed?
2. When Saul is on his way to Damascus, what amazing thing happens?
3. What does Jesus tell Saul to do?
4. What instructions does Jesus give to Ananias, and how is Saul able to see again?
5. By what name does Saul become known, and how is he used?

Additional questions:

1. *Read Acts 8:1-4.*

How did the wave of persecution that struck the newly formed Christian congregation serve to spread the Christian faith, and what similar thing has occurred in modern times? (Acts 8:4; Isa. 54:17)

2. *Read Acts 9:1-20.*

What threefold mission did Jesus reveal that he had in mind for Saul? (Acts 9:15; 13:5; 26:1; 27:24; Rom. 11:13)

3. *Read Acts 22:6-16.*

How can we be like Ananias, and why is that important? (Acts 22:12; 1 Tim. 3:7; 1 Pet. 1:14-16; 2:12)

4. *Read Acts 26:8-20.*

How does Saul's conversion to Christianity serve as an encouragement to those with unbelieving mates today? (Acts 26:11; 1 Tim. 1:14-16; 2 Tim. 4:2; 1 Pet. 3:1-3)

Story 109

Peter Visits Cornelius

1. Who is the man bowing down in the picture?
2. What does an angel say to Cornelius?
3. What does God make Peter see when he is on the roof of Simon's house in Joppa?
4. Why does Peter tell Cornelius that he should not bow down and worship him?
5. Why are the Jewish disciples with Peter amazed?
6. What important lesson should we learn from Peter's visit to Cornelius?

Additional questions:

1. *Read Acts 10:1-48.*

What do Peter's words found at Acts 10:42 show about the work of preaching the good news of the Kingdom? (Matt. 28:19; Mark 13:10; Acts 1:8)

2. *Read Acts 11:1-18.*

What attitude did Peter display when Jehovah's direction regarding Gentiles became obvious, and how can we imitate his example? (Acts 11:17, 18; 2 Cor. 10:5; Eph. 5:17)

Story 110

Timothy—Paul's New Helper

1. Who is the young man in the picture, where does he live, and what are the names of his mother and grandmother?
2. What does Timothy say when Paul asks him if he wants to join Silas and Paul in preaching to people far away? .
3. Where is it that Jesus' followers are first called Christians?

4. After Paul, Silas, and Timothy leave Antioch, what are some of the cities they visit?
5. How does Timothy help Paul, and what question should young ones today ask themselves?

Additional questions:

1. *Read Acts 9:19-30.*

How did the apostle Paul show discretion when he faced opposition to the good news? (Acts 9:22-25, 29, 30; Matt. 10:16)

2. *Read Acts 11:19-26.*

How does the account recorded at Acts 11:19-21, 26 show that Jehovah's spirit is guiding and directing the preaching work?

3. *Read Acts 13:13-16, 42-52.*

How does Acts 13:51, 52 show that the disciples did not allow opposition to discourage them? (Matt. 10:14; Acts 18:6; 1 Pet. 4:14)

4. *Read Acts 14:1-6, 19-28.*

How does the expression "they committed them to Jehovah" help to relieve us of any undue anxiety as we assist new ones? (Acts 14:21-23; 20:32; John 6:44)

5. *Read Acts 16:1-5.*

How does Timothy's willingness to submit to circumcision emphasize the importance of doing "all things for the sake of the good news"? (Acts 16:3; 1 Cor. 9:23; 1 Thess. 2:8)

6. *Read Acts 18:1-11, 18-22.*

What does Acts 18:9, 10 indicate regarding Jesus' personal involvement in directing the preaching work, and what confidence does that give us today? (Matt. 28:20)

Story 111

A Boy Who Fell Asleep

1. In the picture, who is the boy lying on the ground, and what happened to him?
2. What does Paul do when he sees that the boy is dead?
3. Where are Paul, Timothy, and those traveling with them going, and what happens when they stop at Miletus?
4. What warning does the prophet Agabus give Paul, and how does it happen just as the prophet says?

Additional questions:

1. *Read Acts 20:7-38.*

(a) How can we remain "clean from the blood of all men," according to Paul's words recorded at Acts 20:26, 27? (Ezek. 33:8; Acts 18:6, 7)

(b) Why should elders be "holding firmly to the faithful word" when teaching? (Acts 20:17, 29, 30; Titus 1:7-9; 2 Tim. 1:13)

2. *Read Acts 26:24-32.*

How did Paul use his Roman citizenship in fulfilling the preaching commission he had received from Jesus? (Acts 9:15; 16:37, 38; 25:11, 12; 26:32; Luke 21:12, 13)

Story 112

Shipwrecked on an Island

1. What happens to the boat Paul is on as it passes near the island of Crete?
2. What does Paul say to those on the boat?
3. How does the boat get broken into pieces?
4. What instructions does the army officer in charge give, and how many people get to the shore safely?
5. What is the name of the island they land on, and what happens to Paul when the weather gets better?

Additional questions:

1. *Read Acts 27:1-44.*

How is our confidence in the accuracy of the Bible record strengthened when we read the account of Paul's voyage to Rome? (Acts 27:16-19, 27-32; Luke 1:3; 2 Tim. 3:16, 17)

2. *Read Acts 28:1-14.*

If the pagan inhabitants of Malta were moved to treat the apostle Paul and his shipwreck companions with "extraordinary human kindness," Christians should be moved to show what and especially in what way? (Acts 28:1, 2; Heb. 13:1, 2; 1 Pet. 4:9)

Story 113

Paul in Rome

1. Who does Paul preach to while he is a prisoner in Rome?
2. In the picture, who is the visitor at the table, and what is he doing for Paul?
3. Who is Epaphroditus, and what does he take with him when he returns to Philippi?
4. Why does Paul write a letter to his close friend Philemon?
5. What does Paul do when he is set free, and what happens to him later?
6. Whom does Jehovah use to write the last books of the Bible, and what does the book of Revelation tell about?

Additional questions:

1. *Read Acts 28:16-31 and Philippians 1:13.*

How did Paul use his time while imprisoned in Rome, and what effect did his unwavering faith have on the Christian congregation? (Acts 28:23, 30; Phil. 1:14)

2. *Read Philippians 2:19-30.*

What expressions of appreciation did Paul make regarding Timothy and Epaphroditus, and how can we imitate Paul's example? (Phil. 2:20, 22, 25, 29, 30; 1 Cor. 16:18; 1 Thess. 5:12, 13)

3. *Read Philemon 1-25.*

(a) On what basis did Paul urge Philemon to do what was proper, and how does this serve as a guide for elders today? (Philem. 9; 2 Cor. 8:8; Gal. 5:13)

(b) How does Paul's expression found at Philemon 13, 14 show that he respected the conscience of others in the congregation? (1 Cor. 8:7, 13; 10:31-33)

4. *Read 2 Timothy 4:7-9.*

Like the apostle Paul, how can we have confidence that Jehovah will reward us if we remain faithful to the end? (Matt. 24:13; Heb. 6:10)

Story 114

The End of All Badness

1. Why does the Bible speak of horses in heaven?
2. What is the name of God's war with bad people on the earth, and what is the purpose of this war?
3. From the picture, who is the One who will take the lead in the fighting, why does he wear a crown, and what does his sword mean?
4. Looking back at Stories 10, 15, and 33, why should we not be surprised that God will destroy bad people?
5. How do Stories 36 and 76 show us that God will destroy bad people even if they claim to worship him?

Additional questions:

1. *Read Revelation 19:11-16.*

(a) How do the Scriptures make clear that Jesus Christ is the rider on the white horse? (Rev. 1:5; 3:14; 19:11; Isa. 11:4)

(b) How does the blood sprinkled on Jesus' outer garment confirm that his victory is decisive and complete? (Rev. 14:18-20; 19:13; Isa. 63:1-6)

(c) Who are likely included in the armies that follow Jesus on his white horse? (Rev. 12:7; 19:14; Matt. 25:31, 32)

Story 115

A New Paradise on Earth

1. What conditions does the Bible indicate we will enjoy in the earthly Paradise?
2. What is the Bible's promise for those who live in Paradise?
3. When will Jesus see to it that this wonderful change takes place?

Jesus was on earth, what did he do to [...]at he would do as King of God's Kingdom? [...]at will Jesus and his heavenly corulers [...] sure of when they rule over the earth from [...]ven?

Additional questions:

1. *Read Revelation 5:9, 10.*
Why can we have confidence that those ruling over the earth during the Millennial Reign will be sympathetic and merciful kings and priests? (Eph. 4: 20-24; 1 Pet. 1:7; 3:8; 5:6-10)

2. *Read Revelation 14:1-3.*
What is signified by the fact that the name of the Father and the name of the Lamb are written on the foreheads of the 144,000? (1 Cor. 3:23; 2 Tim. 2:19; Rev. 3:12)

Story 116

How We Can Live Forever

1. What do we need to know if we are to live forever?
2. How can we learn about Jehovah God and Jesus, as shown by the little girl and her friends in the picture?

3. What other book do you see in the picture, and why should we read it often?
4. Besides learning about Jehovah and Jesus, what else is needed to gain everlasting life?
5. What lesson do we learn from Story 69?
6. What does the good example of little Samuel in Story 55 show?
7. How can we follow the example of Jesus Christ, and if we do, what will we be able to do in the future?

Additional questions:

1. *Read John 17:3.*
How do the Scriptures show that taking in knowledge of Jehovah God and Jesus Christ means more than merely memorizing facts? (Matt. 7:21; Jas. 2:18-20; 1 John 2:17)

2. *Read Psalm 145:1-21.*
(a) What are some of the many reasons we have for praising Jehovah? (Ps. 145:8-11; Rev. 4:11)
(b) How is Jehovah "good to all," and how should this draw us ever closer to him? (Ps. 145:9; Matt. 5:43-45)
(c) If Jehovah is dear to our heart, what will we be moved to do? (Ps. 119:171, 172, 175; 145:11, 12, 21)

Would you welcome more information?
Write Jehovah's Witnesses at the appropriate address below.

ARGENTINA: Casilla de Correo 83 (Suc. 27B), 1427 Buenos Aires. **AUSTRALIA:** Box 280, Ingleburn, NSW 1890. **BOLIVIA:** Casilla 6397, Santa Cruz. **BRAZIL:** Caixa Postal 92, 18270-970 Tatuí, SP. **BRITAIN:** The Ridgeway, London NW7 1RN. **CANADA:** Box 4100, Halton Hills (Georgetown), Ontario L7G 4Y4. **CHILE:** Casilla 267, Puente Alto. **COLOMBIA:** Apartado Postal 85058, Bogotá 8, D.C. **COSTA RICA:** Apartado 187-3006, Barreal, Heredia. **CUBA:** Ave. 15 No. 4608, Playa, Ciudad Habana. **DOMINICAN REPUBLIC:** Apartado 1742, Santo Domingo. **ECUADOR:** Casilla 09-01-1334, Guayaquil. **EL SALVADOR:** Apartado Postal 401, San Salvador. **FRANCE:** B.P. 625, F-27406 Louviers cedex. **GERMANY:** Niederselters, Am Steinfels, D-65618 Selters. **GUATEMALA:** Apartado postal 711, 01901 Guatemala. **HONDURAS:** Apartado 147, Tegucigalpa. **ITALY:** Via della Bufalotta 1281, I-00138 Rome RM. **JAPAN:** 4-7-1 Nakashinden, Ebina City, Kanagawa Pref., 243-0496. **MEXICO (also Belize):** Apartado Postal 896, 06002 Mexico, D. F. **NICARAGUA:** Apartado 3587, Managua. **PANAMA:** Apartado 0819-07567, Panama. **PARAGUAY:** Casilla de Correo 482, 1209 Asunción. **PERU:** Apartado 18-1055, Lima 18. **PUERTO RICO 00970:** P.O. Box 3980, Guaynabo. **RUSSIA:** P.O. Box 182, 190000 St. Petersburg. **SPAIN:** Apartado 132, 28850 Torrejón de Ardoz (Madrid). **SWITZERLAND:** PO Box 225, 3602 Thun. **TRINIDAD AND TOBAGO, REP. OF:** Lower Rapsey Street & Laxmi Lane, Curepe. **UNITED STATES OF AMERICA:** 25 Columbia Heights, Brooklyn, NY 11201-2483. **URUGUAY:** Casilla 17030, 12500 Montevideo. **VENEZUELA:** Apartado 20.364, Caracas, DC 1020A.   www.watchtower.org